LANDSCAPES OF MODERN SPORT

Sports, Politics and Culture
A series of books from Leicester University Press

Series editors: **Stephen Wagg**
Department of Sociology, University of Leicester
John Williams
Sir Norman Chester Centre for Football Research,
University of Leicester

Published:

Rogan Taylor   *Football and its Fans*

John Sugden &   *Sport, Sectarianism and Society in a Divided Ireland*
  Alan Bairner

Grant Jarvie &   *Scottish Sport in the Making of the Nation*
  Graham Walker

Forthcoming titles:

Stephen Wagg   *Football and Society in Different Continents*

LANDSCAPES OF MODERN SPORT

JOHN BALE

LEICESTER UNIVERSITY PRESS
LEICESTER, LONDON, NEW YORK

DISTRIBUTED IN THE UNITED STATES AND CANADA BY ST. MARTIN'S PRESS

Leicester University Press
(a division of Pinter Publishers Ltd)
25 Floral Street, Covent Garden, London, WC2E 9DS

First published in Great Britain 1994

British Library Cataloguing in Publication Data
A CIP catalogue record for this book is available from The British Library

ISBN 0 7185 1458 0 (hbk)
     0 7185 1464 5 (pbk)

Typeset by Saxon Graphics Ltd, Derby
Printed and bound in Great Britain by Biddles of Guildford and King's Lynn

FOR MY NORDIC FRIENDS

Neatness, symmetry and formal patterns had always been the distinctively human way of indicating the separation between culture and nature.

(Keith Thomas, *Man and the Natural World*, 1983: 256)

More and more, each sport resembles all sports; the flavor, the special joys of place and season, the unique displays of courage and strength and style that once isolated each game and fixed it in our affections have disappeared somewhere in the noise and crush.

(Roger Angell, *The Summer Game*, 1962: 282)

Those who race are different from ordinary people. To hide their feelings, they dress in strange outfits. Their helmets are designed to hold their heads in place. Their goggles are cut to ignore what can not be counted. They have left their hearts at home, for otherwise they cannot be objective. They feed on a diet of certainty and they get upset by ambiguity.

(Gunnar Olsson, *Birds in Egg/Eggs in Bird*, 1980: 198)

CONTENTS

LIST OF FIGURES

LIST OF TABLES

PREFACE

In this book I want to try to provide a broad and interpretive study of the sports landscape and hence begin to fill an obvious lacuna in a major area of both sports and cultural-geographic studies. A wide variety of approaches is available to an author bent on exploring the landscapes of sports and in order to make my own approach clear from the outset a brief autobiographical statement may be necessary as my cultural, academic and sporting background must have inevitably informed my approach. I have adopted an unashamedly eclectic approach and recognise the dangers of the academic quagmire which eclecticism invites. I also recognise that as a white, British-educated, heterosexual male, the contents of this book will be thought of, by some feminists, as 'male-customed' or 'masculinised'. While including aspects of the sporting milieu which relate to gender I have, nevertheless, found it impossible to produce a 'bilingual' or 'trilingual' approach. A feminist perspective on the landscapes of sport requires another book.

My academic background in human geography certainly informs this study even if I have increasingly felt that the rigid disciplinary boundaries of the traditional academy have little to offer the advancement of our knowledge of the cultural phenomenon known as sport. I have found that much of my reading, listening and discussion has introduced me to scholars from a wide variety of 'disciplines' who share a common interest in the serious study of serious sport and I have been surprised to find how many of them have had so much to say about space, place, landscape and environment – themes with which a human geographer (or more accurately, these days, a geographical humanist) should feel at home. The pages of this book, therefore, bring together the ideas of writers from what, at first sight, might appear to be an unlikely academic alliance – sports studies and cultural geography. The book also includes allusions to many other forms and fields of knowledge. I cannot claim to have favoured any single theoretical focus and I have adopted a number of positions in order to present the variety of 'readings' which can be made of the landscapes of sport. I hope to show that a 'landscape approach' to sport, fuelled from a number of theoretical standpoints, has much to commend it in illustrating sport's essential modernity (but also its ambiguity) while, at the same time, showing how the environments of sports are among the most human, though not the most humane, of landscapes.

Equally, my particular sporting interests have inevitably influenced my choice of material in this book. British themes dominate but my all too brief experiences of sporting environments in north America and various countries of mainland Europe have resulted in case study material which is not too parochial. Two or three sports probably receive a disproportionate amount of attention, the result of my own interest and involvement. During my childhood I was immersed in football – Saturday afternoons, thanks to my father, at Ninian Park overcoming the pressures to conform to the rugby union culture found throughout the South Wales grammar school environment of the late 1950s. Later, track and field athletics came to assume a ridiculously important part of my life. My extremely modest athletic achievements were totally disproportionate to the amount of effort I expended in practice but training took me to a variety of landscapes – sand dunes and forests, city streets and cinder tracks – the legacy of which may, in part, be found in some of the pages which follow. I have had a love-hate affair with cricket, its pace of play being a little too slow for my taste, but living as I now do in an English village with its own rustic cricket ground, where on summer evenings I can hear the sound of leather against willow and the gentle ripple of applause, together with the bells of the parish church, I find myself living inside the stereotype. So while seeking to interpret the landscape of sport from an 'academic' perspective, I can also claim a degree of insider knowledge which not only provides a point of identification with my subject but also informs and influences my interpretation of it. I apologise to readers whose interests lie in sports not covered in the pages which follow but they may be able to draw their own analogies from the examples which are.

This book, while at one level a synthesis of much diverse existing literature, scattered across a range of academic disciplines, is also an essay – perhaps a speculation – rather than a definitive statement. It could hardly be that, being the first book on this particular subject . Having written it, therefore, I hope that it will provoke other scholars to think seriously about the hitherto neglected subject of the landscape of sport and to respond accordingly.

ACKNOWLEDGEMENTS

I would like to acknowledge the following who have made their work available for reproduction in this book: the National Museum of Wales for Figure 2.2; Olof Moen for Figures 2.4, 4.5 and 4.8; Robert Price and Aberdeen University Press for Figure 3.4; Grafton Books for Figure 4.1; the National Baseball Library and Archives, Cooperstown, New York for Figure 4.3; *The Guardian* for Figures 4.6 and 8.4; Laila Ottesen for Figure 4.9; Edition Liepzig for Figure 5.2; the editor of *Track and Field News* for Figure 5.4; the editor of the Stoke *Evening Sentinel* for Figure 6.3; Rick Everitt and *Voice of the Valley* for Figure 6.4; Dyersville Area Chamber of Commerce for Figure 6.7; Ling's Cards for Figure 7.1; Penguin Books for Figure 7.2; J. Sainsbury plc for Figure 7.3; *The Independent on Sunday* for Figure 7.8; Esto Photographs and Hellmuth, Obata and Kassabaum, Inc., Sports Facilities Group for Figure 8.1; Caddyshacks Inc. for Figure 8.2. A small number of copyright holders, including some from the former German Democratic Republic, have been impossible to trace. If any such omissions can be located I will be very happy to include them in any subsequent editions of this book.

An earlier form of Chapter 5 first appeared in *The International Journal of the History of Sport* (10 (2), 1993) and I am grateful to the editor, Tony Mangan, for granting permission to reproduce it here in modified form. An even earlier version of Chapter 7 appeared in *Sport Place* (2 (2), 1988) and thanks are likewise given to Dick Pillsbury.

Some of the work that appears in the pages which follow represents a re-working of material which was first presented at various conferences, seminars and colloquia. For the invitations, the engineering of the necessary financial assistance, and the provision of hospitality necessary for me to attend those meetings I must thank Roman Horak, Pierre Lanfranchi, Søren Riiskjær and Otmar Weiss. Most of all I owe an incalculable debt to John Rooney for not only acting as a host and friend in the United States but also for inspiring me to embark on the 'geographical' study of sport in the first place.

This book is the culmination of several years of library research and field studies at sports places far and wide. During its preparation I received help in my research, and assistance in recognising my priorities, from many people. I would therefore like to acknowledge the help of the following: Anthony Bale, John Ball, Tim Brighouse, Allen Guttmann, Andrew Huxtable, Gary James, David Jenkins, Bruce Kidd, Olof Moen, Jack O'Neil, Anu Oittinen, Laila Ottesen, Chris Philo, Karl Raitz, Charlotte Wilhelmsen, and Bruce Young.

In the last six or seven years I have learned a great deal from several stimulating academic visits to Denmark and Finland, two nations in which some of the most interesting work on sport, landscape and nature is currently being done. These adventures were greatly enhanced by the company of a number of people. I dedicate this book to them all but would single out one or two in particular. Søren Nagbøl in Copenhagen helped in more ways than simply introducing me to Brumleby and Café Nick. Also in Denmark, Henning Eichberg has been a constant source of stimulation and ideas while Niels Kayser Nielsen read various drafts of the present text. With his great breadth of knowledge across the social sciences and humanities, Niels was able to offer invaluable suggestions on how my text might be improved and his lengthy epistles are greatly appreciated. He also acted as a very kind host and extremely congenial guide and companion in Jylland and Fyn. In Finland, I must thank Kalevi Olin, Kimmo Suomi, Kari Puronaho and especially Heikki Herva and Tuija Lyytinen who helped make my visits to Jyväskylä very valuable, both academically and socially.

I found difficulty in thinking of appropriate people from various disciplinary perspectives who I could ask to read the entire final manuscript and to offer criticisms. I could not have found better critics than Otto Penz and Soile Veijola and I therefore want to thank them sincerely for commenting incisively and constructively. Many (but not quite all) of their suggestions have been happily incorporated into the text. Maralyn Beech and Andrew Lawrence, photographer and cartographer respectively in the Department of Geography at Keele University, did a magnificent job in transforming an assortment of prints and rough sketches into polished plates, maps and diagrams. Finally I must thank Ruth for her willingness to visit more sportscapes than she would freely choose – and for much else. Despite the help and encouragement of all the above, I alone take responsibility for what follows.

John Bale
Keele
October 1993

1

INTRODUCTION: LANDSCAPE AND SPORT

Considerable controversy surrounded events near the Québec community of Kanehaasatak/Oka in the summer of 1990 when local members of the Mohawk nation discovered that, as part of a golf course development, plans were afoot to destroy a century old pine wood, planted by their mothers and fathers, containing a cemetery and regarded by them as ceremonial land. So concerned were the indigenous Americans that they took up arms to prevent the appropriation of their space. On July 11 Québec police opened fire on the protesters and the Canadian army was dispatched and surrounded the Mohawk communities until September 26. Land colonisation by sport led local people to confront developers over potential landscape changes which would have affected the quality of their lives.

Emotions had also been running high four years earlier when, in the London (England) borough of Greenwich, local football fans learned that their club, Charlton Athletic, was to leave its historic home ground, 'The Valley', and start ground-sharing with another club 12 kilometres away. So incensed were the fans that they fought against the decision to leave their 'home' stadium to the demolition team and, as a result of a number of explicitly political activities – to the extent of forming a political party to contest the local elections – eventually persuaded their club to return to the cultural landscape that they loved.

At about the same time residents of the Bristol suburb of Kingswood became alarmed, not about losing a football stadium but by the prospect of having one constructed in their neighbourhood. They formed an action group and commissioned studies to ascertain the impact of the stadium on their lives. They contacted local Members of Parliament, feeling as they did that the stadium would negatively affect the quality of their lives and lower the prices of their property. For them, the proposed stadium constituted a latter day landscape of fear. Such responses to the promise, or threat, of sports landscapes as neighbours are common throughout the modern world.

After a relatively sedentary day in my office I often go running in the countryside of north Staffordshire. One of my routes takes me along undulating country lanes and, coming to the crest of a gentle hill in the clear air following heavy rain showers during the day, the early evening summer sunlight seems to accentuate and enhance the colours of the light and dark greens of the fields and woods, the red bricks and grey tiles of the farm buildings on the horizon and the different blues and greys of the sky. They seem to stand out in sharp contrast to the dreariness of much modern life, a possible illusion induced by the joy of free movement. Running in such a landscape can become more than running; it is almost a spiritual, sensual, poetic experience which, in large part because of the landscape, undeniably enhances in a small but important way the quality of my life.

These four vignettes show that, in various ways, sports landscapes do matter. Sport is a pervasive cultural form which is not only obvious in the vernacular landscape but also of importance economically and in terms of planning and land use change. Sports landscapes of various kinds are also regularly communicated to us on television. They range from a few square metres (a squash court) to many square kilometres (a golf course) in area; they may be urban or rural; they can be almost natural or totally artificial. As my initial paragraphs showed, such landscapes also have an effect upon people's emotions and as a result, and in many small ways, they contribute to our quality of life, good landscapes improving it, bad ones reducing it.

This book is an essay into the character of a modern type of landscape which has received limited academic attention. My basic thesis is that sports have emerged as highly rationalised representations of modernity which, as much as (and arguably more than) any other form of culture, possess the potential to eliminate regional differences as a result of their rule-bound, ordered, enclosed and predictably segmented forms of landscape. In addition, the geographical 'sameness' of sports space is encouraged by its synthetic and technological character. This is not to say that the sports landscape has reached such a degree of rationality that place to place differences have been totally eliminated, nor that sport as a collective outdoor ritual (or spectacle) has been replaced by individualised indoor entertainment. And while I will show that this may be the general direction in which things are going, I will also emphasise how some sports landscapes are sufficiently ambiguous to force us to question our preconceptions about modern sport and even to apply the term 'post-modern' to some of the landscapes which currently exist.[1] My interpretation of sport is relatively narrow and that of landscape relatively broad. I mean things like stadiums and golf courses, not national parks and wetlands when I talk about *sport land-scapes* and later in this chapter I will spend a little time elaborating on what I mean by each of these two key terms. Before doing so, however, I want to highlight the relative paucity of previous work on the subject of this book.

SPORT, LANDSCAPE AND CULTURAL GEOGRAPHY

Where might we most obviously expect to find written explorations of the sports landscape? Three possible sources come to mind. First, there are planning and land use studies commissioned by urban governments which exist in large numbers. They quantify the amount of land given over to sport and recreation and suggest areas where additional space might be acceptably colonised by such land uses. But they are in no way interpretive and are essentially tools or products of the planning profession. A second group of publications are those of a literary, journalistic or 'coffee-table' nature, designed generally for the sports enthusiast. These cover a vast spectrum – from glossy collections of often stereotypical colour photographs of much-loved golf courses, cricket grounds, ballparks or race courses, to more sensitively constructed descriptions aided by appropriate visual images. Some examples of excellent works in this latter genre come to mind from British and north American literature – the brilliant *Football Grounds of Great Britain* by Simon Inglis (1983); *The Grounds of Rugby League* by Trevor Delaney (1991) (a self-published labour of love by a genuine enthusiast); *Grounds of Appeal* by Aylwin Sampson (1981), an evocative book, among many others, about the cricket grounds of England; and among several studies of the ball parks of the USA two recent and stunning books, one by the photographer Danielle Weil et al (1992), *Baseball – the Perfect Game*, and the other, *Green Cathedrals* by baseball *aficionado* Philip Lowry (1992).

A third group of explorations has come from scholars in such fields as sports studies, history, architecture and geography who might be expected to go beyond descriptions – clinical or sensitive – of sports places and begin to explore the nature of the sports landscape, seek to understand its meaning for people and to 'read' it as a kind of 'text'. But the 'spatial environment in research' in sports studies has been recognised as a 'really alarming deficiency' (Digel, 1991: 136)[2] and although some good books on sports architecture do exist (e.g. Lyngsgård, 1990; Wimmer, 1976), they understandably tend to concentrate on the buildings themselves and fail to include the overall environmental ensemble which makes up the broader landscape. Historians, while often alluding to sports landscapes in passing, have failed to give them one-tenth of the attention given to equivalent forms of high culture such as landscape gardens. Tantalisingly brief references to the changing landscapes of sports are usually found in histories of particular sports and of particular periods of time. A significant exception is the work of the German historian (who these days regards himself more as a Danish 'cultural sociologist'), Henning Eichberg, whose book, *Leistungsräume* (1988), is concerned with the way in which sports places and scenery have changed over time in response to the underlying achievement and record orientation of modern sports, and how sport can be viewed as an ecological problem. Eichberg is a prolific and provocative author whose work I shall refer to many times in the pages which follow.

Even if it is only half true, as Douglas Porteous (1990: 3) somewhat quaintly avers, that 'geography is, above all, the study of the landscape', it seems reasonable to assume that geographers might be the most likely group of scholars to have addressed the landscape of sport.[3] Yet in the broad field of cultural geography sport is much ignored. Some diffuse articles on aspects of the sports landscape do exist but they tend to be found in rather fugitive journals (e.g. Adams, 1987; Adams and Rooney, 1984; Bale, 1985; Raitz, 1987a; 1987b) or in interdisciplinary publications (e.g. Oriard, 1976; Neilson, 1986; Winters, 1980). Jay Appleton's (1975) *The Experience of Landscape* makes some fascinating but frustratingly fleeting forays into sport in a landscape context but in books whose titles might lead the reader to reasonably expect at least some coverage of such a widespread form of cultural landscape – for example, *The Iconography of Landscape* (Cosgrove and Daniels, 1989) or *Rational Landscapes and Humanistic Geography* (Relph, 1981) – it is found to be totally absent. Even in Donald Meinig's *The Interpretation of Ordinary Landscapes* (1979a), an excellent collection of essays upon which I will draw later in this chapter, the landscapes do not turn out to be all *that* ordinary. Authored mainly by Americans, they certainly do not include the ordinary landscapes of the quintessentially American sports of baseball, basketball, ice hockey and football, sports where the exploration of landscape impress and imagery have been left to informed journalists, photographers, literate ex-players, and scholars from other disciplines (see respectively, for example, Angell, 1984; Axthelm, 1970; Dryden and MacGregor, 1989; Winningham and Reinert, 1979).

One book by a geographer which does address the sports landscape directly is an excellent study of *Scotland's Golf Courses* by Robert Price (1989) but the author's background and expertise in geomorphology, while informing our understanding of the Scottish cultural landscape in terms of the variety of physical landforms colonised by golf, prevents him from looking at its broader meaning and its landscape iconography.

Each of the key words in this book, sport and landscape, is ambiguous and neither is easy to get to grips with. Each word's connotations have changed over time and there is little agreement about their meaning. Let me first briefly state how I interpret the notion of sport.

THE NATURE OF SPORT

A number of philosophers have applied their insights to the question 'what is sport?' (e.g. Hyland 1990; Osterhoudt, 1973; Vanderzwaag, 1972; Weiss, 1968) and some of their ideas will be referred to in subsequent chapters. Although George Bernard Shaw (1915: xi) was alluding to 'blood sports' when he noted that 'sport is a difficult subject to deal with honestly', he could quite easily have been dealing with sports *per se*. The notion of 'honesty' (or at least, 'telling the truth') in dealing with any subject presupposes an awareness of a number of points of view, many of which may be unknown to those reared on *status quo* ideology. One can only be honest about what one knows and, as a result of simple bias, sport is generally regarded as 'a good thing', critical evaluation coming almost only from the field of sports sociology. The critique may sometimes be over-generalised or strident as, for example, in early neo-marxist work (Brohm, 1978; Rigauer, 1981; Vinnai, 1973). In later chapters I will seek to adopt a critical perspective, though in a far from unqualified way. One of my reasons for caution is that I believe the experience of sport is highly fractured, partly as a result of the wide variety of people involved but also because of the variety of activities in the total syllabus of sports. And the landscapes within which sports take place are themselves perceived differently by the people involved.

Despite the philosophical attention which sport has received, Stone (1972: 5) has noted that games and sports 'simply cannot be differentiated analytically'. And 'any right definition presupposes that the phenomenon can be reduced to the kind of manageable proportions required for the isolating of its "essence"... [but] ... language is social and changing; meanings depend upon the context in which words are used and there is no reason to suppose a common core of meaning can be attached to a single word' (Holt, 1989: 361). So in the end, sport – which does not seem to be reducible to a single essence – is regarded as what we make it; or it is the kind of thing that sports writers record on the sports pages of the newspapers. Sports can therefore be regarded as 'those practices defined as sports by those institutions engaged at any time in defining them' (Wickham, 1992: 220).

A BODY-CULTURAL TRIALECTIC

Rather than start by trying to define the amorphous word 'sport' an alternative is to start with the *body*, an approach widely used by Henning Eichberg (1983; 1988, 1993a; 1993b), to whom I referred earlier. I will attempt to illustrate his basic idea by using the example of the various forms of running. These, for want of better terms, can be described as play, physical education or sport and are three possible configurations of the *movement culture* or *body culture* of running which in Eichberg's terms, make up a body cultural *trialectic*. If the philosophical underpinning of the body culture is achievement-oriented with the primary objective of running being absolute or relative victory (that is, winning or achieving a personal record, however that might be measured) it is clearly something different from running when the emphasis is placed on exercise, hygiene and fitness, or on play, frolic and gambol. Each philosophical starting point results in the malleable human body assuming a different form, resulting from different kinds and degrees of disciplining. Each also results in the malleable surface of the land assuming a different form. The same *trialectic* could be applied to swimming, football, ice skating, gymnastics, cricket, tennis, and all other forms of human and animal movement.

These interpretations of sport can be summarised with reference to Figure 1.1. This illustrates a 'sports trialectic', which stresses the ideological under-pinnings of each configuration of a body culture (Eichberg, 1983; 1988; 1990a; 1993a; 1993b). It avoids focusing on the dichotomised or dualistic approach of establishing what is sport and non-sport – *A* and *not-A*; in such a focus there is no *B* or *C*. Figure 1.1 indicates the possibility of not only including *B* and *C* (and potentially *D* etc.) but also the changing emphasis between each form of body culture at different points in time or space. So elements of play and sensuousness may creep into serious sport; likewise, serious sport may be incorporated into hygienicist or welfare body culture (as in physical education). Neither is it *inevitable* that serious sport should be the dominant body cultural

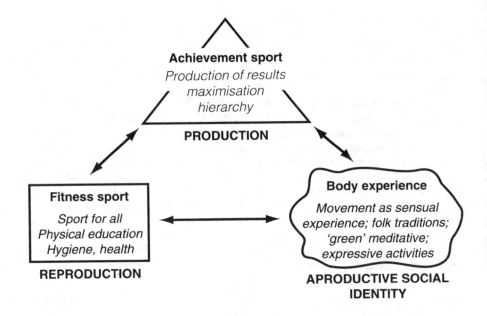

Figure 1.1 An interpretation of various forms of movement culture. (After Eichberg, 1989a, 1990a; 1993b)

model, or even the only *modern* model of body culture (Eichberg, 1991: 122-3).

According to this view recreation and sport are two different things though not necessarily mutually exclusive; recreation may adopt sport-like characteristics and vice versa. But recovery and leisure (that is, re-creation) are required following serious sporting activity, be it training or competition. Some sports may, in fact, be contrary to good health and the number of injuries and even deaths which are a possible outcome of some are unlikely to be considered as serious risks to be encountered in play and physical hygiene. The kind of 'sport' I have been describing so far is better termed achievement sport and sometimes élite-sport or show-sport. I say 'sometimes' because sport can be serious even if it involves only modest levels of performance. Who is to say that the 3 hour 30 minute marathon runner is any less serious an athlete than her élite compatriot who can run an hour faster? Achievement sport (*Leistungssport*) is often (but not necessarily, as my above example makes clear) professional and is additionally characterised by a specialisation of roles (including the separation of genders), competition, quantification, record-keeping, record-breaking and bureaucratisation (Guttmann, 1978; 1988). These characteristics are also usually taken to distinguish modern sports from their pre-modern equivalents.

Each type of body culture has its own ethos; contrast 'winning is everything' with 'enjoyment is what matters'; or 'racing for the record' with 'frolic in the forest'. As a result, each type can be said to create not only different kinds of people/bodies but also, and of central significance to this book, different types of landscape and architecture (Wickham, 1992; Eichberg, 1993b). Landscapes of achievement contrast with those of social hygiene and sensual experience. Whether a particular form of body culture is play, recreation or sport has, therefore, important implications for the kinds of landscapes we see around us. Recreation and play do not require spatially demarcated areas, often of monoculture; nor, necessarily, does training for sport; but sporting competition does. Such specialised areas may be used for sport competition, training, or both and although the training landscape is not prescribed in any official set of rules it is often the same as that used for competition. A society uninterested in achievement sport (Maoist China, for example) would require few of the present day facilities for football, running or swimming and, as a result, its landscape would be quite different from ours.

The bureaucratisation of sports included the specification and administration of the various sites and landscapes upon which sporting action takes place but these landscapes may be regarded as highly masculinised in the sense that while claiming to be 'the norm' they have a long tradition of excluding or ignoring women. For example, the Olympic Games excluded women until 1920; in Britain relatively few women play football; in Kenya there are many more male than female runners. In addition, the men who initially organised sports were generally members of the upper and middle classes. Sports diffused 'down' the social hierarchy and the working classes were often required to adopt professionalism in order to compete on more equal terms with the leisured amateurs. Versions of the same sports were usually adapted for women later with the spatial parameters and the athletic performances often being adjusted and related to an implict masculine norm (Rose, 1993: 44; Willis, 1982: 122). Women's sports have gradually mimicked their male equivalents, though many sports landscapes remain unevenly populated in terms of gender and social class. The relative underpopulation of this landscape by women results less from their active opposition to incorporation into an activity dominated by men than from the widespread view that sport is still basically a masculine activity.

FROM DISPORT TO SPORT; FROM PLAY TO DISPLAY

Although it might be possible to claim renaissance Italy as the home of modern sport it is more often regarded as an eighteenth and nineteenth century English invention, an accompaniment of industrialisation, rationalism and modernity. Before that most 'sport' was closer to its etymological root – disport – but with modernisation it became less like play and more like display (Stone, 1970). 'Play' became 'work' and spectators became more numerous than participants, encouraging the spectacular. The modal decades of sports development were those of the late nineteenth century when activity after activity became rulebound and governed by a male-dominated bureaucratic organisation which meticulously maintained records and results. Swimming, running, kicking, hitting, fighting, twisting and turning – and various folk games – were all forms of movement culture which became 'sportised' or 'sportified'.

In Britain, the precursors of sports were invariably local games of various kinds but in other European countries, notably in Germany and Scandinavia, sports also emerged from physical exercises with an educational and hygienic, rather than a competitive rationale. Gymnastics, for example, initially placed greater emphasis on 'style' and principles of hygiene and posture; only later with the adoption of points to produce a ranking system did the emphasis shift to winning and it too became a sport. Similar sportisation took place in diving and judo.

It is a plausibe claim that 'the first laws ever to be voluntarily embraced by men (sic) from a variety of cultures and backgrounds are the laws of sports' (Mazrui, 1976: 411) and these laws are crucial to the contents of this book. Without laws which were accepted over large areas, inter-regional competition was difficult if not impossible and the laws of sports were drawn up to make competition between geographically dispersed teams more meaningful. To enforce these laws, national (or in large countries, regional) bureaucracies (i.e. sports associations) were set up. In western nations the cumulative frequency curves for the growth of such associations display a pattern of initially slow but subsequently rapid (late nineteenth–century) growth, characteristic of many cultural innovations (Bale, 1989: 45, 50-56).

As sports diffused internationally the formation of national governing bodies was followed by similar *global* organisations but western sports did not simply take root in virgin soil; they were often firmly implanted – sometimes ruthless-ly – by imperialists, while in other cases indigenous élites sought to imitate their masters in order to gain social acceptance. Such sports-colonisation was at the expense of indigenous movement cultures and as cultural imperialism swept the globe, sports played their part in westernising the landscapes of the colonies – tennis and golf courses, race tracks and football pitches becoming permanent features of the cultural environment while evidence of indigenous games often became relict features of the landscape.

The laws drawn up by the sports bureaucracies almost always included the spatial parameters within which the sporting action was to take place. It is this explicitly spatial character of the globally applied rules of sport which has such an important impact on the sports environment since it facilitates global 'body trading' (Shilling, 1993: 20), permitting people from different cultures to make sense of the sports landscape by encouraging 'sameness' wherever it might be in the world. Although the 'globalization of culture is not the same as its homogenization' (Appadurai, 1990: 307), the globally enforced rules of sport encourage sameness, homogenisation and placelessness to an extent not so commonly found in such global common denominators as tourism, leisure or work. Even if one was to accept the rather unconventional view that modern sport is essentially the same as its antecedents in that each are 'the ritual sacri-fice of physical energy' (Sansome, 1989: 37), the modernity of sport (in the sense that word is used in this book) is demonstrated by its standardised spatial and environmental forms. Today, a squash court or a running track is essential-ly the same whether it is in London or in Lagos. Sports, therefore, are versions of what Appadurai (1990) calls 'technoscapes', each having roots in a number of multi-national organisations (sports' governing bodies) which, with the help of modern technology insist on certain standardised landscapes within which sport is allowed to take place. I will return to this fun-damental *spatial* character of sport later but, in passing, note that the spatial characteristics of the earth's surface have tended to be analysed by scholars from several academic fields, but notably from geography, geometry, architecture and horticulture. Each is also central to sport and I draw on work from these 'disciplines' in the pages which follow. Each is also central to the concept of landscape, the subject to which I now turn.

CONCEPTS OF LANDSCAPE

Like 'sport', landscape is a slippery term. It appears that it was originally applied to paintings from sixteenth century Italy (Cosgrove, 1985: 52), though more frequently associated with Dutch landscape painting which signified beautiful natural scenery. Later it came to refer to 'pleasing prospects' themselves, rather than to pictures of them (Olwig, 1992: 16) and later still was used as a verb meaning to 'prettify'. It has therefore been argued that the word traditionally connoted 'rural-*Gemeinschaft*-good' (Pugh, 1990a: 1) but this hardly applies to landscapes of sport which are mainly urban-*Gessellschaft* – and often bad. The sports landscape is certainly not necessarily the result of 'prettification'.

Sports are not natural forms of bodily movement. The landscape upon which such body culture takes place is therefore generally regarded as part of the *cultural* landscape and, for the purposes of this book, will be taken to include everything we see around us, including people and buildings in a sports context; it is more or less synonymous with the scenery of sports. The sports landscape is one of many ordinary or vernacular landscapes which have tended to be ignored by students of the cultural scene (Cosgrove, 1989a: 133) and few people think of ski-slopes, golf courses or hockey arenas as landscapes (Lewis, 1979: 11). But these are among the most human of landscapes, making up part of our 'unwitting biography, reflecting our values, our aspirations and even our fears in tangible, visible form' (Lewis, 1979: 12). These can be counted among what have been termed 'alternative landscapes' – or 'the taken-for-granted landscapes of our daily lives' (Cosgrove, 1989a: 131) whose symbolisms are waiting to be de-coded. These landscapes stand in contrast to those of high or dominant culture – the landscaped gardens of country seats, the grandeur of cathedrals and palaces, or the national seats of power in our great cities. Whether reflections of high or low culture, however, landscapes can 'take on the very character of human existence. They can be full of life, deathly dull, exhilarating, sad, joyful or pleasant' (Relph, 1985: 23). Sports landscapes are no exceptions.

The broad interpretation of landscape outlined above allows me to explore it from a number of different perspectives. It has been suggested that the landscape can be researched by the use of three possible paradigms (Punter, 1982: 102). These are:

(a) the perception paradigm which explores the links between vision, perception, comprehension, preference and action in attitudes towards landscapes;
(b) the landscape quality paradigm which focuses on the visual and formal qualities

of the landscape, often using quasi-scientific forms of 'landscape evaluation' to evaluate landscape quality; and

(c) the interpretation paradigm which explores the meanings imputed to landscape and its social and cultural content.

Although not totally ignoring the second of these approaches, the contents of this book are, in part, devoted to the perception approach (in relation to landscape preference) but mainly to the interpretive approach. I regard the sports landscape, therefore, as a sign of something beyond itself (Tuan, 1971) and in more ways than one, therefore, I want to explore 'the lie of the land'.

Ten Views of the Sports Landscape

Any landscapes, including those of sports, can be broadly interpreted in different ways and the 'ten versions of the same scene', adopted by Donald Meinig (1979b), can be readily applied to the sports landscape. How might it be viewed?

1) SPORT, LANDSCAPE AND HABITAT

Because sport is a cultural and social phenomenon it is self-evident that sports landscapes are not natural and have been interpreted as basically anti-nature (Galtung, 1984: 14), a theme I return to in Chapter 3. However it is possible for sports participants to encounter and utilise natural landscape for certain sports events and, when the event is over, never return to it. They remain landscapes and never become sportscapes. In sports like orienteering, sailing, white water canoeing or cross country running, nature can be used for sport but not 'sportised' in any permanent sense. Athletes may also come into close contact with nature during their training. Here, the human impact is less than in the case of competitions and the athlete is able to enjoy nature much more than in a competitive situation when the senses are more narrowly focused on achievement. Running, swimming or skiing in a natural landscape invariably enhances the sporting experience. Impressions of nature and environment are important elements of the athlete's experience, relations with nature being full of emotions and memories (see Chapter 6).

2) SPORT, LANDSCAPE AND HABITAT

To an extent, the sports landscape can be regarded as part of the human habitat, a conscious decision having been made for slopes, soils, elevations, sites and routes, fields, channels or relief features to be used as homes for sport. In such cases humans rearrange nature into various sport-related forms in a harmonious way – an adjustment to nature but not the overwhelming conquest of it; the sport landscape, therefore, becomes a blending of humanity and nature, analogous to a garden (see Chapter 3).

3) SPORTS LANDSCAPES AS ARTIFACTS

Humanity's power to modify the surface of the earth has changed dramatically over time. Virtually none of the present-day British landscape can be strictly termed 'natural', such has been the human impact on it. Today many sports landscapes seem to disregard the natural or semi-natural landscape upon which they are found. This view sees humankind as the conqueror, not the modifier of nature, with sports landscapes made of concrete, plastic and glass totally destroying and providing no evidence or legacy of what went before. Many sports seem to have a fixation with the environment so that in many sporting environments nature has been neutralised by a totally flat synthetic surface in an indoor arena.

4) SPORTS LANDSCAPES AS SYSTEMS

The stadium, the swimming pool or the route of a cycle race may be landscapes given over to sport but they can also be viewed as but part of intricate econom-ic or physical systems. A sports stadium, for example, does not exist in isola-tion; it generates flows of people and spatial interactions over an area much greater than that of the stadium itself (Bale, 1992b: 82). The *Tour de France* generates economic multiplier effects on the places through which it passes; it is part of an economic system. Sports events are also part of physical systems; an absence of snow may affect performances at ski events; rain may deter attendances at team sports; altitude can affect performance in track events. This view of the sports landscape, therefore, sees it as an 'immense input-output matrix' (Meinig, 1979b: 38).

5) THE SPORTS LANDSCAPE AS PROBLEM

The observer who views the the the sport landscape as having 'gone wrong' and needing correcting in some way sees an excessive dominance of sport over nature leading to social or environmental pollution, erosion and visual blight. Such problem landscapes occur in a variety of sports and in quite different ways. Traffic congestion and crowding resulting from the hosting of a sports event in an inner city stadium is one example (Bale, 1992b); another is the ero-sion of soil and plant cover on ski pistes in alpine regions. The former are tem-porary but annoying to many people; the latter are permanent but, paradoxical-ly, annoying to few. When the sports landscape becomes perceived as a prob-lem it can lead to political activism and the rejection of sporting events which might have induced landscape change. The sports landscape can therefore be interpreted as being the result of political contestation. Sports landscapes, like other cultural landscapes, do not 'just happen'. They are often the result of the exercise of power by one group over another – the imposition of 'territoriality' (Sack, 1986) whereby certain people can be excluded from a prescribed geo-graphic space. Power may be reflected in landscapes where a strong degree of control is needed over people, as in football stadiums in Britain (Bale, 1992b) or where exclusion is on the basis of social or economic criteria as in élite sports landscapes such as the rowing regatta milieu at Henley-on-Thames or its socially-related seascape at Cowes. Sports landscapes may also generate the exercise of power against authority so that while some new sports landscapes may be welcomed by some interest groups others may contest them by the use of various forms of political activism. These views of the sports landscape will also be alluded to in later chapters.

6) SPORT LANDSCAPE AS WEALTH

Except possibly in the case of golf or in the pastoral myths (Chapter 7) sur-rounding sports like baseball or cricket, it is difficult to accept the view that 'built into the idea of landscape is a conservative resistance to capitalism, espe-cially financial capitalism (and that) the power of landscape (is) to give the impression that far from being implicated in the commodification of land and any attendant class tensions, it represented a world of nature, or a world where land and life were in harmony' (Daniels, 1989: 206). The sports landscape is more accurately represented by the widely held view that land is a raw materi-al, one of the economists' factors of production. The notion of the possibility of a financial return on landscapes of sport is not new. But it is not only the long term returns on landscapes given over to sport that are important; one-off events can generate large amounts to local areas. The 1978 Open Golf Championship, for example, created receipts amounting to £3,231,000 for the St. Andrews region (Blake et al.: 1979, 20). City, regional and national boosters have long seen sports as a form of place-boosting for purposes of attracting investment. Stadium landscapes are often developed by municipalities, banks or corporations with a view to rental profits and golf courses are these days rarely constructed solely with the golfer in mind. The sports landscape is lit-tered with advertising hoardings and other evidence of corporate sponsorship. The sport landscape does not only generate wealth itself; it can effect the wealth of others – positively and negatively. Prices for similar types of housing tend to be higher if they are adjacent to golf courses than if next to football sta-diums (Bowen: 1974).

7) SPORT LANDSCAPE AS IDEOLOGY

The sports landscape can be viewed as a reflection of various ideologies. In some countries the sports landscapes are very explicit responses to nationalism, new national sports being 'invented' in order to distance themselves from more dominant neighbours. A cultural viewpoint might see the 400 metre synthetic running track as a reflection of the achievement ideology – the desire to achieve better and better (i.e. faster and faster) performances. The synthetic nature of the track, the massive television screens sited at each end of the stadi-um instantly presenting replays of each event, the timing equipment recording performances to one-hundredth of a second, the 'container architecture' of the sports hall, and the concrete stadium might also be seen as the triumph of mod-ern sport over nature – a reflection of modern technocentric ideology. The sports landscape may also reflect, in its design, a more explicit political ideolo-gy. Who can visit the landscape of the 1936 Berlin Olympics and not still be struck by its Nazi iconography?

The human occupance of the sports landscape also reveals, through its highly gendered character, the dominance of men in sport and its organisation. Sports landscapes can therefore be read as masculine landscapes (see Chapter 4). Few gender specific sports have been formulated and organised by women and women's sports are mainly mimetic versions of the activities of men. In addi-tion, the rational, straight-lined, quantified landscapes of sport are associated by many feminists with 'dominant masculinities' (Rose, 1993: 7).

8) SPORT LANDSCAPES AS HISTORY

'A landscape is the most solid appearance in which a history can declare itself' (Inglis, 1977b: 489) and it is possible to see the present day landscape of sport as the result of a cumulative process of historical evolution. Sports landscapes are often accumulations. To adapt a quotation from Meinig (1979b: 43), the size, shape, material, decoration, outbuildings and position of a stadium may tell us something about the way people experienced sport. Just as each stadium has a builder, however, each landscape can be interpreted as having an 'author' and a historical/economic context. Sport can therefore be seen as a 'world of authored landscapes' (Samuels, 1979: 67) where the hand of individuals, their ambitions, and their perceptions become important in explaining the present day scene.

9) SPORT LANDSCAPE AS PLACE

Although landscape and place are often distinguished on the basis of geographical scale, the former being broader and less prescribed than the latter (Norberg-Schultz, 1979), in much humanistic geography the term landscape has been replaced by the existentialist concept of *place* (Punter, 1982: 106). This view sees landscape as a locality, possessing particular nuances and unique flavours possessing a 'sense of place' – our lives being affected in a myriad of ways by the particular localities in which we live (Meinig, 1979b: 45, 46) For the sports participant – performer or spectator – the experience of place, therefore, could be argued to contribute to the overall sporting experience or, indeed, the sports performance.

10) SPORT LANDSCAPE AS AESTHETIC

The fact that a sense of place will vary between different landscapes implies that such landscapes possess aesthetic qualities predisposing the observer towards one and against another. Some sports landscapes, like all landscapes, will find favour with some fans and lack of favour with others. The aesthetic quality of, say, golf courses is said by golfers to vary considerably but the same is also said about more spatially confined spaces like football stadiums, cricket grounds – even ice hockey arenas. Aesthetics are clearly related to the 'artistic quality' of the sports landscape. But sports landscapes are not only portrayed in earth and vegetation, concrete and timber. They are also shown in paint, film, photograph and print. The sport landscape can therefore be interpreted as one which is sometimes *projected*, subsequently *perceived*, and *interpreted*. It is quite possible, of course, the sports landscapes as portrayed are accurate representations of what actually exists in the physical landscape. But it is also possible that such landscape icons are mythical landscapes, projecting a particular image, sometimes with an explicit purpose in mind. The landscapes of British cricket and American baseball, for example, are frequently projected as natural, rural idylls despite their widespread urban presence and highly technologised practices (Chapter 7).

OVERVIEW

Having outlined my interpretation of sport and landscape it is time now to pre-
view what follows. In this book I will develop further several of the views of
the sports landscape briefly described above. My broad aim is to identify the
nature of the highly rationalised character of the landscapes of modern sport,
how they are (mis)represented and what they mean. Given my loose definition
of landscape, the contents of the book are wide-ranging. To an extent, each
chapter stands independently of the others; they are virtually separate essays
which could be read in any order the reader chooses. Although the approach is
inter-disciplinary, in most of the chapters the basic ideas and inspirations have
been drawn from the writings of a small number of cultural geographers.

In Chapter 2 I briefly describe the antecedents of the modern sports landscape. I want to see if the landscapes of body cultures found in selected pre-
modern societies were fundamentally different from those of the modern period
which I cover in more detail in subsequent chapters. The chapter is simply
intended to set the scene for what follows and ends with the emergence of a
recognisably *modern* sports landscape.

Chapters 3 and 4 respectively explore the impact of artifice and geometry on
the sports landscape, each, therefore, treating the sports landscape as artifact,
though artifice and geometry are often used to politicise and control the landscape and to transform it into sources of wealth. Chapter 3 examines the fundamental anti-nature character of sport, the growth of artificiality in the sports
landscape and the impact of technology upon it. The sports landscape is thus
presented as being analogous to a garden – a cultural rather than a natural landscape. I will mainly use ideas developed by the geographer Yi-Fu Tuan (1984)
to illustrate some of the ways in which the sports landscape reflects the power
of human beings over nature – in other words, landscape as ideology.

If Chapter 3 is about sport's conquest of nature, Chapter 4 is about its standardisation, control, delimitation, and segmentation in space. It examines the
character of the spatial parameters within which sports take place and hence
defines the margins of the landscape of sport. The demarcation of space
marked a crucial break with the pre-modern traditions of sport and is interpreted as 'segmentation' or 'territorialisation' of the sports landscape, again drawing on the work of Tuan (1982) and cultural geographer Robert David Sack
(1986). It will be stressed, however, that the spatial limits of sports vary in
specificity and we may therefore conceive of a typology of sports ranging from
those with 'hard' to those with 'soft' spatial limits. The ambiguous character of
modern sport is teased out by comparing it with the world of theatre and by
emphasising the liminality of many of its boundaries.

Because of its achievement orientation, sport is a constituent of another
series of landscapes which make up 'achievement space' (*Leistungsräume*) –
perhaps a variant of a landscape of wealth or productivity – and this forms the
basis of Chapter 5. The modern sport landscape is often a landscape of speed,
facilitating the minimisation of time between two points in space, just like the
landscapes of modern transport – motorways, high speed railway tracks and
international airports. The pressures to produce 'placelessness' in the sports

landscapes invites an exploration of the ideas of Edward Relph (1976; 1981) and I do this with reference to the global sport of track and field athletics. This chapter also highlights, by exploring its landscape, the extent to which this particular sport displays what we might expect of a truly *modern* form of movement culture.

Chapter 6 focuses on the way that sports landscapes, though tending towards placelessness, can nevertheless generate a sense of place – *genius loci* (Norberg Schultz, 1979) or 'topophilia' (Bachelard, 1969; Tuan, 1974). This reflects Meinig's notion of landscape as place and shows that despite the pressures to produce placelessness, noted in Chapters 2 to 5, many sports places remain much-loved elements of the cultural scene. At the same time, of course, it is possible for sports milieux to engender fear and distaste and sports places may also, therefore, provide sources for topophobia. Examples are taken from many sports but particular emphasis is placed on team sports in Britain and America.

Interpretations of sports landscapes by treating them as texts and applying to them the notion of myth (Barthes, 1973) forms the basis of Chapter 7. This approach has attracted the interest of several cultural geographers who see the landscape as a collection of icons (for example, Cosgrove and Daniels, 1989) or 'representations' (Barnes and Duncan, 1992; Daniels, 1993; Duncan and Ley, 1993). From media of various kinds, we obtain mental images which carry many hidden messages of various sports landscapes. Allusions in this chapter are made to British football and American baseball but particular emphasis is placed on English cricket. These are sports in which the idea of myth is, perhaps, most aptly applied, given their strong association with urban/industrial landscapes on the one hand (British football) and rural and idyllic landscapes of summer (baseball and cricket) on the other.

A concluding chapter speculates about the possible nature of sports 'futurescapes' or the landscapes of 'post-sport'. Natural landscapes are, with the help of technology, often reduced to sports 'blandscapes' – even a world of simulations. But science has also created new, flexible uses of space, while, at the same time, providing the means of creating the last sports landscape. These ideas are illustrated by a series of allusions to several environments ranging from those which have continued the tendencies towards immurement to those which have taken to the open air. But, as in other chapters, the ambiguity of *modern* sport is consistently stressed.

NOTES

1. Berman (1983) notes that paradox and contradiction are central to *modern* life. Among the many books on post-modernism, I have found Harvey (1989) and Rosenau (1992) especially useful.
2. The limited number of 'geographical' studies of sport is more apparent than real (Bale, 1992a; see also Riiskjær 1993).
3. 'Sports geography' has not entirely ignored the sports landscape (Bale, 1989; Louder, 1991; Rooney, 1975; Rösch, 1986), but this book seeks to provide the broad synthesis to which Collins (1990: 32) has alluded.

2

THE LANDSCAPE ANTECEDENTS OF MODERN SPORT

What interpretations can be placed on the landscapes of modern sports and in what ways are they different from those of the pre-modern period? These questions form an underlying theme of this book. The sports landscapes of modernity can be fully appreciated only by being aware of what preceded them and for this reason I will use this chapter to briefly explore the landscapes of sport-like activities which existed up to the late-nineteenth century, by which time such activities were beginning to become 'sportised' and to assume most of their modern characteristics.

The pre-modern period was characterised by different attitudes to time and space from that following, first, the Renaissance and secondly the Newtonian revolution. Some observers view the emergence of modern sports as 'the slow development of an empirical, experimental, mathematical *Weltanschaung*' (Guttmann, 1978: 85). In other words, it was part and parcel of (the Eurocentric notion of) modernisation (Lee, 1988: 302) with its associated rationalisation, commodification and differentiation. Western and later non-western society became more time and space conscious – there was to become a time for work and a time for play; and spaces for work and spaces for play, along with a division of labour. Nevertheless, it should be stressed that such 'developments' did not 'just happen' as 'an abstract evolutionary process'; instead a 'more open-ended set of limits, pressure and struggles' (Gruneau, 1993: 87) existed – and continue to exist – out of which the sports landscape has grown.

A paradox of the division of time and space was that work and leisure became more like each other (Thrift, 1981: 64) to the extent that some observers today argue that 'it would be as well to abandon the common sense categories of "work" and "leisure"' (Moorhouse, 1989: 28). This is certainly relevant to the landscapes in which sport is played/worked, being, as they are, ambiguous spaces which always contain elements of 'work' and 'play' at the same time. With the growing segmentation of time and space it might be reasonable to assume that broad changes were taking place in the sports landscape amounting to a shift from a multicultural use of space to one of sport monoculture or 'sportscape'. In other words, the various urban and rural spaces of pre-sportised movement cultures happened to be used for sport-like corporeal activities whereas modern sports landscapes are given over solely to the cultivation of sport, implying a separation of roles (player-spectator) and an associated segmentation of space. It is an exploration of this trend (if trend it be), from landscape to the beginnings of sportscape, that forms the basis of this chapter.

If I adopt the interpretation of sport as outlined in Chapter 1, it is not really possible to describe pre-modern movement cultures as sports and they are usually called folk-games. Historians of sports have paid a good deal of attention to when, how and by whom such games were played, but they say relatively little about where, and in what kinds of places they took place. The notion of sport monoculture as a modern phenomenon is stressed by Eichberg (1990b: 129) when he notes that the sportisation of movement culture in the nineteenth century meant 'the rise of a new world of stadium architecture, of sports halls and sports places with their monofunctional facilities like the synthetic track of standardised length'. Of course, monofunctionalism and standardisation need not be shared characteristics of a landscape. In other words, it is possible to have spaces designed and designated specifically for sport-like movement cultures without them necessarily being standardised to satisfy the requirements of the 'ritual of the record'.

Perhaps the most widely cited folk-game/modern sport dualism is that proposed by Dunning and Sheard (1979) who, among fifteen contrasting properties of folk games and modern sports cite (at least) three which are of particular relevance to the cultural landscape upon which folk-games were, and modern sports are, 'played'. First, whereas modern sport has 'formal and elaborate written rules, worked out pragmatically and legitimated by rational-bureaucratic means' folk-games had 'simple and unwritten customary rules, legitimatedby tradition' (Dunning and Sheard, 1979: 33). Leading on from this is a second dichotomy, namely the contrast between national and international standardisation of rules of modern sports and the regional variation in rules of the folk-games. This is related to a third difference, that is the spatially defined boundaries of modern sports in contrast to the absence of any fixed limits on the territory of folk-games. These dichotomies are taken from a book on the history of British rugby football and it is not clear to what extent they are meant to apply to other sports.

The Dunning-Sheard classification also gives the impression that modern sports are the outcome of a process of evolution which in some way implies that they are superior to, or an 'advance' on, folk games. Eichberg (1991) has suggested, however, that sports are simply different from folk-games (this is implied in his 'trialectic' – see Figure 1.1) and that traditional games may not simply become permanently 'sportised' versions of their former selves but could re-assert themselves in various forms. This denies an evolutionist view, therefore, and later in this chapter I will outline an alternative perspective, that of various 'waves' in sports landscape history. This, of course, also invites a look into the future, a subject reserved for my final chapter.

PRE-MODERN SPORTISH LANDSCAPES

The simple dichotomisation of landscapes into enclosed and open, multi- and mono-cultural, natural and artificial and their respective associations with pre-modern and modern landscapes may encourage an unexamined form of dualistic thinking (Sayer, 1989) and in so doing oversimplify a complex mélange of sporting milieux in both time and space. Such complexity is accommodated, however, by Eichberg's more fluid approach (Figure 1.1) which I outlined in the previous chapter. This is not to say, of course, that no dualisms or polarities exist in the history of sports but I believe that the simple dualisms of open/enclosed and multi- /monofunctional and their identification with pre-modern/modern when describing the history of sports landscapes is an over-simplification. An implication of the modernisation thesis is that few places would have existed in the pre-modern period which were specifically designated for sports, though this is not to say that sophistication was lacking in the spatial organisation of such places. It seems that in some, but not all, pre-modern periods there were, in fact, permanent features in the landscape used for movement and body cultures of various kinds though in the absence of governing bureaucracies standardised spatial parameters were generally absent. The absence of any agreement about the nature and dimensions of sport space meant that in some cases rules had to be mutually agreed among participants before the game could start.

In exploring the complex nature of such pre-modern environments of games I will use some brief case studies of 'tribal', ancient, and pre-industrial games, basing my evidence on information from the hunter-gatherer societies of the Kalahari Desert, from the Greco-Roman world, the tribal nations of north America and from pre- and early-modern Europe.

Games and landscapes in a non-competitive society: the case of the !Kung

During the period of human existence, it has been estimated that over 90 per cent of all people who have ever lived have engaged in hunting and gathering as a means of livelihood (Lee and DeVore, 1968: 3). In other words, the modern period is a tiny stage in the total history of humankind. As written evidence of movement cultures for most of human time remains unrecorded, I am dependent on the evidence of anthropologists, working in the environments of the few remaining hunter-gatherer groups, for extrapolations back in time regarding the impact, or lack of it, that our distant ancestors had on the environment and landscape. I will choose one particular group, the !Kung San of the Kalahari Desert in what is today Botswana.[1]

A fundamental characteristic of !Kung village life is that space is 'undifferentiated as to function' (Draper, 1976: 202). This is reflected in the spatial organisation of their physical games (it is impossible to use the word 'sports' in this context). It has been observed that !Kung games do not involve competition, rules or complex strategies, though this is far from saying that no skill is involved. For example, while watching a game called *zeni*, involving the throwing of a weighted feather (zeni) into the air, catching it before it lands and then re-throwing it, the anthropologist Patricia Draper (1976: 203) never observed participants counting the times a player threw the zeni without missing it. It appeared that the players took part solely for enjoyment or for practicing their individual skills. The players were of mixed age and gender, hence making rivalry meaningless. Such a lack of competitive spirit is, of course, reflected in the sites of such games so that, for example, in stick throwing they throw from approximately the same spot but no marker or line is made on the ground to record the distance thrown (Marshall, 1976: 322). Natural features like anthills are used for certain games but most are played in any open space large enough to accommodate the players. Little evidence exists for competitive sports among the !Kung (Whiting, 1968: 339) except in the case of tug-of-war. The !Kung landscape does not appear to be sportised in any way and in zeni played by young people up to about 15 years of age, it has been noted that players:

> ... reveal a lack of interest in manipulating the environment in order to facilitate the goal of the game. Far from setting the game in a cleared area where the player could have an optimum chance of reaching the zeni as it comes down, the game goes on in the middle of the village or on the periphery just behind the huts. When they play inside the village, the children stumble into huts, narrowly avoid stepping into smouldering hearths, and so forth. When they play on the periphery, they are in the open, unimproved bush and have to dodge around holes in the ground, thorn bushes, anthills, and fallen logs. As one used to the orderly progress of games played according to rules on a green, graded field, I wondered that the children derived as much satisfaction from throwing the zeni as they did. (Draper, 1976: 204)

Sport-like landscapes of Greece and Rome

Given the Greek concept of 'the whole man' and the absence of any distinction between the body and the soul, 'it was as natural for the polis to have gymnasia as to have a theatre' (Kitto, 1951: 173). Hence, an assumption that the games of Greece and Rome were characterised by an absence of specialised facilities and of fixed limits on the territories of games would be quite incorrect. The Greco-Roman world contained many artificially created and often costly arenas, amphitheatres and stadiums. Though used for a variety of purposes, including such events as feasts, banquets, military training, gladiatorial exhibitions and religious ceremonies, it seems probable that at least some of them were constructed primarily with sport-like activities in mind and considerable information exists, for example, about the nature of the environment of what today would be called track and field athletics. But even if the stadiums were built primarily with sports in mind and displayed a considerable degree of sophistication, notably in the remarkably 'modern' notion of a mechanical starting gate (the *husplex*) – yet to be incorporated into twentieth century human racing events – to prevent false starts (Harris, 1973: 28), the events themselves lacked the modern characteristic of standardisation of the distances over which races were run (Gardiner, 1930: 128). The basic unit of distance used in Greek athletics was the *stade*, a distance of around 190 metres and the length of the straight sprint track. Other races were multiples of the *stade*, but were not standardised and various middle and long distance races ranged from 7 (about 1.4 kilometres) to 24 *stades* (about 5 kilometres). In practice, however, standards of measurement differed from place to place and courses therefore varied considerably in distance (Table 2.1). As Guttmann (1979: 43) notes, 'the Greeks, and certainly the Romans, were technologically sophisticated enough to have standardised these distances, but they chose not to'. The pre-modern characteristic of unstandardised spatial parameters for the running courses was matched by the lack of standardisation in the discus, with many variations existing in the weight and size of such implements (Gardiner, 1930: 156).

Table 2.1 Track measurements at selected Greek stadiums; each distance refers to one *stade*

Location	Distance (metres)
Pergamum	210.00
Olympia	192.27
Epidaurus	181.30
Delphi	177.50

Source: Gardiner, 1930: 128

Stadiums also assumed a variety of shapes though the Greek stadium was usually a long parallelogram, the track being rectangular. Races of more than one stade involved the athletes in making sharp turns around a socket or turning point placed on a raised spine (*spina*) along the centre of the course. Preparation of the natural land surface was also required for the long jump, where participants, in Greek games, used jumping weights in each hand in order to aid performance. The long jump had a hard take-off (the equivalent of the modern take-off board) and in front of the board the ground was dug up and levelled to make it soft enough for safe landing and for the feet to make an impression so that the jump could be measured by rods. Individual jumps were marked with pegs (Gardiner, 1930: 144) but rank order of performance seemed to be of greater significance than the absolute distance which was jumped. The stadiums may, or may not have been constructed mainly with physical games in mind. What is clear, however, is that courses and sites were far from being natural landscapes; special places were used for these activities and in some cases specialised sites were prepared with considerable care. Indeed, special sites were also prepared for training purposes. These were often surrounded by trees to provide shade or were, in other cases, training tracks covered by a portico (Harris, 1964: 145).

There seems to be less ambiguity about whether or not facilities were constructed solely for movement culture in the case of the ball-court (*sphairisterion*)and swimming pool. The former, 'a place *specifically dedicated* to ball-play' according to Harris (1973: 84, emphasis added), were common in Greek and Roman times. They were often attached to Roman public baths. The wealthy among the population had private ball-courts, sometimes warmed by a hypocaust for winter play while in the 'luxurious country mansions' of fifth century Roman Gaul the well-to-do 'had *special places* for ball play' (Gardiner, 1930: 234, emphasis added). All ball-courts seem to have been open-air enclosures (Harris, 1973: 85). As wealth grew in the Roman Empire 'natural swimming facilities were supplemented by artificial swimming pools' (Harris, 1973: 118). An indoor swimming pool built in Rome by Maecenas was said to have been maintained to a high standard. It is very questionable, however, whether these ball-courts and swimming pools were used for much more than play and recreational swimming. Evidence of competitive swimming does exist (Harris, 1973: 122) but it was not attractive enough to be a spectator sport and the impression is that the ball games and swimming that took place in these specialised facilities were more akin to play or hygiene than to anything approaching serious competitions.

Much more typical of the pre-modern model of sporting land use was Greek horse racing. This took place on land ordinarily used for agricultural purposes and all that was needed to 'prepare' for races was to remove stones from the course and to install two turning posts (Harris, 1973: 162). In the more affluent Roman Empire, however, the racecourse became housed in majestic structures, the most famous being the Circus Maximus which had a capacity of over 250,000 people (Harris, 1973: 186). Geometry, a characteristic of the modern sports landscape (Chapter 4), was present in equestrian events, the Greeks using staggered starts for their horse races while in Roman chariot races the lanes were marked out with chalk (Harris, 1973: 189).

This brief sampling of Greco-Roman sports space indicates that far from movement cultures taking place in natural landscapes and unenclosed environments, a high degree of specialisation and spatial organisation characterised the stadium and the later hippodromes. On the other hand, these landscapes were in no way standardised; immediate victory over an opponent rather than a lasting reputation as a 'record holder' seems to have been more important; the nature of the performance did not require a landscape of performance.

Game landscapes among native Americans

Of tribal groups, perhaps the most documented in terms of their games and sport-like activities are the indigenous Americans who practised many potential sports as 'occasions for interaction with the mysterious realm of the sacred' (Guttmann, 1988: 14). In other words, they were not secular in the modern sense; as with Roman and Greek 'sports', they were intimately bound up with ritual and religion. Only one, lacrosse, seems to have developed – or have been developed – into a modern sport. Though the basis of this section is the detailed nineteenth century descriptions – both literary and visual – of native American sport-like activities by Catlin (1973) and Culin (1907) it is reasonable to assume that they had remained unchanged for many centuries (Penz, 1991: 56).

It is difficult to generalise about the spatial and environmental character of the games of native Americans, not least because of the extreme geographical variations found in the north American continent and the wide variety of pre-American nations that existed there. From the many tribes of present day

Mexico to the Inuit in the Arctic regions, a rich variety of games have been recorded. All I can do in the space available here is to take selective examples which illustrate my general contention that among native Americans the preparation of sport-like sites was greater than that of the !Kung but less than that of the Greeks.

Of native American games from what is today the southeastern United States, two illustrate the tendency towards some kind of provision for sport-like activities in the landscape, though it must be recognised that the places in which games were played may have had religious, as much as sporting significance. In the early colonial period the most popular game in the southeast was known as chunkee. This was a variety of pole and hoop game in which a small, wheel shaped disc of carefully polished stone was rolled and as it was rolling players cast their poles in order to hit the ground as near the stone as possible when it came to rest. The game involved considerable running as players sought to 'encourage' their poles, in much the same way as modern-day bowlers follow bowls. The game was not played at random sites or locations. Within the plaza of the major Creek towns of the eighteenth century, the largest structure in terms of area was generally the chunkee yard with its smooth surface 'often covered with packed sand' (Hudson, 1976: 423) with banks of earth surrounding it (Catlin, 1973: 222). The size of such yards varied considerably; one near Wilson, Arkansas, measured 46 by 31 metres (Morgan, 1980: 70) while a Choctaw yard recorded by Hudson (1976: 423) was only about 30 by 4 metres. The symmetrical and geometric forms of native American architecture were typified by these yards and although obviously unstandardised, the descriptions noted above confirm the view that a chunkee facility was a '*specially prepared* playing field' (Culin, 1907: 485, emphasis added), both in terms of its shape and playing surface. What is more, in the central plazas of the larger towns of prehistoric America, they were prominent and permanent (or semi-permanent) features of the landscape (Figure 2.1).

Among other major sport-like activities of the native Americans were a wide variety of ball games, several loosely resembling lacrosse. These were usually played on sites similar to that described by Hudson (1976: 409) when describing a Chicksaw ball ground: 'a cleared stretch of river bottom land, and each end of the field was marked by a goal consisting of two poles driven into the ground'. A shinny game is described as being played on a level ground with two low mounds of earth being heaped at either end, the object of the game being to drive the ball between the mounds of the opponent (Grinnell, 1972: 325). Alternatively the goal was marked by vertical posts often with a cross bar. The width and height of the goal varied considerably, as did the length of the playing area. A sample of recorded field sizes shows that their length could range from 100 to 500 metres and their breadths from 150 metres to 200 metres. It has been suggested that in games of extreme importance the area used for shinny could extend as far as 12 kilometres (Oxendine, 1988: 53) though there is a strong suggestion that they became smaller following colonisation by Europeans (Hudson, 1976: 409). The spatial separation of spectators from these ball games appears to have been unenforced and no fencing or roping of fields is in any way evident from Catlin's sketches and oil paintings.

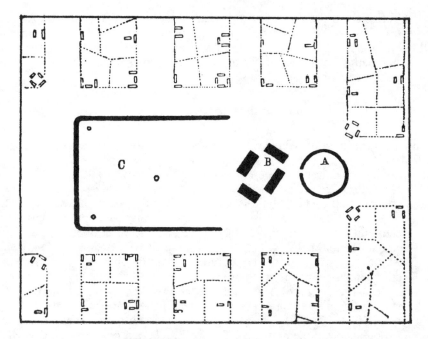

Figure 2.1 The chunkee yard (C) was a major feature of the Creek town landscape, together with (A) the town house and (B) the summer council house. (*Source*: Hudson, 1976: 222)

The running traditions of many native American nations did not, in general, produce running fields akin to those described for chunkee nor to tracks like those of the Greeks. Rituals did encourage certain spatial characteristics of running courses, however, and in Jicarilla society the 'running tracks' tended to lie east-west (Nabakov, 1981: 47). Some modest preparation of tracks also took place; among the Pueblo, 'early on race day the track was scrupulously swept' (Nabakov, 1981: 91). Tracks varied in size, from 300 metre straights recorded in the Crow nation to a 5 kilometre track 'formed like a giant horseshoe, so that start and finish lines were but a hundred yards apart' (Nabakov, 1981: 84). In the Osage nation a four kilometre training track was 'constructed' in order to keep warriors fit (Nabakov, 1981: 84). It also seems likely that in some native American nations, monofunctional running tracks existed. For example, a report of a three mile race course used by the Mandan tribe in 1892 noted that 'it was a level prairie and was cleared of every obstruction and kept in condition *for racing purposes only*' (quoted in Oxendine, 1988: 81, emphasis added).

It is clear from this brief sample of descriptions that native American movement cultures did make some impact on the natural environment and that specific sites were constructed for certain ritual sport-like activities. Unlike the !Kung, the native American nations often exhibited a fierce competitive spirit in their games. Scoring systems existed and a winner was found in some of the most simple of games. This greater seriousness with regard to movement culture is reflected in the greater prominence of the landscape provision for such activities. Chunkee courts remain as archeological features in the landscape (Morgan, 1980), hence showing the fixed nature of such sites. At the same time, such activities differ greatly from the landscapes of modern sports in the sense that they were not standardised.

Stones, fields, courts and houses

In an intriguing paper on early Scandinavian stone labyrinths, Eichberg (1989b) speculates that such arrangements may have been the world's first 'sportsgrounds'. Though greeted with scepticism by some observers (e.g. Hansen, 1991), Eichberg's basic idea, that the labyrinth originated as a place of dance, riding, ball games, running and ritual fighting exemplifies further the point made in my discussion of native Americans, that some pre-modern tribal movement cultures did not simply take place anywhere but favoured particular sites and locales and that physical structures, rather than 'open space' may have been used to 'contain' sport-like activities, even though they may not have been constructed solely with that purpose in mind.

As a general rule, however, it seems likely that the 'sports' of the medieval and early modern period were less specialised than those of Greece and Rome (Guttmann, 1978: 37). The folk-games of the later period covered a vast spectrum of rough and tumble activities. The medieval countryside, as evidenced by written records and in the many paintings of Pieter Bruegel for example, show physical games and various movement cultures going on in village streets and town squares, in fields and woodlands, in rivers and on frozen lakes. This tradition of outdoor physical activity had existed from the tenth century. From Scandinavia we know of archery and spear throwing, skiing, skating, running, swimming, jumping and various fighting 'sports'. Ball games were common throughout the British Isles and France, a wide range of jumping events in Germany and various forms of wrestling were found from Iceland to Switzerland.

In the French ball-game "choule" or "soule", church portals, walls, field boundaries and even puddles were chosen as "goals" and the use of church yards for folk-games was common, as were the streets of towns and commons of the countryside (Eichberg, 1986: 101). Though the character of 'soule' varied with location it can be inferred from descriptions of the game that common characteristics were the necessity of hitting a target made up of a vertical surface (for example, a church porch) and throwing or kicking from a horizontal surface (the town or village square). In some cases the vertical target was a pond or lake where the ball had to be pushed down (rather than thrown up as in the case of the porch). We can still see these vertical and horizontal dimensions in modern rugby (Quilis, 1991).

It was not simply the mass of the population whose games were practised in unconfined spaces in the open air. The Florentine nobility took part in a form of football known as *calcio* which was played on the frozen Arno and in the Piazza Santa Croce and other squares. Such examples would support the view that the environment of pre-modern movement culture was an existing landscape with the various forms of games taking place in the open air on sites not designed specifically with sportive activities in mind. This mixed use of space was one of the classic characteristics of the pre-modern period. But this is not to say that the environments of medieval sportive activities lacked geometric characteristics. Indeed, some historians argue that exact measurements were applied to medieval and especially Renaissance sports places. Even the usually-regarded rough games of English folk football are believed by some to have possessed certain modern characteristics. For example, it has been claimed that near Newark in the mid-fifteenth century a game of football was played in which spatial boundaries 'had been marked', the inference being that this was an activity 'conducted within some framework of acceptable rules' (Young, 1968: 19).

Much firmer evidence of some form of rudimentary sportisation is provided, however, from the fifteenth and sixteenth century Italian renaissance. In a book by Antonio Scaino on ball games, published in 1555 and described as a text 'which bristles with numbers', are the dimensions of small and large tennis courts (McClelland, 1990: 57) while in a treatise on the 'ideal standard form of *calcio*' written in 1580 by Giovanni Maria Bradi, the dimensions of the playing area are explicitly stated (McClelland, 1990: 55). Such spatiality in Renaissance sport displays 'modern' characteristics with respect to landscape and place, notably the elimination of the possibility that one of the teams would be unfamiliar with the size of the playing area (McClelland, 1990: 56) and can be seen as part of the Renaissance task of perfecting God's creation (Cosgrove, 1989b: 194). Likewise, the sixteenth century Venetian noble, Daniele Barbaro, proposed a hierarchical ranking of 'public drama into *theatre*, properly so called, an enclosed structure for the performance of scripted plays and musical recital, *amphitheatre* for athletics and feats of physical prowess and *circus* for the performance of gladiators and animals. Each should have its own appropriate building and location in the city' (Cosgrove, 1990b: 235, emphasis added). Interestingly, the degree of 'enclosure' in each kind of movement culture was related to social class, the closed and covered space being reserved for the 'highest orders', away from the 'vulgar eyes' which watched athletics and animal sports in the open arena (Cosgrove, 1993: 238). Such a locational strategy and the tightening social and spatial order is again reminiscent of modernity and the precepts of town planning.

The medieval country house and court, as well as the city square and countryside, accommodated Renaissance sport-like activities. One sport which may have achieved the status of having specially designed spaces was tennis. Originally played in the courtyards of castles and monasteries, tennis players would have encountered doorways, windows, and projecting roofs. When the courts 'began to be designed and built *solely for playing purposes*, formerly functional details were incorporated into them because they had become part of the game' (McClelland, 1990: 63n, emphasis added; Eichberg, 1982: 53). In 1590 it was reported that in Paris there were 250 ball courts (Eichberg, 1986: 103) though many of these were likely to have been uncovered (Ross, 1898: 457). In London in 1615 there were said to be only 15 (real or 'royal') tennis courts (Eichberg, 1986). In addition to tennis a number of forms of movement culture such as gymnastics, fencing and indoor equestrian activities took place in the geographically confined, though unstandardised and non-specialised, spaces of halls and rooms in country mansions, stately homes and chateaux of much of sixteenth and seventeenth century western Europe.

The increasing degree of spatial enclosure of the tennis court can be interpreted in various ways (Eichberg, 1982; 1986). First, the indoor courts provided protection from the elements; secondly, the territorial boundaries defined by indoor courts were marked out by the nobility at the expense of commoners who were, literally, put in their place; and thirdly, as noted earlier, the new architecture became part of the game itself.

It is clear from the above examples that seventeenth century Europe contained a number of places specifically designed for body-cultural activities. The examples of the Roman stadiums, medieval ball courts and Creek-American chunkee yards further confirm the pre-modern traditions of such specificity. For the mass of the people, however, the landscapes occupied by sports up to beginnings of the modern age were not specialised; they were multi-cultural rather than mono-cultural. At the same time, I have shown that definitions of the playing area were, in some cases, defined spatially though given the limited geographical interaction between different regions, the rules would have necessarily been local in nature. This tradition continued into nineteenth century Europe but the landscapes of sport were soon to become as specialised as those of other, increasingly rationalised, activities.

SPORT LANDSCAPES IN EIGHTEENTH AND NINETEENTH CENTURY EUROPE

The rest of this chapter describes the developments in the sports landscape in the period immediately before the emergence of monocultural and standardised sportscape in both town and country. I will be careful to show, however, that the enclosure of space for sport did not 'just happen'. Indeed, such spatial confinement was vigorously contested in both town and country – and continues to be contested at the present time as the opposition to all-seat football stadiums in Britain clearly shows (Bale, 1992b). What is more, it cannot be said that monoculturalism and enclosure are the only trends since these are being opposed by contrary tendencies towards openness and the rejection of immurement, themes which I discuss later.

The use of commons, streets and squares

The urban street continued to be used for football and other sportive activities until it began to assume its modern form as an artery for transport in the late nineteenth century. Eighteenth century folk football was a game which took place wherever the ball could be kicked or thrown. Many examples of the spatial freedom of such games and their total lack of geographic confinement could be cited from the numerous historical surveys of the character of football in its early days (e.g. Dunning and Sheard, 1979; Magoun, 1938; Marples, 1954; Young, 1969). For example, in a game between Hitchin and Gosmere (played in Hitchin, Hertfordshire) in 1772, the ball was 'drowned for a time in the Priory pond, then forced along Angel Street across the Market Place into the Artichoke beerhouse, and finally goaled in the porch of St. Mary's Church' (Magoun, 1938: 68). In Derby in the 1800s, football matches, having started in the market place, 'surged at random through the streets, down alleyways, across gardens, in and out of the River Derwent, with the object of reaching the goals situated at opposite ends of the town' (Delves, 1981: 89). These descriptions appear to differ hardly at all from those of street football during the fourteenth and fifteenth centuries. Football was not the only sport-like activity which utilised the street. Pedestrianism took place 'on public highways and when it attracted crowds of spectators it could be seen as a public nuisance' (Golby and Purdue, 1984: 80).

If football was a street game, cricket occupied commons and fields. Agricultural and cricketing land use were far from mutually exclusive and cricket 'usually had to wait for its field until after the first haymaking', the start of the cricket season at any particular place being influenced by its latitude (Brailsford, 1983: 42). Often, fields used for a variety of sports were owned by an adjacent inn which provided changing facilities as well as refreshment. They would often be used for boxing matches, nineteenth century pugilism depending largely on the services of the hostelry (Brailsford, 1991).

In Britain attempts to suppress sport in unenclosed public spaces had existed for centuries. During the seventeenth century the Puritans had attempted, with limited success (Brailsford, 1969: 122-57), to restrict folk-games, using the word of God as an argument. In the nineteenth century the elimination of games such as football from streets and cricket from agricultural land was the result, on the one hand of these sports interfering with economic activities, and on the other from pressures to improve the surfaces and standardise the spatial dimensions of the fields of play. It was a case of growing economic rationality on the one hand and of sporting rationality on the other, though these two were to become inextricably intertwined. Enclosure of land and its resulting effects on folk-games has been well-documented by Malcolmson (1973) and the details of the large numbers of commons, squares, fields and streets on which athletic activities of many kinds became forbidden need not be detailed here (see Malcolmson, 1973: 108 *et seq.*). The town centre location of many folk football games posed a particular threat to the growing commercial imperatives of urban life. 'The centrality of the market-place in playing the games is apt; it is a geographical expression of the underlying forces which were determining and reshaping working class leisure experience' (Delves, 1981: 92). It was often the case, however, that 'where customary playing spaces were nullified, no new alternatives were available' (Malcolmson, 1973: 110). This was to change as the century progressed.

Before the enclosure of sport space in the mid to late nineteenth century, sport and space were not yet specialised. Although certain places may have had vaguely sporting associations, a wide variety of sporting practices took place on them, often taking occupation for short periods of time and leaving no permanent imprint on the landscape. Boxing was often an additional attraction at race meetings or bull-baiting. 'Sports' events consisted of running, horse racing, sailing and cock-fighting, all taking place at the same venue on the same day (Brailsford, 1991: 78).

Just as common and agricultural land was increasingly becoming enclosed, so too was the newly defined sporting land – and for much the same reasons, that is, efficiency and profitability. Space would be made to pay its way. Spatial parameters would not only be placed on the fields of play in the form of visible white lines enclosing the actual playing space but in the broader arena, including the spectators, who also had to be contained. This was not always easy with space-extensive sports such as horse racing and the first enclosure of horse racing events occurred at the course at Sandown Park as late as 1875 though access to grandstands had been restricted earlier, resulting in physical segregation by social class from the first half of the nineteenth century (Delves, 1981: 112). Cricket matches were enclosed by rope or fencing from the 1740s but in Britain the first enclosed sporting arenas on any scale were for pedestrian events from the 1820s (Brailsford, 1992: 81). The first fenced baseball field was at Brooklyn in 1862 (Furst, 1986: 206).

I have dealt in some detail with the spatial enclosure of football elsewhere (Bale, 1992b; 1993) and will here simply illustrate my claim that the territorialisation of sport was a major index of its modernisation in the late nineteenth century by briefly citing a number of examples. Without a line to visibly separate the skilled performer from the less skilled spectator, mixing between the two could easily occur, as was the case with football in England in the early 1880s. As Marples (1954: 163) noted, early modern football continued to involve the considerable mixing of players and spectators at the edges of the field of play, even though the ground itself may have been enclosed. Following the initial codification of major sports like football and cricket there remained very little, if any, spatial distinction between 'players' and 'spectators'. Early games of golf were not necessarily incompatible with the use of land for people taking country walks. Nineteenth century prints and paintings of cricket show spectators and players almost randomly interspersed. It was the drawing up of the boundary lines between players and spectators, the creation of specialised, monocultural sports space, that signalled the end of the period of pre-modern sport. Intermixing of sport and non-sport uses, and that of players and non-players, was clearly a residual form of the folk-games of the pre-modern period but the straight white line heralded a basic characteristic of modern sport, the prohibition ('the ultimate foundation of social space') of the mixing of different groups in geographic space (Lefebvre, 1991: 35).

Rules insisting on a clear and physical (that is, visible) definition of the spatial parameters of sports landscapes were usually drawn up somewhat later than the initial formulation of rules, sometimes by as much as a century or more. The Football Association rules were written in 1863 but the length and breadth of the field of play were initially marked only by corner flags, the touchline not being introduced until 1882. In cricket, the Marylebone Cricket Club (MCC) rules drawn up in 1744 defined the length of the 'wicket' to be 22 yards but the boundary line was not formally included in the game's rules until 1885. In rugby the respective dates of the initial rules and the dead ball line were 1871 and 1891. Other kinds of spatial rules were introduced in this late nineteenth century drive towards geometric regularity; in the American 'gridiron' football game, for example, the minimum yardage gain rule was introduced in 1882 (Riesman and Denney, 1971). As noted in Chapter 1, spatial rules were the crucial factor encouraging – indeed, enforcing – the geographical standardisation of sports places.

Although certain specialised and enclosed facilities such as swimming pools and running tracks were being provided from the 1820s, 1830s and 1840s, the nineteenth century witnessed the gradual increase in provision of spaces in cities with municipal parks and playing fields being provided for various sporting activities. This development coincided with a period of rapid sportisation, in the sense that sports became more codified than previously, including the specification of their precise, and hence replicable and predictable, spatial requirements. A regional example illustrates the pace of such change. Before 1870 there were no enclosed sports grounds within the 320 square kilometres of the east Northumberland coalfield in the north of England, sport taking place on highways, beaches and moorlands. By 1914 over 200 grounds had been enclosed, including 50 football grounds, 16 cycle tracks and eleven private cricket grounds (Metcalfe, 1993: 108). Sponsors of such grounds were often innkeepers, though the agencies involved in the emergence of such specialised facilities were many and varied, both within and between particular regions.

As local parks were providing the specialised land use for mass (male) sport, at the level of the more accomplished performer who people were prepared to pay to watch, the late nineteenth century witnessed the (re)emergence of the stadium which was to become the primary container of the modern urban crowd. A precursor of the modern stadium, in miniature form, accommodated smaller crowds; it was the cockpit. Although cock fighting had been a major recreational diversion of the eighteenth century, it continued to be very popular into the nineteenth (Cuming, 1933: 372). Though often held in conjunction with race meetings or as organised fights in village churchyards, pits were constructed either indoor or out and while not standardised, specialised and purpose-built amphitheatres were built, often in the yards of public houses (Figure 2.2).

The larger stadiums, dominated by those for football and specifically devoted to serious sport grew rapidly from the late nineteenth century. Initially, football clubs used grounds which, during summer, were used for cricket or even horse racing, the football pitch occupying only a relatively small part of the green sward and hence making spectating difficult from certain parts of the ground. Other clubs occupied grounds which included running and cycling tracks, again reflecting a pre-modern tradition of multi-functionality but, at the same time, a considerable distancing between player and spectator (Bowden, 1994). But as football, especially, became more businesslike 'grounds' were claimed by clubs as their 'homes'. They were not initially stadiums, however, but grew, willy-nilly in an unplanned way. Stoke City's Victoria Ground has been the club's home since 1878 and, like many others developed later, grew incrementally before assuming its present fully enclosed form. A typical sequence of events, applied to cricket and football, would probably have been as follows:

Figure 2.2 Cockpit from the yard of the Hawk and Buckle Inn, Denbigh, now found at the
Welsh Folk Museum near Cardiff. (*Source*: Welsh Folk Museum)

(1) roping and subsequently fencing-in of the field, with gates where spectators
    could be charged admission;
(2) sloping banks, sometimes built with rubbish, ash and cinders, were built
    around the pitch so that people could obtain a better view;
(3) small wooden grandstands were built on the half-way line on the western
    side of the field for businessmen who had invested in the club;
(4) further banking and stands were incrementally developed and re-developed
    (Inglis, 1983: 12-3), a process which is still going on today.

A sequence of baseball park development suggested by Shannon and Kalinsky
    (1975: 9; see also Riess: 213-22) includes:

(a) the game being played in open fields;
(b) enclosed wooden ballparks characterising the baseball landscapes from
    1862 to 1909;
(c) the commencement of the concrete and steel era until 1960; and
(d) the development of 'superstadiums' including domes and synthetic sur-
    faces to the present day (see Chapter 8).

Of course, baseball, cricket and football in its various codes continue to be
played on fields of all kinds, often unenclosed, but even in the smallest places
the permanently placed icons – the diamond, goal posts, or sight screens –

remind us of what the place is used for.

On land, therefore, the late nineteenth century witnessed the gradual enclosure of sport and its spatial standardisation. These were intrinsic characteristics of 'fair play' and record orientation but were further encouraged by commodification. But achievement-orientation was not viewed solely in economic terms since sports in which no fortunes were to be made or for which money was rarely taken at the turnstiles or entrances, were also becoming increasingly rationalised.

Water, space and body culture

Apart from washing in domestic baths, today swimming is almost certainly the most popular form of activity in water. Competitive or achievement sport, however, is not the only form of swimming though it has replaced a number of other forms over the last century or so. As a result, the landscape of swimming has changed dramatically.

The movement of the human body in water courses such as the sea, lakes or rivers was far from unknown in pre-modern times though other forms of mobility were favoured. Swimming did not possess the utilitarian value of walking though it undoubtedly was used for purposes of survival (Brailsford, 1969: 184). It was often encouraged as a form of military training (Brailsford, 1969 : 18), as a means of relaxation in hot weather (Brailsford, 1969 : 194) and as a cure for melancholy (Brailsford, 1969 : 165). It may have been incidental to folk football, as, for example, when the ball was carried across rivers during the course of a game.

'Record'-oriented swimming existed in Denmark in the early 1800s. Whereas swimming in Scandinavia had tended to place emphasis on style and decorum in the tradition of physical education, 'during the summers of 1809 and 1810 long distance swimming became a sport' (Kayser Nielsen, 1993a). The body now overshadowed education, swimming becoming achievement for the sake of achievement with competitions involving the longest time it was possible for swimmers to remain in the water. When a swimmer died of over-exertion, however, a limit was placed on swimming time and distance but without recourse to a purpose-built swimming pool. The first swimming club in Germany was formed in Berlin in 1876 and, typical of such early clubs, was as much concerned with health and fun as with competition. Until the end of the nineteenth century swimming festivals among the growing number of German clubs were of a social nature but by the early years of the present century competitions became increasingly standardised and sportised (John, 1986-7). This kind of transition is shown in more detail in Table 2.2 which summarises the three basic kinds of swimming clubs in late nineteenth and early twentieth century Lyon. Whereas the three forms ('festive', 'demonstration' and 'competitive') were of more or less equal significance in the 1880s, festive and the demonstrative forms of swimming declined in relative terms as sportised swimming came to dominate not only the number of clubs but, necessarily, the nature of the swimming landscape.

Table 2.2 Configurations and characteristics of swimming clubs in *fin de siècle* Lyon.
(After Arnaud, 1989: 250)

	FESTIVE	DEMONSTRATION	COMPETITIVE
Characteristics of club's activities	convivial, playful, fun	militaristic, civic pride, educational	performance, champions, fixtures
Types of practice	games, utilitarian	quadrille, breast stroke	speed, crawl, races.
Qualities required	courage, endurance, solidarity, audacity	courage, obedience, solidarity, discipline	competitive, endurance, speed, resistance
Location and landscape	riverine; many clubs on banks of Rhône and Saône.	town centres, urban and rural zones	dispersed, special spaces, standardised

In Britain the first public swimming pool was built in Liverpool in 1828 (Harris, 1975: 99), slightly earlier than the first running track, but almost all early serious competitions took place in unenclosed natural water courses or artificial lakes designed for non-sportive purposes. The flavour of early sport-swimming in England is illustrated by the activities of the Cambridge University Swimming Club, which was set up in 1855 when a bathing shed was built, having a frontage of 120 feet to the Granta. It accommodated 120 male bathers and had a committee room, behind which was an enclosed area of grass with various items of gymnastic equipment. A diving stage existed with platforms at various heights. The racing course had 'a fairly straight reach of 120 yards' with all races of that distance being swum down stream, those of longer distances being swum up and down stream. The notion of the 'record' was already present as it was reckoned that times in the river were about 5 seconds faster per hundred yards than in a swimming bath (Sinclair and Henry, 1893: 329-30). The first national governing body was not set up until 1869, the year in which its initial championships were held in the River Thames (Arlott, 1977: 900). The swimming events at the 1896 all-male Olympics were 'arranged in a somewhat ramshackle fashion in the harbour of the Peiraeus' (Harris, 1975: 100) and those of the 1900 Games at Paris in the River Seine; pollution and 'current assistance' characterised the events (Guttmann, 1992: 22). As I will show in some detail in Chapter 5, rationalisation of sport space did not occur overnight and in the case of swimming, residual characteristics of the early sports landscape continued into the mid, even late, twentieth century.

Figure 2.3 The district swimming championships near Uppsala, Sweden, taking place in a natural water course, 1946 (*Source*: Moen, 1990: 278)

the early sports landscape continued into the mid, even late, twentieth century. Rivers, lakes and coastal waters continued as the locations for quite important swimming competitions. But increasingly water was becoming spatially contained and controlled. In Copenhagen, for example, organised swimming races took place during the first quarter of the present century in the sea at Helgoland where a wooden structure enclosed several open air salt water basins (Lyngsgård, 1990: 115-6; see also Nagbøl, 1991). A considerable amount of serious swimming and diving took place in natural water courses into the 1950s, for some age categories national championships taking place in coastal waters, separated from the open sea by wooden beams and floating walkways. I can recall seeing the Welsh junior championships taking place in the sea at Tenby in Pembrokeshire in the late 1950s. Elsewhere, championship events took place in lakes and rivers with permanent structures such as changing rooms built alongside (Figure 2.3). Although displaying a number of characteristics, such as bureaucratisation, record-keeping and record-seeking, and internationalisation, the sports landscape clearly retained a number of pre-modern features.

In most cities of the western world, swimming clubs and indoor pools had grown rapidly in number by the mid twentieth century. In so doing a shift had not only occurred from the festive and demonstrative to the sportised forms of swimming but also from natural waterscapes to the rectangular and regular 25 metre or 50 metre pools as required by the competitive forms of swimming. It was not until the last quarter of the twentieth century that the geometric regularity of rectangular pools – designed for achievement sport but widely used by less serious swimmers – was challenged by the growth of 'water worlds' and the different bodily experiences associated with them (see Chapter 8).

The machine, the body and its enclosure

Much of what I have described already has been primarily focused on athletic competition and not on the training which is a necessary requirement for participation in performance-oriented sport. Although training can, and often does, take place in exactly the same environment as the competition, it is not required to do so and athletes, therefore, often undertake training and exercises indoors for competitions which might take place in the open air. I have already noted that real tennis had a tradition of specifically designed indoor spaces from the mid sixteenth century. But by the early eighteenth century the marketing of the body became increasingly connected to the marketing of fitness equipment (Borgers, 1988). The period not only witnessed the immurement of body cultures; it also began to witness the development of 'motion-machines' which enclosed the body in a different way. As early as 1735, for example, a tract dealing with a 'riding machine' was published in Leipzig while vaulting horses, parallel bars and springboards all served to 'intensify production' of German gymnastics (Eichberg, 1986: 48). Specifically technical sports were also emerging during the late nineteenth century – cycling and motor sports being the most obvious examples – where the machine served as an extension of the body and satisfied the sporting urge for strength and speed. In a late nineteenth century Alfred Jarry observed the man-machine relationship, describing the bicycle as an 'external skeleton' (Hoberman, 1992: 9) while in a French novel about cycling (*Vocie des ailes!*, Maurice Leblanc), one of the characters comments that cycling was not a case of *man and machine* but one of a *faster man* (Kern, 1983: 113). Although the mechanised body was able to become increasingly mobile and speedy, body machines in places of spatial confinement have, of course, continued to the present day with fitness studios and video-aerobics being the successors of the earlier machines for 'static motion'. Body-machines put a new gloss on the notion of modernity as – in this case literally – 'an iron cage of conformity'.

Not for nothing has the late nineteenth century been labelled 'the Age of Calibration' which witnessed a 'mania for measurement' (Hoberman, 1992: 5) and in sport, as elsewhere, the enclosure of space was matched by an enclosure of time. Built into the rules of sports were time limits as well as space limits and an important item of a referee's equipment in football and other team sports became the increasingly reliable stop watch or arena clock. The growing sophistication of timekeeping in sports, however, is best illustrated from events which involved racing, notably athletics. Matches against time in running necessitated reliable watches. Times of sporting competitions were measured to the half-minute in the 1670s, to the second by the 1750s, and to quarters of a second in the 1880s, reducing further to one-hundredth of a second a century later (Eichberg, 1982: 47). Quantitative data collected from horse racing events began to be studied scientifically from the 1880s, extrapolative mathematical analyses being applied in order to predict future performances. The prediction of future human athletic records was likewise made from 1906 onwards (King, 1986-7: 306-7). The stopwatch 'became a symbol of the new combination of striving for achievement, measuring that achievement, and the dynamics of time: a symbol of increase, growth and progress' (Eichberg, 1982: 47).

GREEN WAVES?

The evolution of the sports landscape is usually interpreted as a linear form of 'development' towards one of increasing rationalisation. For one form of movement culture (that is, sport), it is difficult to deny that this has taken place in the last one hundred years. The dominant form of sport at present seems to be one which shows a 'tendency towards an all-embracing and totalizing industrailization and commercialization [which] will prevail in the immediate future' (Rigauer, 1992: 68). This is not to say, however, that this need be the only form of 'sport' (for want of a better term) or that the 'sportisation' of movement culture is inevitable or that it has been one of linear 'development'. Nor does it mean that all sports fully adopted an unequivocal modernity at the same time, witness the example of the outdoor swimming championships in natural water courses into the 1960s. Neither does it mean that there is an absence of countermovements against an unambiguously modern form of sport, nor that all 'folk-games' simply died out (Tomlinson, 1992: 194). These subjects are dealt with later and for the moment I will simply outline one view which opposes the linearity of the traditional approach.

A non-linear pattern involving 'waves' or periods where outdoor activities were superceded by movements indoors and back again into the open air, with resulting landscape implications, is suggested by Eichberg (1982, 1986, 1988) and while not fully accepted, even by historians in his adopted country of Denmark, it nevertheless provides an interesting alternative interpretation to the views of mainstream sports historians, and, perhaps, the implicit approach of this chapter so far.

The essence of Eichberg's 'green' model of the sports landscape is that its history should not be viewed solely in terms of 'progressive' tendencies – especially at the present time when, as Chapter 8 will show, 'interest is being directed toward counter-tendencies – and for good social reasons' (Eichberg, 1982: 52). Undoubtedly, Europe in the fifteenth and sixteenth centuries was characterised by outdoor body cultures, including those of the nobility. But the feudal nobility sowed the seeds of a period of immurement during the seventeenth and eighteenth centuries, during which the games of the nobility began to take place in enclosed spaces. Spatial segregation, social divisons and the exclusion of children each constituted a new landscape of movement culture; the indoor hall, the fencing and riding schools, gymnastics and indoor tennis paralleled the dancing of the minuet and the insertion of the apron stage typifyied a further form of spatial segregation (see Chapter 4).

This period of interiorisation of the body was followed toward the end of the nineteenth century by a decline of the indoor recreational culture of the nobility. The celebrated riding schools gradually closed their doors, ending with Dresden (1848) and Hanover (1863). The only one to persist, in almost museumised form, was the Spanish Riding School in Vienna. Instead, people turned to outdoor activities, to formless speed-riding in the open, to fox hunting and coursing in the English style and to steeplechasing and horse racing (Eichberg, 1986: 103-4). Ball courts also lost their attraction. Just as horses were taken to the outdoors so were humans. The early nineteenth century phil-anthropic German educationalists, for example, argued for exercise in the open air. J. C. F. GutsMuths believed that education 'thrives best in the bosom of nature...Our gymnastics should, as far as possible, be the outdoors' (quoted in Eichberg, 1986: 104). His views were amplified by Friedrich Ludwig Jahn who established the first gymnastics school in 1811, emphasising uncontrolled play in the open air. Eichberg (1986: 106) notes how, originating in England in the nineteenth century, sport-like activities broke out of the confines of the halls, taking the form of running, rowing, cycling, and winter sports.

The green revolution in movement culture, if it can be so described, of the late eighteenth and early nineteenth century, did not last. Indoor gymnastics, swimming pools, large commercial halls such as Madison Square Garden in New York, the Albert Hall in London and the Sportspalast in Berlin all emerged from the 1850s onward. Such interiorisation of the human body was mimicked at around about the same time by the fascination with the *encase-ment* of plant and animal life in the Victorian middle class home – exotic fern gardens enclosed in glass cabinets and containers of fish, snails and plants (Fuller, 1988: 20; Rees, 1993: 159-63).

As such immurement was taking place, however, the germs of another reac-tion were spreading through western Europe. The late nineteenth century did not only witness a series of non-sportive movements into the open air – tourism, sea bathing, nudism, alpinism, the German *Wandervogel*, scouting – but also a form of popular gymnastics and the rapid emergence of the classic English out-door sports, noted earlier in this chapter. The forms assumed by the landscapes of such sports are described in the chapters which follow.

Eichberg's notion of 'green waves' is an attractive and provocative counter-view to the traditional historical trap of 'linearity' or 'progress'. But it is difficult to know if it is over-stated and at times it comes close to being a simplistic form of dualism. The notion of sport taking to the outdoors in the late nineteenth century may be literally true, but its spatial confinement in straight lines and its increasing rule-boundedness made it as constrained as any game played in the ball courts. The white lines around the field constituted invisible walls. If the present day is considered, it can be seen that no one trend seems to dominate. The number of new indoor sports which are being formulated is probably similar to that for sports taking place outdoors while, at the same time, movements are taking place which seek to neutralise the signif-icance of having special sites at which sports should take place. In addition, different tendencies are occurring within the same sports as subsequent chapters show.

Resistance to territoriality

Before concluding this chapter I think it is important to stress that 'spatial and temporal practices are never neutral in social affairs. They always express some kind of class or other social content and are more often than not the focus of intense social struggle' (Harvey, 1989: 239). Such opposition is implicit in Eichberg's 'green waves' but it is likely that these were new movements in themselves, rather than oppositional strategies targeted at existing forms of movement culture. Nevertheless, many instances of resistance have been recorded, most notably in England in the context of the enclosure of the commons and the appropriation of the streets. For example, several attempts to put down folk-football in Kingston-on-Thames in the 1790s were successfully resisted (Malcolmson 1973: 139). Half a century later at Derby, where in the eighteenth century there had been several unsuccessful attempts to ban Shrovetide football, efforts were made to territorialise street football by banning it from the town centre and re-locating it outside the town – the players being offered financial inducements to do so (Delves, 1981: 90). In 1846, cavalry and special constables confronted football players as a game took place in opposition to mayoral suggestions for more 'rational' recreation. Territorialisation as a solution to street football was also practiced at Alnwick in 1827-8 where 'the Duke of Northumberland provided a convenient meadow for its refuge', a similar locational strategy being adopted in Twickenham in 1840 (Malcolmson, 1973: 142). The movement of eighteenth and nineteenth century football spaces, out of the streets and into peripheral meadows, resulted in the games losing 'much of their peculiar appeal' (Malcolmson, 1973: 142) as is the case with current relocational strategies among British football clubs. Various forms of resistance continue today as the opening paragraphs of Chapter 1 clearly showed.

CONCLUSION

An interesting view of the final triumph of the pre-modern over the modern in a vaguely 'sporting' context has been interpreted as having taken place in December, 1911 when the Norwegian, Roald Amundsen defeated the Englishman Robert Falcon Scott in the 'race' to the South Pole. The criteria used by Katz and Kirby (1991: 260) in this interpretation are based on the fact that for Amundsen the race was 'an expression of an intimate relationship with nature' and that the Norwegians 'had accomplished the task using the materials of everyday life: wooden skis, leather boots, reindeer furs' (Katz and Kirby: 1991, 259), in contrast to Scott's adoption of modern technologies.[2] In subsequent 'races' of this kind, modernity would triumph. If these kind of criteria were applied to more conventional sports it would be interesting to see what date could be placed on the end of sport's pre-modernity. The Renaissance *calcio?* The 1896 Olympics? The Stockholm Olympics of 1912? Or the end of the swimming championships held in natural water courses in the 1950s?

What can be said with some certainty is that on the eve of the present century the sports landscape was already becoming more specialised, it was colonising other landscapes, it was commodified and slowly becoming standardised and technologised. These trends might also be interpreted as a symbolic 'masculinisation' of the landscape, part of which was a growing voyeurism of performance. Certainly by the 1920s 'intimate relationships with nature' and 'materials of everyday life' were disappearing from the world of achievement sport. As early as 1921 the author of a book on the sociology of sport saw the crisis in sport reflecting the 'tendency towards rationalization' to be found in the broader (capitalist) society (Risse: 1921, quoted in Bathrick, 1990: 114) with all the landscape implications this possessed. And it is the inter-war period in which Hoberman (1984: 123) sees sport emerging 'as nothing less than a modern style'. Certainly, by the 1920s a modernist style of sport seemed to have arrived. Sport had become a 'living metaphor of modernity making the world measureable, making the human being productive; "developing" space under the dominance of "dynamic" time. Rationality finds its expression in pure form in the time-place patterns of sport' (Eichberg, 1993c: 4). This is not to say that all folk-games had totally disappeared (see pages 97-99) nor that modern sportscape is without its ambiguities and paradoxes as subsequent chapters will show.

This chapter ends, therefore, with the emergence of the physical culture of an achievement oriented industrial society which did not only 'produce exercises of the body. It also necessitated the establishment of a separate environment in which to pursue them' (Eichberg, 1986: 101). Such 'separate environments' were not unknown in earlier times but the characteristics of modern sports are undeniably different and it is the separate environment of sportscape which forms the subject of the rest of this book.

NOTES

1. The term 'San' is used in preference to the more commonly used, but derogatory, sexist and racist 'Bushman'.
2. As Scott and Amundsen were each motivated by the 'race' to the south Pole it could be argued that there was less difference between them than Katz and Kirby imply (Simpson–Housley and Scott, 1993). Indeed, the intense seriousness of the competition seems decidedly modern.

3

STADIUMS AS GARDENS, ATHLETES AS PETS

In what is arguably still the most sustained case for the centrality of geography in the analysis of sports, the cultural geographer Philip Wagner (1981: 94) noted that 'there is nothing natural about a sports event'. There is, therefore, nothing natural about sportscape, made up as it is of 'an entire class of very closely defined *conventionalized* places' (Wagner, 1981: 92, emphasis added; see also, Giamatti, 1989: 54-5). I will return to the spatial character of such conventional – not, notice, unique or unconventional – places in the next chapter and at this stage will simply note that it is the conventions of sport (or its underlying ideology) which create its own cultural landscapes. It could be argued that being a cultural and not a natural phenomenon, sport imposes itself on the natural landscape and therefore, at root, is anti-nature. Such an imposition (as with so much in modern life) goes far beyond simply killing plants or animals (including humans) for survival; sport is one of the many things that are done once survival is assured and is a plausible reality 'only to people who have satisfied their more pressing needs' (Tuan, 1984: 18). Put more strongly, and implying an excess of human power, the sports landscape could be said to reflect 'the way in which the links between nature and everyday life have been battered by modernity [so that] for the most part, nature and society are now perceived to be counterpoised' (Katz and Kirby, 1991: 261). The crucial points of this chapter are that, because of its inherent character, sport inevitably dominates nature and that some sportscapes result from the application of excessive human power over the natural world. However, my use of the the garden as an analogue reveals the sports landscape as an ambiguous category, between nature and culture – and the ambiguity of power itself.

The previous chapter implied that during the eighteenth and nineteenth centuries the landscape of sport became increasingly artificial as science and technology 'improved' the cultivation of sports, just as they were improving the cultivation of wheat, barley, sheep and cattle. Improvement in urban areas was reflected in the greater efficiency of roads, railways, factories and offices. Such improvement was, of course, also found in the emergence of *sportscape* – a manifestation of sport's fixation with neutralising or altering the effects of the physical environment, and producing a landscape given over solely to sport. A more explicit exploration of the structures of sport provides a base upon which to explore sports' fixation with improving on nature and artificialising the landscape in its quest for the optimal sporting milieu.

SPORT AS ANTI-NATURE

In order to understand what I mean by 'deep structures' it may be useful to identify different ideologies with respect to the natural environment *per se* and the implications of such ideologies for the sports landscape. Ideologies relating to environmentalism (more or less the same thing as 'landscapeism', except that landscape and environment are never thought of as being synonymous) range from the technocentric or utilistic to the ecocentric or naturistic ends of a rather wide spectrum (O'Riordan, 1981: 376; Pietarinen, 1991). At the technocentric/utilistic end lie members of society who can be termed cornucopians. In relation to sports, the cornucopian ideology would accept that the *citius, altius, fortius* model of achievement sport is compatible with – or, at least not in any serious conflict with – the domination of the natural environment. Cornucopians basically believe that humankind will always find a way out of difficulties. Hence, problems resulting from continued construction of, say, sports landscapes for the Winter Olympics in mountain and forested regions with resulting soil erosion and the depletion of forests, or problems of motor sports which further the depletion of natural fuels and the emission of pollutants, are capable of being resolved by technology, science or politics. At the naturist/ecocentric (or catastrophist) end of the spectrum lie the deep ecologists who lack faith in large-scale technology and élitist and detached expertise. They advocate bio-rights and the conservation of nature as close to its primordial condition as possible and hence see degradation and pollution in the development of sports as denials of the intrinsic importance of nature for the human race. Deep ecologists would go so far as to argue that 'the satisfaction of the need for outdoor life and the need for machine oriented technology cannot take place simultaneously' (Naess, 1989: 178). According to this view, therefore, it would be quite inconsistent to use a gasoline-driven car in order to take part in an orienteering or cycling event (Figure 3.1).

Between these two extremes lies the technocentrist position. This is the taken-for-granted or most widespread attitude (O'Riordan, 1981: 376) and consists of two less radical groups, the accommodators and the self-reliants (or soft-technologists). Two alternative intermediate ideological categories may be identified as humanism and mysticism (Pietarinen, 1991: 583-5). Technocentricism is an ideology which recognises sport in its present, technologised form as a 'good thing'. Most of us have internalised this perspective from an early age and in order to provide an alternative to this *status quo* view, therefore, it is with the more ecocentric or deep ecological view that I will start this chapter. Without an awareness of this approach, any subsequent discussion of the landscape of sport would be incomplete.

In the previous chapters I described the role of men in the emergence of the

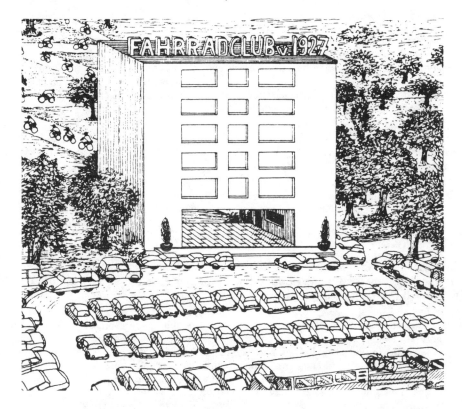

Figure 3.1 Sport and the environment (Source: Eichberg, 1988)

sport and I will note in the following chapter the implicit 'masculinity' of sportscape. It is worth noting that many feminists have commented on the opposition between masculine Culture and feminised Nature (see Rose, 1993: 68-9). Nature has long been viewed as passive and female and later I will draw attention to the way in which nature and women can be viewed as having been controlled and exploited in the interests of an essentially masculinised sport. For the moment I will focus on the idea that the notion of sport as a form of athletic 'production' sets it against nature. Indeed, once nature is separated from self the stage is set for nature's exploitation (Lash and Urry, 1994: 293).

The notion of sport being anti-nature is perhaps most emphatically put by Johann Galtung who notes how the landscape of sport is a 'carrier of deep culture and structure', a reflection of western conceptions of our relations to nature. He adds that :

> ... nature is there to be controlled, to be used – with 'abused' being just around the corner. The consequence of this is highly visible in the ecological crises of the world today: the decrease of maturity in ecosystems; depletion and pollution. In this field *sport plays a minor role, but the inclination is in the same direction.* Sporting events decreasingly take place in natural surroundings, and increasingly in special places made for the purpose,

with an overwhelming amount of concrete rather than just pure, uncontaminated, unma-
nipulated nature. The sports palace and the stadium, Olympic or not, are anti-nature and
have to be so because they are near-laboratory settings in which the unidimensionality of
competitive sports can unfold itself under controlled conditions. Pure nature has too
much variation in it, too much 'noise'. .... Although the human body is nature and nature
also is the human body, the distance between sport and nature in itself seems to be ever
increasing. (Galtung, 1984: 14, emphasis added)

Similar sentiments have been expressed in a discussion of twentieth century
sports development, where it is noted that:

... for sports facilities, trees were not planted ... but rather torn down. Tennis courts
behind high chain fences mimic the spatial divisions and one-dimensionality of the
industrial areas, in which they are located – concrete swimming pools and synthetic running tracks are eating their way into the few green areas left to us – the environment of
sports has once again become the opposite of nature. (Eichberg, 1982: 54)

Likewise, in a discussion of the problems of sport, ecology and progress, it has
been noted how the human body and nature are each scientifically modified in
order to fulfil the ideology of sport. The:

... 'correcting' of nature is justified according to requirements of sport, confirmed by the
general ideology of growth and progress. Whenever our body or nature is not given the
biologically necessary periods of maturation and recreation this is artificially effected. In
the eyes of sports representatives, a further 'improvement' of nature is necessary when
the basic conditions for training and competitions have to include equal chance for all
competitors. Equal chance and tensions as constituting elements of sport require constant
conditions throughout a certain period ... Nature with its processes of growth, its variabil-
ity and its biologically determined regeneration periods, is not equipped to comply with
these conditions ... These elements of uncertainty of man [sic] or nature have to be extin-
guished to attain the scientifically calculated goal. (Peyker, 1993: 73)

It has also been observed that in sport:

... real play and enjoyment, contact with air and water, improvisation and spontaneity all
disappear. These values are lost to the pursuit of efficiency, records, and strict rules.
Training in sports makes of the individual an efficient piece of apparatus which is hence-
forth unaquainted with anything but the harsh joy of exploiting his [sic] body and winning. (Ellul, 1965: 383).

Note again, the allusion to the exploitation of human, as well as physical,
nature (see pages 62-65).

The formal landscaping of sports places 'reveals the human need to dominate' (Tuan, 1984: 22). Others have implied that such a 'need', if it is one,
should be kept in check and that serious sport and the future of the environment
are incompatible. For example, Naess (1989: 178), widely regarded as the
founder of deep ecology, prefers 'exuberance in nature' and an economically
responsible *friluftsliv* ('open air life') which would resemble the physical activity found in the !Kung hunter-gatherer societies described in Chapter 2. This is

not 'passive adaptation' to nature – which would view humans as totally subordinate to nature – but 'active adaptation' (Sandell, 1991), acknowledging that survival depends on some control over nature but, at the same time, showing respect for the landscape and leaving 'traceless passages' through the countryside and wilderness, obviously the antithesis of of planned sports courses, tracks, trails and zones. The deep ecology movement would view competitive sports as creating self-realisation for the select few (Faarlund, 1973). The concept of sport presupposes 'losers' whereas in the the the kind of *friluftsliv* advocated by Naess one's own self-realisation would be satisfied by that of others. In a 'naturist' world, 'not much room for sport would be left' (Pietarinen, 1991: 586).

These deep ecological views about the exploitation of natural landscapes by sports involve a number of ethical questions relating to such things as biorights and the ethics of destroying wild flowers as well as forests. It is difficult to deny, however, that sport as a form of culture 'takes a bite of nature each time we can make it function in such a way that we can repeat and control that function' (Larsen, 1992: 117). To allow for a humanised world we 'use power to change nature for own benefit and delight' (Tuan, 1986: 128) – to break a tree to make a spear in order to kill an animal for survival – or to cut grass in order for a ball to roll smoothly as in football. As Cosgrove (1989b: 190) notes, 'humanism has always been very closely aligned in practice with the exercise of power both over other human beings and over the natural world'. The problem seems to be that although a humanised world may be inevitable an over-humanised world need not. A humanised world can give great pleasure but an excess of humanism can paradoxically produce a dehumanised landscape (Relph, 1981). If, therefore, the founder of the modern Olympics was correct in believing that sport 'tends inevitably towards excess' (quoted in Hoberman, 1992: 159), then landscapes of excess might by expected to characterise those of sport. Excessive power over nature in a sporting context therefore moves away from pleasure and delight to extravagance and wastefulness.

SPORTSCAPES AS GARDENS

Of course, sport is far from unique in using nature for its own ends and it is helpful, therefore, to use analogous contexts to inform my feelings about the sportscapes. In doing so I move towards an arguably more sensitive and less unambiguous view than that propounded by the deep-ecologists.

Among the most perceptive of cultural geographers since the late 1960s has been Yi-Fu Tuan (1974; 1979; 1984; 1986; 1989) whose work has consistently bucked the positivist trend of post-war geography and who has promoted a more phenomenological view of place and landscape by means of his 'descriptive psychological geography' (Tuan,1984: ix). In one of his more pessimistic essays, *Dominance and Affection: the Making of Pets*, Tuan (1984) approaches the landscape as a reflection of the exercise of human power over nature in botanic and zoologic contexts (though in doing so he cannot be said to fully embrace a deep ecological view). It could be argued that such power is simply part of nature, all human enterprise indirectly or directly affecting all other living things and that civilisation, and hence sport, 'could only emerge through the mastery of nature' (Tuan, 1984: 173). Human power over nature therefore seems inescapable. In western societies this reflects the widely held view that the world and its bounty had been created for humankind and that all other biological species were to be subordinated to human wishes and needs (Thomas, 1983: 17). This is essentially a Christian perspective; whereas the pagan world possessed 'cave cults' and animistic beliefs, the Christian destruction of these 'made it possible to exploit nature in a mood of indifference to the feeling of natural objects' (Tuan, 1968: 178).

Tuan's ideas are undoubtedly relevant to the sports landscape. Whereas, at a certain level of simplicity, the domination of nature in the production of arable and pastoral landscapes result from the basic need for human survival, the golf course, football field, sports hall, ski jump, tennis court and swimming pool – like ornamental gardens and artificial lakes – are landscapes which have been transformed in order to provide pleasure once the necessity for food has been secured. They are, therefore, forms of power or domination but do not seem to derive from a hatred of nature but, rather, from a desire to civilise it (Tarasti, 1988: 41). They may be forms of what Tuan (1984: ix) calls 'playful domination' and are often treated with affection. Indeed, like gardens, sports places are often viewed as 'cultural models of the good life' (Tuan, 1986: 25). This illustrates the ambivalent nature of power and the relationship between dominance, on the one hand, and affection on the other, and throughout *Dominance and Affection* Tuan stresses that dominance is not the opposite of affection but is, in fact, dominance with a human face. 'Dominance may be cruel and exploitive, with no hint of affection in it. What is produced is the victim. On the other hand, dominance may be combined with affection, and what it produces is the pet' or garden (Tuan,1984: 2), nature being viewed as a well-loved servant (Wilson, 1992: 33). In a sports context the victim may be an exploited human, animal or landscape. The sportscape or athlete to which we show affection is the athletic analogue of the garden or the pet. As Tuan (1984: 5) notes, 'affection mitigates domination, making it softer and more acceptable, but affection itself is only possible in relationships of inequality'. Put another way, even if we appear to be kind to nature we still exert power and dominance over it.

It is this softer form of power (that is, affection) which, I believe, is often (though far from always) reflected in the landscape of sport and I will illustrate these ideas with examples ranging from sports landscapes which, while illustrating the exercise of power have minimum impacts on the natural landscape, to those where the power relation is one of true dominance (Table 3.1).

An environmental fixation

The emergence of serious sports resulted in a radical change in the relationships between movement culture and nature. In contrast to the pre-modern play and games culture 'the opponent in competitive sport is normally an artificial impediment or situation, whose creation requires preparation and development

Table 3.1 Dominance and affection in various landscapes of sports

'Nature'	*Affection*
Orienteering course	
Golf course	
Skiing piste	
Race course	
Football field	
Tennis court	
Stadium	
Sports Hall	
'Culture'	*Dominance*

of the natural environment' (Vuolle, 1991: 598) and the dominance and power over the natural landscape in a modern sporting context can be regarded as part of an environmental fixation. Since the beginning of the present century, sports bureaucrats have made concerted attempts to modify or neutralise the natural elements of the earth's surface, the soil, vegetation, climate and the relief of the land. It is sometimes said that sport should ideally take place in 'environmentless' situations. As noted on page 42, 'fair play' logically involves athletes competing in the same environments, as well as keeping to the same rules, and sports bureaucracies have constantly sought to alter physical irregularities – climatological as well as geomorpological – in the earth's surface in order to achieve such fairness. This has meant that most environments for sport are 'developed natural environments' or 'built environments', rather than 'genuine natural environments' (Vuolle, 1991: 599).

As broadly interpreted in this book, the sports landscape includes the air above it. Sports meteorologists such as Lobozewicz (1981) and Thornes (1977) have shown how the weather as well as the surface of the land interferes in sports and discriminates against some athletes more than others, even during the course of a single event. Sports such as football or cricket for which the weather creates interference 'are ideally suited to "weatherless" days' which contrast, of course with those sports such as skiing and sailing which might be defined as 'specialised weather sports' but as I will show later, even these are undertaken in far from 'natural' conditions. The same applies to what Thornes (1977: 261) calls 'weather advantage sports', that is, sports like track and field or golf where the weather can create an advantage for some players, but not others, even in the same event. A classification of sports could probably also be drawn up in relation to topographic effects, similar to the three-fold division based on weather effects.

The reaction to, and the fixation with, natural environmental interference has resulted in sports bureaucracies:

(1) making allowance for it and taking it into account in evaluating athletic performance (e.g. by disallowing a record if it is achieved on a downhill track or with wind assistance);

(2) artificialising or improving it in order to improve performance (e.g. by creating smoother surfaces or more rational slopes, to make snow for skiing when none naturally occurs); and

(3) neutralising its effects (e.g. by taking sports indoors).

Although statistical data could be (and will be) used to illustrate the damage done to nature as well as to human and other animals in the name of sport, it also needs to be stressed that in sport, as in play, 'the abuse of power is evident less in any quantitative measure as in the character of change – in the ways that power has been used to distort plant, animal and human nature to aesthetic [and sporting] ends, and the ways that animals and humans ... [as athletes] ... have been used to suffer indignities and humiliation' (Tuan, 1984: 4, brackets added). It is this distortion of nature in the name of sport that forms the substance of the rest of this chapter.

Taming the field of play; the stadium and other sportscapes

Orienteering is widely regarded as an imaginative sport involving running with map and compass through wooded – often natural – landscapes, finding or not finding information provided at various points *en route*. Other sports which take place over the more natural forms of landscape include cross country skiing and running (Table 3.1), though the latter has responded to commercial imperatives in recent years and increasingly uses cultural landscapes (e.g. race courses, golf courses, pastures) of various kinds. These kinds of sports leave virtually no lasting changes on the landscapes on which they take place (Mützelberg and Eichberg, 1984) and top level athletes (men and women) in orienteering and cross country skiing sometimes cite 'nature' as the primary motive for taking part in such sports (Herva and Lyytinen, 1993).[1] But despite such sports participants' apparently benign use of the natural landscape, they do, nevertheless, use it (Tuan, 1984: 176) and even orienteering can temporarily damage vegetation, though most of it recovers quickly (Breckle, 1992; Douglas, 1990).

Increasingly, however, landscapes designed specifically with sport in mind, like 'formal landscaping reveals the human need to dominate' (Tuan, 1984: 22). The domination and possession of nature for sport, as with other land uses, occurs in three stages. Prospective sportscape is first *mapped*, the landscape being summarised cartographically for purposes of marketing it to the world of various sports businesses; secondly, it is *mythologised* as being ideal or 'natural', as, for example, with golf courses, marinas, ski-pistes or stadium complexes. Thirdly, it is *aestheticised* by landscaping, the use of exotic plants or novel architectural forms (Katz and Kirby, 1991: 265). In many cases, however, aestheticisation is unconvincing and landscape and nature become dominated by sport to such an extent that it causes considerable controversy. For the 1992 Winter Olympics at Albertville in France ski runs were carved out of mountain leaving permanent scars, rare high mountain marshland was damaged by cross country skiing pistes, and an environment-friendly ski-jump was rejected and replaced by a controversial facility driven into the mountainside with 300 giant piles (Lean and Keating, 1992). Such examples illustrate the clear and brutal dominance of sport over nature.

Dominance in more benign form may be illustrated by the stadium and other sportscapes which share almost every basic characteristic of the garden or park. The green enclosures of sports may also be reminiscent of university court-yards and quadrangles, but seem to me more redolent 'of the garden world, the condition of leisure where all play aspires to paradise ... a green expanse, complete, coherent, shimmering, carefully tended, a garden' (Giamatti, 1989: 69-70). Stadiums, ski slopes, lawn tennis courts and golf courses, for example, are classic blendings 'of nature and artifice: they are the product of horticulture and architecture. On the one hand, they consist of growing things; on the other of walls, terraces, statues, ...' (Tuan, 1984: 21). It should be stressed, however, that while the words 'park' and 'garden' are frequently applied to sportscapes, they are often used in a purely euphemistic way, sometimes having plastic carpets instead of grass and concrete towers and terraces instead of trees. The visitor will look in vain for grass in an American 'fieldhouse', for flowers at Villa Park, or for shrubs at Maple Leaf Gardens. In constructing such facilities human beings display power to spare, in no less a way than in the desire of interior designers to bring indoors the most pleasing aspects of the garden world outside, in public winter gardens, domestic green-houses, conservatories and Wardian cases (Rees, 1993: 147-65).

Although landscape gardeners – and their suburban hobbyist equivalents – have been deadly serious about the scientific improvement on nature, the garden has always been associated with playfulness (Tuan, 1984: 29). But 'the garden is not only a product of play but also an arena for play' (Tuan, 1989: 91) and, as a result, in one or two cases modern sports actually grew out of playful activities traditionally associated with the garden. Tennis and croquet come most readily to mind; but in such cases the activity was hardly playful enough to leave nature unaffected since a flat surface and a meticulously maintained lawn were required. Developed from the indoor 'real' or 'royal' tennis, the burgeoning suburban gardens of early twentieth century England formed the focal points for the growth of not only individual grass courts on back lawns but suburban tennis clubs with eight or more courts, sheltered from both summer sun and the intrusive gazes of the lower classes by a luxuriant foliage of trees (Holt, 1989: 126). The London suburb of Wimbledon is, perhaps, the perfect home for the most suburban of sports – at least in England (Bale, 1982: 98-9) while Flushing Meadow ('home' of US tennis) is hardly redolent of the inner city.

CRICKET AND ITS FIELD

The cricket field is a paradigm example of the 'improvement' of nature in the name of sport. Although the eighteenth century had witnessed a general tenden-cy to 'remove any local variations on the way the game was played' (Brailsford, 1983: 38), in order to provide a fairer basis than hitherto for betting and gambling (a variation on the 'fair play' theme), by the early nineteenth cen-tury playing surfaces were still generally uneven and unkempt. Traditionally the preparation of the cricket pitch was managed by sheep and the roughness of these early grounds produced notoriously low scores. In many early nineteenth century village games a rough pitch was actually encouraged in order to make the bounce of the ball unpredictable for opposing batsmen. At least one village in Hampshire 'was reputed to spend the winter coaxing plantains or bents to grow about the length spot of their main fast bowler' (Arlott, 1984: 69). But an improved playing surface was a 'necessary condition for the development of cricket in its modern form' (Allison, 1980: 11) and although from 1849 it became 'legal' to sweep or roll the pitch before an innings, the absence of fierce, overarm bowling meant that there was little incentive to further tend the pitch. But 'without a good 'wicket' – a closely mowed and rolled playing surface – it was not possible to have either large scores or overarm bowling, both of which added immeasurably to the glamour and popularity of the game' (Allison, 1980: 11). With the legalisation in 1864 of the overarm technique, it became necessary for the surface on which the game was played to be transformed and to be reclaimed totally from nature.

In 1864 the first groundsman was appointed at Lord's cricket ground in London. Even village teams started to expect proper facilities and cheap labour was available to prepare the grounds and even full-time groundsmen were sometimes employed (Cole, 1982: 2). The stadium and the garden became almost homologous by the expertise of those who tended them; groundsmen actually *were* gardeners. The groundsmen of late nineteenth century England, those whose job it was to perfect the surfaces upon which sports were 'played', were fully familiar with horticulture, often bringing their expertise from the environments of country houses to those of urban stadiums. Consider, for example, the case of Percy Peake who, in 1874, went to Lord's Cricket Ground and commenced the task of making it famous the world over for the quality of its playing surface. Peake:

> ... had been a gardener and a keeper of lawns before he first made a name for himself as a cricket groundsman at Brighton. He was an expert in agriculture, horticulture and geology although he never pursued formal training in those disciplines. His careful and empirical study of soils, grasses and marls gradually produced a surface at Lord's that became the envy of every county club. He wrote many articles on the preparation of pitches and spent his last years laying down several cricket grounds across the country. (Sandiford, 1984: 279)

In the new landscapes of sports, the domination of gardener-grounds*men* such as Peake produced a field of perfection, lacking in decorative detail, smooth of surface, and subjected to 'turf management'. Such a masculine 'garden', produced with sport-as-achievement in mind, can be symbolically contrasted with the domestic garden – 'small-scale in design, fashion conscious [in its] concern with colour, and the importance of flowers', all signifying its femininity (Ford, 1991: 154).

The introduction of the heavy roller (first used at Lord's in 1870) further served to standardise the playing surface and the late nineteenth century saw the growth in production of specialised cricket equipment to aid the gradual levelling and equalising of the cricket landscape in an age of rapidly changing technology (Figure 3.2). By the first decade of the present century the cricket groundsman had technologised the cricket pitch, freeing it from the 'incalculable and unscientific misconduct caused by a rough and entirely unscientific pitch' (Arlott, 1984: 78). Marl and liquid manure were regularly applied to the top class pitches and the governing body, the Marylebone Cricket Club (MCC) felt it necessary to urge club secretaries to have pitches prepared by only applying water and a roller. Groundsmen seem, however, to have become obsessed with producing grass surfaces which made fast bowling difficult, hence encouraging high scoring. According to Neville Cardus (1972: 25) 'the groundsman, the producer or stage manager of cricket, made the mistake of producers in the theatre – he became engrossed in ... the setting [that is, the field's surface] at the expense of the play'. The groundsman was arguably the vital actor in the emergence of the sports landscape for, like the garden, the sportscape has to 'be maintained thoughtfully and systematically; otherwise it will revert to nature' (Tuan, 1984: 19).

Attempts to further eliminate nature from the cricket landscape included the covering of wickets in wet weather, the first experimental covering before matches at Lord's being as early as 1872 (Bowen, 1970: 284). At Edgbaston in Birmingham, a 'motorised cover was introduced in 1982 which protects virtually the whole playing area from rain, and can be rolled back to the edges of the ground, as soon as the weather relents, at the flick of a switch' (Martin-Jenkins, 1984: 183). Beyond the wicket itself, fertilisers and artificial watering have made what had traditionally been virtual deserts in dry weather permanently green. At club level, though not at that of professional cricket, pitches manufactured out of tough plastic have proliferated. Because the pedology of cricket pitches is highly variable (e.g. McIntyre, 1985: 84), many believe that it is only a matter of time before plastic pitches are accepted at the highest levels of a game which has traditionally projected a natural and rustic image (see Chapter 7).

The most synthetic form of cricket is the indoor game. While cricketers have practiced indoors for many years (using barns in nineteenth century England), competitive indoor cricket in its modern guise was initiated in Australia in the 1970s. It is cricket for instant gratification. While the pitch is the traditional 22 yards, the entire 'field' is only 30 yards by 12 yards. In Australia such games are played in air-conditioned halls in suburban 'industrial parks', possessing a placeless style of container architecture. In such situations, the industrialisation of sport is both metaphorical and literal; it is part of the suburban industrial landscape. In Britain, the indoor game is also becoming popular though the number of purpose-built facilities are few. Although its advocates claim that the indoor game is meant to be fun, an Indoor Cricket Federation does exist 'to try to ensure the game is played to standard rules with the best possible facilities' (Hamlyn, 1985).

Improved playing surfaces have also characterised football and other team sports. Whereas games of cricket and baseball stop when rain would spoil a game, football in its various forms continues in rain or snow; fog is the only meteorological variable certain to stop play. Natural or cultivated grass fields tend to get damaged during the course of a season and as a result experiments with synthetic turf have been widespread. Although such experimentation had been tried in connection with indoor football in England (Inglis, 1983: 49), in its modern form it is widely regarded as having been pioneered in the United States during the 1960s when it was found that natural grass would not grow satisfactorily in the Houston Astrodome. Astroturf and other such forms of sur-

Figure 3.2 Changing technology was a major factor in the development of a specialised sports landscape (Source: Pardon, 1876)

face cover (for example, the synthetic running track – see Chapter 5) became highly popular as alternatives to natural surfaces, outdoors as well as in, during the 1970s. They not only maximised the output of sport but also made games more predictable and, in some cases, more dangerous.

THE STADIUM AS GARDEN

The cricket and football fields exemplify the imposition of human power on a natural landscape. The stadium is the outcome of the application of horticulture and architecture which together produce the sporting equivalent – in more austere form – of the garden-quadrangle. I have already reviewed some of the horticultural applications to these kinds of sportscapes but the broader landscape is completed by the work of architects whose structures – the stadiums – enclose the fields of achievement upon which the sporting action takes place. As shown in the previous chapter, stadiums had characterised Greco-Roman athletic contests. They doubled as both sportive and military spaces, a land use relationship which continues to characterise the stadiums of modern times.

An arena or stadium 'may look more like its ancient precursor than anything else in the modern world looks like its architectural ancestors' (Giamatti, 1989: 32-3) and like the garden the stadium 'is power in confident mood – witness the size and masterful layouts of some of its grander specimens' (Tuan, 1984: 32). It is difficult to avoid being impressed by the power symbolised by modern Olympic stadiums. That at Berlin, built for the 1936 Games, was more than a stadium and part of an integrated suburban *Reichssportfeld* which has been described as the first Olympic park complex; it 'also served to glorify the Fascist Germany and feigned a peaceful Olympic state. Its architectonic form was determined by the official state architecture' (Wimmer, 1976: 35). The conglomeration of sports facilities put nature well and truly in its place, somewhat paradoxical in view of early Nazi sport ideology which had been rather anti-competitive and had lauded an Aryan anti-urban ideal of 'green' physical exercise in the open countryside. In addition to the main stadium there was an open air swimming stadium, polo field, hockey stadium, field for equestrian events, and an open air stage surrounded by a large Roman-style open air theatre where gymnastic events were held.

At the same time, however, the architecture of Olympism need not be identified with brutalism. The stadium, (again like the garden) can also display 'power in a whimsical mood – witness the details of design' (Tuan, 1984: 32). The Stockholm Olympic Stadium is a case in point. Designed by Torben Grut for the 1912 Olympics, it was built in the vernacular style with grey-violet brick walls and granite towers. Pierre Baron de Coubertin regarded the stadium highly and 'with its pointed arches and its turrets, its technical perfection, its good order and its purposeful disposition seemed to be a model of its kind' (Wimmer, 1976: 190). It is remarkably human in scale and is today a much-loved element of the Stockholm townscape, 'a stadium part castle, part mansion, part cloister, part pageant but altogether magnificent and built entirely out of Swedish materials' (Inglis, 1990: 238). It is impossible to chronicle the stadiums large and small which have architectural merit and charm or, in the case of small stadiums in country towns, possess an air of innocence (Inglis,1990: 233), often seemingly at one with the landscape out of which they have grown.

Certainly, such stadiums possess a sense of place or *genius loci*, a theme I return to in Chapter 6. My point here, however, is that while being the undeniable result of human power, sometimes evident in a boastful way, such buildings can nevertheless display whimsy and playfulness in design.

The ambitious garden-architect is willing to go to considerable lengths to create magical worlds which constantly surprise the visitor (Tuan, 1984: 35). To what extent can the same be said of those who build stadiums? Although many possess individual differences and some do provide extremely pleasant surprises (Inglis, 1983; 1990), a sports stadium has to be more than a stadium to make it magical. Stadiums with surprises in them are those which are, in themselves, often ambiguous structures. The football stadium in Monaco is one (Inglis, 1990: 110-1); the SkyDome in Toronto is another. In the latter case nature is totally neutralised by artifice, its synthetic 'field' upon which no grass grows and its retractable roof making even the normal dualism between indoor and outdoor ambiguous. But its external mural decorations (Figure 3.3) are at least whimsical while the ability of the Dome to host all manner of events, from football to funfairs makes it magical for at least some people. There are, of course, other interpretations which can be made of such a facility and I will return to these in Chapter 8.

All too often, however, the stadium seems to becoming a bland, containerised structure, one looking more or less the same as any other. In the United States the term 'concrete saucer' is often applied to anonymous bowls which all look the same. In recent decades it has been suggested that in the belief that form should follow function, builders have erected 'huge concrete circles and called them baseball parks. Everywhere the emphasis has been on symmetry, uniformity and keeping everything in balance' (Dickinson and Dickinson, 1991: 27). Such features often have massive car parking provision, further contributing to the dominance of sport over the natural landscape. Where synthetic fields exist the sameness of places is even more in evidence. It is arguably the synthetic running track that has the most human pressure placed upon it to be identical to all others of its type and I will deal with this particular kind of sportscape in Chapter 5.

Landscapes which appear much the same as any other typify what Relph (1976) termed 'placelessness' which, in its purest form involves uniformity – 'an environment without significant places' (Relph, 1976: 143). The concrete bowl stadium with its plastic carpet and the fenced-in tennis court with its synthetic surface typify such environments. In such cases, the attempt to create simple modifications of nature which will accommodate human sporting activities have, like so many gardens, failed to provide that simplicity. Gardens so often become high art and stadiums often become high tech – each 'dependent upon social and technological power' (Tuan, 1986: 115). Simplicity and freedom become endangered by blandness and constraint.

But it must be said that sports landscapes vary in their degree of placelessness; some sports are closer to landscape uniformity than others and I shall develop this theme further in Chapter 4. In many cases the pre-existing landscape is not simply flattened but often sculptured to produce aesthetically pleasing slopes and hills, lakes and woods. Indeed, many people would regard

Figure 3.3 The Toronto Skydome; even the modern, sanitised stadium does not have to be totally boring

them as more visually enjoyable than the landscapes, natural or agricultural, which preceded them. Such sportscapes are classically exemplified by golf courses.

GOLFSCAPES

Golf courses provide an excellent example of the conversion of natural land-scapes to sportscape through the imposition of human power over natural or semi-natural environments. Golf can, in fact, now be played across such a wide range of landscapes that it is difficult to think of the sport as possessing any general landscape characteristics – apart, of course, from holes, greens, fairways and rough. Even some of these are missing, except in simulated form, in the hyper-real world of indoor golf (see Chapter 8). There are over 13,000 conventional golf courses in the USA, in total covering over 1,500,000 acres of land, twice the area of the state of Rhode Island (Adams and Rooney, 1985). In the state of Arizona alone, where the conversion of areas of natural desert to golf courses has given the phrase 'the greening of America' a new meaning, the total maintenance costs of such artificial sportscapes in 1987 alone amounted to $75,752,360 (Barkley and Simmons, 1989: 22). In such sports, the landscape itself becomes a plaything, like the landscaped garden, often 'ingenious and full of surprises' (Tuan, 1984: 34) with the designer being 'a specialist in optical illusions, in the deceptive organization of distances, in the sly concealment of obstacles' (Clay, 1987: 218).

In Scotland, widely regarded as the home of modern golf, the sport has both utilised and transformed a wide range of landforms and natural landscapes. In his exemplary study of the physical geography of sport, Robert Price (1989) has shown how the early golf courses colonised the natural landscapes of the linkslands of coastal southern Scotland. In the United States also, 'many early courses were very primitive, often consisting of several holes on an essentially unaltered natural landscape' (Adams and Rooney, 1985: 421). Many of Scotland's most famous golf courses, including St. Andrews, Carnoustie, Muirfield, Troon, Prestwick and Turnberry, made use of the natural well drained links, typically located on a raised beach or raised marine platform covered with dunes, between 10 and 35 feet above the present sea level. Ten courses existed before the end of the eighteenth century, eight of them occupying coastal links. While earth moving equipment was hardly required for the construction of such courses, the invention of the lawn mower in 1830 had a major effect on the nature of the carefully maintained green.

As demand for golf increased, courses were developed on a wide variety of landforms. Some inland courses were hardly regarded as the real thing but they were often approximations or clever simulations of the coastal linkslands. At Lanark, a course opened in 1850, was well drained and 'located on a spread of fluvioglacial sand and gravel with an irregular surface topography of ridges, mounds and hollows' (Price, 1989: 24). The early twentieth century was characterised by attempts to 'work in all the natural features, not developing them more than was essential but using them fully to provide a course with its own planning' (Hawtree, 1983: 24) and a wide variety of landforms were accommodated by golf courses (Figure 3.4). Today 42 golf courses in Scotland are sited at elevations of over 180 metres (600 feet) and according to Price's (1989: 74) tabulations only 19 per cent of all Scotland's courses are now of the links type (Table 3.2).

Although it cannot be denied that the variety of environments encountered in Scottish golf add charm to playing the game and hence an affection for the courses, the conversion of hillside and moorland to golfscape clearly illustrates the use of nature for sport. In the 1890s, as golf mania began to sweep through England, one observer noted that the resulting landscapes had no relationship with nature (Lowerson, 1993: 134). In England where the linksland environment was less common, the development of inland golf produced a breed of sub-Capability Brown figures who specialised in 'golf course architecture'.

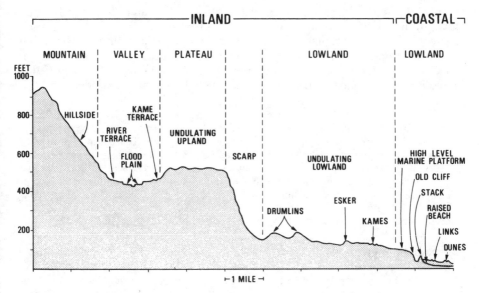

Figure 3.4 Scottish golf landforms (Source: Price 1989: 75)

Table 3.2 Per cent of Scottish golf courses in each landform category (After Price 1989: 74)

Type	Total	%
Undulating	117	28
Links	80	19
Kame & river terraces, sandur	70	16
Hillside	66	15
Raised beaches/platforms	46	11
Drumlins	35	8
Eskers, kames	11	3

The result was an 'improvement' on the wilder Scottish linklands as previously enclosed fields or woodland were turned into carefully simulated heathland. Farmers leased their land to golf clubs and common land was encroached upon (Lowerson, 1993: 135). This typified a different form of power relation – that of an élite golf set over the commoners. The use of commons for golf during the 1870s and 1880s led to disputes with other users of such lands, a further reflection of the deprivation of public space in the countryside as well as in the towns.

Robert Adams (1987) has contrasted the archetypal (and in the light of Table 3.1, stereotypical) Scottish golf course, habitat-like in its relatively natural linksland environment, with the more artificial American course. Indeed, the language of agriculture has entered the US golfing vocabulary with the concept of the 'turf farm' golf course. 'Such courses are highly artificial, humanised constructs where the environment has been restructured in an attempt to smooth or eliminate the irregularities of Nature and the uncertainties that they pose' (Adams 1987: 32). Landscape sculpturing to match that found in the most ambitious of landscape gardens is required in the construction of such courses. Indeed, golf course architecture has assumed the form of landscaping to the extent that it has been suggested that 'Horatio Brown, Humphrey Repton and Uvedale Price would have been the Trent Jones of their time if golf had started its growth much earlier' (Hawtree, 1983: 37). Adams continues:

> The construction of a first-rate turf farm course often begins with moving hundreds of thousands of cubic yards of material to recontour the terrain in order to accommodate the construction of tees, fairways and greens to exact prescriptions. Topsoil, often with additives, is then replaced and seeded with special, non-native strains of grass. The grass is nurtured by the applications of huge quantities of fertilizers, herbicides, fungicides and pesticides and by the construction of elaborate irrigation systems. Mowing is accomplished with sophisticated machinery so that the height of the grass is exactingly controlled. Fairways, and particularly greens, are repeatedly aerated and top dressed. The results are uniform, lush, soft, velvety-smooth carpets of grass. (Adams, 1987: 32)

The manicured green of the superior golf course is sportscape in perfected form – 'the ultimate outdoor artifact – the prototypical American lawn' (Clay, 1987: 219), or 'a state of nature apt to the age: a vast acreage of greenery scrupulously regulated to support a network of tiny, shallow holes' (Sorkin, 1992: 222).

The more natural Scottish courses, where varying physical environments and landscapes intrude, where wind and rain are more part of the game, are inevitably more unpredictable. To Americans this seems 'unfair' and in the United States attempts have therefore been made to neutralise the natural environment in order to produce a consistency of landscapes and playing surfaces. What Americans call 'target golf' (an outdoor form of darts, as opposed to the Scottish game where the ball must be hit short of the target because of unpredictable bounces near the green) is 'a science that is performed in controlled environments where proper execution yields repeatable and predictable results' (Adams, 1987: 35). Yet around the course, more literal garden-like elements are found. A variety of plants can be placed at the limits of fairway and rough, not only to delimit the area of play but also to lend a pleasing prospect to the participants and spectators (Raitz, 1987a: 54). Although such landscapes obviously reflect the dominance of human power over nature, the dominance is ambivalent, as evidenced by the equally obvious affection with which many such landscapes are held.

If the greens on golf courses are what Clay (above) regarded as prototypical domestic lawns, where are the houses? The golf course illustrates not simply the conversion of landscape to sportscape but also the subsequent insertion of residences into the land use of sport. Starting in the US, but spreading to Europe, a late twentieth century form of golfscape is what Adams and Rooney (1984) term 'condo canyon' where real estate development, usually made up of condominiums, takes priority over golf in the course design strategy. What emerges is a golf-based community, at least one 18 hole course, but often 36 or 72 holes being surrounded by residential development. Whereas the traditional course was compact, the 'condo canyon' requires a more extensive use of space for all residents to possess golf frontage. Adams and Rooney (1984: 72) describe Quail Ridge, in Boynton Beach, Florida, as a typical example:

> It was laid out around two 18 hole courses on 578 acres of land. Course construction was accomplished by excavating and filling a scraggy patch of semi-swampy Florida wasteland. Extensive ponds and water hazards were created by penetration of the water table. The materials removed by this process were used to raise the level of the golf courses and the adjacent housing sites. The Quail Ridge development is exemplary of what has occurred repeatedly throughout Florida and the Southeast. Wasteland has been converted to plush fairways, greens, lakes and most importantly, to prime building sites. Paying golf among the condominium homes and apartments is now commonplace. The price extracted from the residents and visitors is high, but construction to satisfy this golf-oriented lifestyle continues at a phenomenal pace.

About half of the new courses being constructed in the USA are of the condominium type. In such golf courses the distinction between sportscape and domestic garden becomes somewhat blurred.

The craze for the conversion of natural or semi-natural landscapes to golf courses is not restricted to north America. Indeed, the country experiencing the most rapid growth in the number of golf courses is probably Japan where the number has increased from 72 in 1956 to over 2,000 at the present time with 3,000 forecast for the year 2000, taking up 0.57 per cent of the nation's land surface (McCormack, 1991: 125; Rimmer, 1992: 1621). In the case of Japan, golf course development not only exemplifies the dominance of nature but also its pollution and despoilation. Golf courses ideally require undulating land near cities which is neither built on nor given over to agriculture. With no such land left, 1 per cent of the nation's forests, usually at the foot of mountains, has been felled for course construction. What is more, legal measures to protect national parks, mountain and coastal environments have been abandoned in the interests of what is known as a 'human green plan' where the 'green' quality 'is achieved by the application of three to four tons per year of herbicides, germicide, pesticides, colouring agents, organic chlorine and other fertilizers including chemicals that are carcinogenic or cause various health abnormalities' (McCormack, 1991: 126-7). Water draining into rivers and lakes has resulted in over 950 places possessing water quality which has been adversely affected by golf development while widespread damage to animal, bird, insect, marine and human life has also been reported (McCormack: 127). In Korea it has been noted that pesticides spread on golf courses can be absorbed into the human body through inhalation or skin contact and 'pesticide abuse' in golf course maintenance is now regarded as a problem which requires serious regulation (Moon and Shin, 1990).

What alternatives exist to the continued colonisation of nature by golf and other land-extensive sports such as skiing? In the case of golf, smaller courses have been promoted by applying a heavier golf ball which travels only half the distance of a normal ball. Perhaps the most well-known example of such developments is known as Cayman Golf, which involves the use of a ball with lower compression than a regulation ball and thus, when struck, travels over shorter distances. A prototype short-ball course, constructed on the Cayman Islands by

Jack Niklaus's Golden Bear Corporation, uses a quarter to one-third of the land required for a regulation course. The reduced use of the space, the faster time to complete 18 holes and the larger number of players able to play during a given time period make this an attractive idea (Adams and Rooney, 1985: 437). A given number of holes can also be completed quicker with the help of the golf-cart, 'the ultimate reconciliation of machine and garden, a benign transport indigenous to leisure' and sport (Sorkin, 1992: 222).

HUMAN POWER AND MOTOR POWER

One of the most dramatic forms of modern sport is the collective group of activities known as motorsports. Such sports illustrate, in extreme form, the cult of speed and power. Through motor sports spectators experience the awe and pleasure of power in one of its most dramatic forms. But in order to experience it, nature may be affected in several ways. Not only are concrete tracks required for racing; a vast amount of gasoline is used, not only to power the racing machines but to get the spectators to the necessarily out-of-town circuits where such races are held. Of the motorsport disciplines practiced in Britain, however, nineteen have been identified as not being dependent on purpose-built facilities (Elson et al. 1986: 11-2). Apart from the huge use of the unrenewable oil resource, noise is a major environmental impact made by motor sports. Noise pollution adds to the impression of power generated by such sports. Of all sport-related noise complaints it is likely that over 42 per cent come from motorsports while other negative impacts include the destruction of flora, the inhibition of floristic regeneration, the disturbance of wildlife, the destruction and compaction of topsoil, and the erosion and rutting of surfaces (Elson et al., 1986: 181-3).

WATER WORLDS

Unlike land-based sports, many competitive water sports continue to take place in natural waterscapes which remain unaffected when the competition is over. Swimming races across the English Channel are more likely to be disrupted by the results of technology than to cause any disruption themselves. At the same time, many water-based movement cultures take place in totally artificial water courses which can be used for little else than for the specialised activity for which they were constructed.

Sailing and yachting do *use* the natural environment and motor powered vessels contribute to water pollution. Those driven by the wind or human energy, however, are almost neutral in terms of their impact on the waters in which they take place. Such water sports can, however, create minor ecological damage at the interface between land and water and the constructions associated with such major events such as the America's Cup can cause considerable negative impacts near to their venues.

Controlling the world of water

Rowing events, while frequently taking place on natural water courses, also occur on specialised water routes designed specifically for rowing at the élite-sport level. By doing so the idiosyncracies of riverine currents are eliminated. Rowing events on natural water courses do continue to take place, as do slalom races on the torrent stages of river courses. When humans use such environments little permanent damage is created. But human power is available to replace these natural waterways with 'water sport centres' and specially designed courses for events such as the Olympics. For the Munich Olympics of 1972 the rowing course at Foldmoching-Oberschleissheim was 140 metres wide and 2,225 metres long, the largest structure built for the Olympic Games. According to Wimmer (1976: 198), 'there are no outer lanes affected by waves because the banks are provided with 2.10 metres wide sloping strips; wind turbulences are ... prevented by 67.50 metres wide free zones alongside each bank'. For the same Games, the canoe slalom course at Augsberg was the first to be ever specially constructed for the Olympics.

As I showed in Chapter 2, swimming races are only one of several forms of movement culture through water. Much recreational and non-sportive swimming continues to take place in coastal waters and lakes though increasing pollution has undoubtedly reduced its popularity. But there has been a further neutralisation of the natural environment in swimming events at all levels and today virtually all races of any seriousness take place in covered, rectangular pools (interestingly, the Barcelona Olympics in 1992 were held out of doors) constructed to standardised dimensions. Natural water courses possess too many vagaries of nature, too many random variables.

Swimming baths control water in typically modern form. In his astonishing book, *Haunts of the Black Masseur*, Charles Sprawson (1993: 274) quotes Joan Didion who noted that a swimming 'pool is, for many of us in the West, a symbol not of affluence but of order, of control over the uncontrollable. A pool is water, made available and useful ...'. Fresh water is not required to fill the pool at regular intervals and, like the garden fountain, it is controlled to circulate and be cleansed without needing to be changed for many months. The rigid geometry of its rectangular shape reflects the essential opposition to nature and serves to encourage achievement-oriented swimming (up and down a regulation length pool in straight lines) rather than more frolicsome water movements which invariably get in the way of serious, sportised swimming.

Snow and ice sportscapes

Snow and ice is water in its solid form and here too sport has created distinctive cultural landforms. Skiing and skating originally took place to aid locomotion. Today snowmobiles can be used to traverse snow covered surfaces more quickly and skating and skiing (and snowmobiling) are chiefly regarded as sports.

Skiing has assumed a variety of forms. Cross country skiing has minimal impact on the natural (or semi-natural) landscapes where it takes place. In the cases of downhill, slalom and ski-jumping, on the other hand, considerable re-shaping of the landscape has been needed. In these sports human interference with the landscape has occurred in three ways, first, by re-shaping landscape; secondly, by denuding land surfaces of their vegetation cover; and thirdly, by creating artificial snow to cover surfaces where it does not naturally exist at the time of the competition. In the case of ice skating, the activity has been removed from the natural landscape completely and major competitions are today held indoors.

RESHAPING THE SKI LANDSCAPE

The micro relief of the natural landscape is changed in two basic ways in order to satisfy the demands of serious skiing. First, earth and rock moving equipment actually change the profiles of slopes in order to make them 'suitable' for downhill skiing. Secondly, for ski-jumping events new structures are erected. Ski jumps have become longer and taller over the last one hundred years, the long-profile of the slope having been progressively steepened (Bale, 1989: 150). On the other hand, and again reflecting the ambivalence of such dominance, the Holmenkollen ski jump in Oslo is visible from many parts of the city and many people admire it as a tasteful landmark.

SKI LANDSCAPES FROM DEFOLIATION

Where the surface geology of an area is neither eroded by machines nor built upon in the interests of skiing, the vegetative landscape is often removed in order to create suitable pistes. It has been estimated that as much as 15 per cent of the surface area of some parts of the Swiss Alps have suffered negative ecological effects from the development of improved skiing facilities (Mossiman, 1985).

HUMAN INDUCED WEATHER

Where the landscape is not naturally covered by snow, recent decades have seen human power being deployed in the covering of such landscapes by artificially formed snow. This is done by various means, but essentially involving various forms of 'snow cannon', the artificial snow having been formed by using various nucleii around which an ice crystal can form. Initially minute polystyrene particles were used but more recently these have been replaced by a bacteria which, when added to compressed air and water acts as a 'crystal inducer'. This method was used at the Calgary Olympics (Burns, 1989: 34).

SKATING

In the Middle Ages Breugel's paintings showed folk skating taking place on natural watercourses such as lakes and rivers. Such environments continue to be used for relatively serious racing, notably in the Fenlands of England and traditionally in the Fresian region of The Netherlands. Outdoor ice skating races in this latter area have diminished since the 1960s when an artificial ice rink, built according to international standards, was constructed (Jansma, 1991: 79). Today it is more likely to find skaters on artificial rinks and speed skaters on tracks.

The first skating rinks were built in the late nineteenth century. In terms of their shape they were frozen equivalents of the swimming pool being rectangular with curved corners and around 60 metres long and 30 metres wide. Although the traditional Olympic ice skating events continue to take place on outdoor tracks, the tendency towards both immurement and speed is illustrated by the growing enthusiasm for indoor short-track skating – spectacular and spectatorial.

The sportscapes described above have covered a wide spectrum and in some respects possess the characteristics of many other modern landscapes. For example, they represent specialised rather than diversified land uses, they are relatively standardised and they are highly technologised. Although golf courses seek to replicate nature to an extent, as do some of the more post-modern water and ice environments, the modern sportscape is frequently difficult to distinguish from a warehouse or factory, such is the containerised architecture in which it is housed. Land and life cannot be said to be in harmony if the land is covered in plastic; the world of nature is hardly represented by concrete stadium walls surmounted with video surveillance equipment and barbed wire.

ATHLETES AS PETS

If sportscapes are analogues of gardens then in Tuan's terms athletes – both human and animal – can be viewed as the sporting analogies of pets. Animals have long been implicated in sports; along with human athletes they make up the overall sport landscape ensemble, adding life and vitality to what would otherwise be an unpopulated landscape and the broad interpretation of landscape adopted in Chapter 1 permits me to include animals, human and other, as part of the cultural landscape. During the nineteenth century and before the word 'sport' acquired its modern connotations, it often involved the hunting and killing of animals, mainly by men. A good day's 'sport' would invariably be associated with the slaughter of 'game', ranging from pheasants to elephants. The killing of animals continues and flourishes at the present time and is most devastatingly displayed in bull fighting. In a standard bullfight six bulls are killed and each year the figure amounts to several thousand with many horses also being maimed.

The dominance of (hu)man power over animal life has long been of significance, though such dominance is not invariably thought of as unethical. Indeed, some believe that because violent death is part of nature, human participation in it is natural and culturally viable (Causey, 1989). Short of killing animals, human power over them is most evidently exemplified in a sporting context where they are trained to race as in dog and horse racing and in other equestrian events involving jumping and dressage. In her anthropological study of rodeo Elizabeth Atwood Lawrence (1982: 134) proposes:

> ... the horse as an archetypal symbol of man's conquering force. The conquest of the animal itself represents the conquest of nature, and it is not difficult to understand why the figure of a man on a horse has throughout history been a sign of conquest. Power and aggressive force have always been associated with the mounted man .... Implicit in the horse-rider relationship is the fact that the rider has already mastered the horse, and his dominance over the animal may be seen as setting the stage for further conquest.

In horse racing this conquest was concerned with overcoming either other contestants or time; other equestrian events concentrated on the conquest of heights or other obstacles. In seventeenth century England horse racing was

already being labelled by the Puritans as cruel because it involved 'overstrain-
ing ... and over-forcing creatures ... beyond their strength' (quoted in Thomas
1983: 158), something which many would still observe to be the case today.
Even the gentle sport of orienteering causes deer to flee (Douglas, 1990). At
the present time the use of animals in any sport can be interpreted as a way of
reducing animals to a means, and therefore to deny them the value they possess, irrespective of whatever we may want from them (Tester, 1991: 10). A
major activity of animal rights organisations is their opposition to various
forms of cruelty in animal sports (Hoberman, 1992: 280-3). This ranges from
the over-racing of greyhounds and the application of 'mechanical doping'
(inflicting pain in horses' legs in training to provoke greater muscular effort to
which the horse may become habituated) to a form of mutilation of horses
known as 'tendon firing' in which tendon injuries are treated by a technique
claimed to be 'comparable to an orthopaedic surgeon pressing a red-hot poker
into a ballerina's tendon' (*Agricultural Science*, August 1985: 3). Yet while
trainers may force horses and dogs to run faster and further than they would
freely choose, even in gambol, the same people undeniably show care (even
love) for their charges, hence further illustrating the two-sidedness of power –
between dominance and affection.

Sportspeople as pets

Human beings have long been treated like performing animals ('freak shows')
and such condescension and cruelty is far from unknown in sports. In the St.
Louis Olympic Games of 1904 which were held in conjunction with a world's
fair, for example, 'anthropology days' were held in which 'a number of "sav-
ages" were rounded up from the fair's sideshows and asked to demonstrate
their native games and to compete among themselves in modern sports'
(Guttmann, 1992: 25-6). Their relatively poor performances were regarded as
confirming their racial inferiority. Although such blatant forms of racism are
not common today, condescending and patronising attitudes are still made
towards athletes, be they men, women or children.

   Just as animals are *trained* to behave according to human whims, as circus
animals are *trained* to perform lovable antics, and as racehorses and greyhounds are *trained* to race, so too human athletes are subject to exhaustive rou-
tines and schedules of *training* in order to achieve their sporting goals. The
manipulation of the human mind and body shows similar configurations to the
manipulation of nature. As Peyker (1993: 72) points out, 'the history of civilization is characterised by a growing control, mastering, management and
domestication of inner nature (instincts, passions, desires and emotions) and
outer nature (environment)'. As we force nature by directing or constraining its
growth we also force humanity through the wearing of certain clothes and by
directing people, notably in sports, into particular forms of bodily movement.
Rail (1991: 748-9) describes more explicitly the exploitation of the natural
body, noting its virtual superfluity in achievement sport, covered as it is with
aerodynamically designed clothes, shaved for speed, locked into ankle, knee
and neck braces, invaded by diuretics, growth hormones, high calorie foods,

vitamins and carbohydrates. The body can also be divided into pieces (plastic surgery) or replaced by artificial parts. Like the natural landscape, the natural body disappears and is made subservient to the record, the performance and the spectacle. When the body (or landscape) gets damaged in sport, efforts are not made to change the sport but to repair the body (or landscape) as quickly as possible (Rail, 1991: 746). The modernist concrete stadium can be seen to have its human analogue – the modernist body – in the steroid-induced functional figure of the athlete. But there is a contradiction here; although athletes, with their aerodynamic outfits, are liberated from the constraints of cumbersome and constraining clothing they are forced to pay close attention to the body via the internalised artifice of diet, drugs and daily training.

Some observers would go so far as to claim that 'the glorification of cruel and grinding ill-treatment is the ultimate rationale of all shades of contemporary sporting ideology' (Vinnai, 1973: 101). Though others might argue that this is an exaggeration, there is little doubt that sporting competition can involve considerable pain. The experiences of sports stars show that: 'it starts to hurt deep in your throat. The blood rushes up. You feel sick, your stomach muscles knot up and your legs feel like lead' (former French middle distance runner, Michel Jazy); 'You have to go beyond suffering. The bruises come out after the match, but the pain is bearable. At the end of a match I have sometimes not even had the strength to get undressed .... Mentally you are prepared but not physically' (rugby player, Walter Spangerro, quoted in Brohm, 1978: 24, 26). It has been suggested that pain-oriented techniques resembling mechanical doping could find its way into the preparation of human athletes when the limits of drug use and more conventional training have been reached (Hoberman, 1992: 282). Social and cultural concepts of order are thus reflected in both humanity and nature. Just like the untidy meadow, the untidy body needs to be *trained*, with all the pain that is implied.

Because no contest is ultimately 'fair' (because no two people are identical), I regard the notion of 'fair play' as an unrealistic ideal. Each 'player' having an 'equal chance' is clearly a charade and the uneven application of human power over others is basic to sport, and continues despite attempts equalise power through various 'rules'. In sports unequal power relations between human beings are reflected in many ways. Dominance may appear in its benign form, as with coaches who kindly and carefully prepare their charges for important high or long jump competitions. Dominance is also displayed by the trainer who constantly exposes a boxer to severe physical punishment. Professional boxing is the human analogue of cock fighting (though it could be argued that the boxer has some sort of choice in the decision to take up boxing). It is not simply human power displayed as two fighters try to over-power each other by punching each other's bodies but also the often exploitative power exercised by the repertoire of agents, managers and promoters. Whereas professional wrestling is close to the carnivalesque, professional boxing is close to – and sometimes actually is – a fight to the death. So too are motor sports. But boxing forms the end of a spectrum of all sports events in which the basic aim is to dominate an opponent.

As sport is dominated by men it is hardly surprising to find that women and children are among those dominated. As I stressed earlier, the sports landscape is highly gendered. Acculturation leads more boys into achievement sports than girls and being basically a configuration of masculinity 'women can learn sport but sport cannot learn women' (Veijola, 1993: 9-10); when women enter sports they are sports built by men for men (Rail, 1992: 746). Indeed, it has been suggested that 'competitive team sport is the ultimate display of male gender' (Veijola, 1993: 9) though this is far from saying that men do not also display power over other men in sports. Power is 'able to reduce humans to animate nature and as such they can be exploited for some economic purpose', as with professional sports players especially in sports like boxing where, as in certain other areas of life, 'the line between condescension and sadistic taunt is thin' (Tuan, 1984: 15). Alternatively they may be treated condescendingly like pets – people being treated like performing animals as in gymnastics.

Women's sport is often dominated by men. 'In patriarchy', writes John Fiske (1989: 34), 'the woman has been constructed as the object of the masculine voyeuristic look, which places him in a position of power over her and gives him possesion of her, or at least of her image'. Are not spectator sports places for looking, 'for possession of the female by the male look'? (Fiske, 1989: 51). Journalists and television cameras continue to place emphasis on the sexuality of female athletes, often before their athletic abilities. Track and field athletics and most notably gymnastics provide voyeuristic opportunities for male spectators, often exploited by television cameras. And can it be denied that male coaches derive sexual gratification through their power over female athletes? Child sexual abuse through sports is only now beginning to emerge from the taboo status which this subject has traditionally possessed.

For girl gymnasts it has been argued that 'cruel and unusual peril is now enshrined in the customary rules of the game' (Blue, 1987: 156), the result of highly dangerous somersaults, twists and turns. What is more, many girl-women gymnasts suffer from anorexia nervosa, the result of the fetish for low body fat, implicitly encouraged by participation in serious sport from an early age – an example of inadequate preparation for adolescence (Turner, 1984: 192). It is a kind of (self) control of (human) nature (Turner, 1984: 193). It is also believed that drugs are widely used in order to retard the onset of puberty in many young gymnasts with the aim of minimising body weight in the interests of maximising performance. In such cases the human pet is, literally, 'a diminished being' (Tuan, 1984: 139). But it is with women athletes' use of anabolic steroids that the imposition of masculinity is arguably the most sinister. It has been noted that as a performance-enhancing substance

> ... the anabolic steroid is nothing less than an expression of male biology as power, since there is no female hormonal derivative that can match its ability to promote muscle growth and endurance. The historical background of this chemical asymmetry is, of course, the prestige of maleness that has been an important part of our cultural heritage for millennia. In this sense, testosterone and steroids have exercised a kind of gender tyranny by requiring female athletes to accept the risk of virilization – for example, hirsutism, deepened voice, male pattern baldness – as the price of improved performance. In addition, these side-effects seem to be reversible in males but not in females. From a strictly biological perspective, then, the uninhibited pursuit of athletic performance is esentially a *male* project to which females may subscribe voluntarily or even involuntarily (Hoberman 1992: 146)

The map of the physical landscape may be symbolically 'masculinised' with the linearity and power of sites of achievement (see Chapter 4) but the 'map' of the female athlete's body is literally made more masculine by the adoption of extreme pharmacological aids.

Resolving the paradox of dominance and affection

Sportscape has emerged as an environment of power and illustrates as clearly as any other cultural landscapes the dominance of human power over nature. At the same time it should be noted that 'people who exploit nature for pleasure and for aesthetic and symbolic reasons seldom realise that they they are doing harm to plants and animals' (Tuan, 1984: 167). It is only recently that the ecological and landscape impacts of mega-events such as the Olympics have been well publicised. The deep cultural norms of western societies which encourage individuals to compete fiercely against each other in so many walks of life is perfectly complemented by sports which also encourage the production of more and more records and competition, not simply between individuals but between collectivities, be they schools, cities or nations. In such competition, the landscape and other human beings are inevitably implicated. The significance given to sport, has, as I have already pointed out, led to the colonisation of much land in the form of sportscape. In its own small way, therefore, sport contributes to pollution and ecological problems. Unlike factories or nuclear power stations which also create such problems, those associated with sport not only bring pleasure to thousands of people but are also often aesthetically pleasing. For this reason it is highly unlikely that sport could take a lead in de-emphasising the impact of human power evidenced in the brutal effects of sport-related concrete, gasoline and noise on the landscape.

The resolution of the tension between sport and human power relations is not likely to be solved easily. Power over plants and animals is inevitable, simply to survive. In the modern world people do not regard themselves as part of nature and there is too much investment in sport for big business to easily let go. But in the final lines of *Dominance and Affection* (Tuan, 1984: 176) and in the third of Eichberg's body movement configurations in his sports trialectic (see page 6) there does, perhaps, lie some hope. Affection is a benign form of power and, arguably, in the form of play it 'ideally mixes dominance with affection, control with nurturing care' (Tuan, 1984: 175). A rejection of serious sport and its replacement by more play-like body cultures may be exceptionally difficult – but not impossible. This comes close to Faarlund's (1973) view that outdoor life in the sense of exuberant living in nature presupposes the self-realisation of others to achieve one's own (that is, a presentation of self which does not separate the individual from nature). There are even hints that it is beginning to take place with some 'post-modern' forms of movement culture, green movements and new age philosophies.

NOTE

1. Although 'nature' was the least common motive for overall participation among the five sports in the Herva and Lyytinen (1993) study, 10 per cent of orienteers and about 5 per cent of cross country skiers did claim nature as their prime reason for participating in sport. No athletes from track and field, baseball or (not surprisingly) volleyball mentioned this motivating factor.

4

PURE SEGREGATION? SPORT AND SPACE, GEOMETRY AND TERRITORIALITY

In the previous chapter I explored the triumph of sport over nature and the resulting landscapes of artifice. I now want to consider the place of arithmetic, geometry, enclosure and segmentation in the triumph of sport over space as a further part of its rationalisation. Sportscape is often a landscape of flat (or at least) smooth surfaces, its paradigm being the isotropic plane of the theoretical geographer, Walter Christaller, upon which are constructed 'machines for sport' in the metaphorical style of the modernist architect, Le Corbusier. Compared with the notion of 'feminine' nature, such rationalised, western, 'objective' space has been coded by some observers as 'masculine' (Gregory, 1994: 129-31; Lefebvre, 1991: 243). The formal design exhibited in sports places celebrates the control of nature in the same way as such formality displays power in 'improved' landscape gardens (Gold, 1984: 17-8; Daniels, 1988: 63-4). To a large extent, the sports landscape is made up of straight lines, rectangles, right angles and semi-circles, all subjected to precise and accurate measurement. The geometrication of sport, like the rectangularisation of much of the modern settlement pattern of North America or that of the planned modern city, reflects the imposition of order on the landscape. Berman (1983: 177) quotes from a Russian poem about such 'new order':

> geometry has appeared,
> land surveying encompasses everything.
> Nothing on earth lies beyond measurement.

Modernity is the context of the map or of Cartesian geometry; modern space is objective space (Lash and Urry, 1994: 55). This was nowhere more apparent than in sportscape. Indeed, it has been suggested that 'the reduction of space to geometry, the abstraction of what is concrete, real and tangible in nature, is carried to the ultimate extreme in sport' (Brohm, 1978: 74). Of course, there are many sports where such geometric regularity is not very obvious – indeed, it is all but absent in some – but a boundary (even if liminal in character) invariably separates such sport from non-sportised space. Sportscape and landscape are rarely, these days, overlapping sets. In all sports played in regularly demarcated spaces, with accurate measurements and the associated meticulousness of timing, the isotropic surface is the ideal and the geometric character of the sports landscape is obvious. And segmentation and segregation are not reserved for the players and their separation from the audience; indeed, they are often more rigidly enforced among spectators and although the early part of this chapter is concerned with the landscape of the players, the second half focuses on that of the fans. What is more, at the level of the city, sportscape has become segregated from other urban land uses with the emergence of leisure complexes, sports zones or sports parks. At the same time, however, I try to show how the various boundaries in sports are not as unambiguous as the straight lines on a plan or map may imply.

The term 'time and motion', while usually applied to business and industrial efficiency in the style of the pioneer of time and motion studies, Frederick Winslow Taylor, is also highly apt for a description of sports where time-minimisation and output-maximisation (comparable with the *citius-altius-fortius* philosophy of the Olympics) within spatial constraints are key themes. Indeed, it can be argued that modern sports (and many of their problems) derive from the adoption of modern industrial technology (Hoberman, 1992), requiring as it does, noted Vinnai (1973: 47) in a book comparing factory processes with the 'production' of a modern game of football, 'increasingly complex labour processes and an increasing regulation of individual behaviour at the workplace'. I find it interesting, therefore, that Taylor, the founding father of 'scientific management', should have been a sports fanatic who applied his management principles to the world of sport, reducing it to its mechanical elements. Among a number of inventions, he fashioned a special kind of tennis raquet to improve his backhand and invented the winch to tighten the net. 'His object was simply to achieve results' (Relph, 1987: 94). The Taylorisation of sport has proceeded apace since the turn of the century with spatial constraint, rationalisation and standardisation producing not only increased output (i.e. more sport) but also what many regard as a superior 'product' (i.e. better performances). But the technologies of sport and work appear to be symbiotic: the application of the stop-watch to time and motion studies showed sport influencing work – the transfer 'of the body techniques of sport into work rationalisation' (Eichberg, 1990d: 120). Likewise, the concrete car-racing track was the prototype of the *autobahn*. The link between Taylorism and sport is not surprisingly drawn by the neo-marxist observer, Bero Rigauer (1981: 20), when he notes that 'implicit in both top-level sport and social labor is the demand that we continually raise the level of our achievement. This demand manifests itself in the establishing of goals which are continuously corrected upwardly'. It can be argued that sports tactics are 'like spatiotemporal planning models [where] it is a question of reaching a game-specific goal (goal, basket, finishing point etc.) with the greatest economy of effort, that is, by the shortest route' (Rigauer, 1993: 289). The landscape is, of course, implicated in all this and sport appears to be fixated with spatial as well as environmental considerations in order to raise achievement and reach 'optimal output'. I will develop this theme in what follows.

ORDER ON THE LAND AND SPATIAL FIXATIONS

Sports are eminently spatial phenomena; they are struggles over space, possessing 'elaborate spatial strictures' where 'the detection and restraint of spatial infractions and the measurement of spatial progress in play are of great importance' (Wagner, 1981: 95). Sports are 'dramas acted out within minutely prescribed spatial frames' (Wagner, 1981: 85), requiring 'exactly specified and formalized environments, for in most cases the contest explicitly concerns dominance of territory or mastery of distance' (Wagner, 1981: 92). But sports hardly ever take place in theoretically infinite space though I cannot be dogmatic about this as I will show by citing the inevitable exception later. I would argue, however, that in addition to the long-established environmental fixation discussed in the previous chapter, sports also possess a long established fixation with space. The spatiality of sport has led the various governing bureaucracies to produce standardised spatial environments where exact measurements, involving the most modern technology, is part and parcel of the rationalisation process. Such a desire to achieve exactitude in measurement is most apparent in sports involving the conquest of distance, that is by various forms of racing and in events involving throwing and jumping. Constant refinements in measuring techniques have been matched by refinements in timing, as was shown in Chapter 2.

THE SPATIAL FINITUDE OF SPORTS

Non-sportised configurations of body culture do not require spatial specificity. For children, writes Tuan (1986: 15), 'life is joyous in its vitality, and vitality is motion during which time is forgotten, space becomes freedom'.[1] For sports participants, however, time is of central significance and space is an obstacle and a constraint. Take the case of walking. In its recreational form there are relatively few spatial limits which prescribe where it must take place, though this is not to deny that restrictions on freedom of movement and access have increasingly been imposed. In its sportised form, however, it takes place either on a prescribed and measured route along a road or on a standardised 400 metre track. Parallels could be drawn with say, swimming and ball kicking. As Rigauer (1981: 59) has noted, 'sports events cannot take place just anywhere; they only take place under standardized circumstances. Anyone who insists on using his own irregular equipment or unmeasured stretches and places simply excludes himself [sic] from the system of comparable measures of achievement'. In most other areas of our lives time and space limitations are rather opaque whereas in sport they are made thematic and integral (Hyland, 1990: 132). In our daily lives we often try to avoid finitude – especially, of course, temporal finitude (that is, death) – but in sports we bring to the forefront those modes of finitude which we usually try to avoid. In sports, temporal and spatial rules limit us in more arbitrary ways than in everyday life (Hyland, 1990: 129). While much of people's lives is governed by rules, sport is different in so far as 'the rule-governed element and the finitude it entails is made an explicit theme of the activity itself' (Hyland, 1990: 130). Indeed, sports illustrate perfectly a way in which space and time are condensed down to scales at which participants can adequately perceive them (Ullman, 1974: 135). One manifestation of finitude, present throughout our lives but central in sport is our bodily limitation. Sports with their explicitly delimited boundaries most clearly illustrate a spatial fetish and finitude but less rigorously delimited sports also have boundaries, the nature of which will be noted later in this chapter.

TIME, SPORT AND SPEED

It would be possible in some sports to trade time against space. For example, in track and field athletics the track events tend to seek minimisation of time (the same applies to swimming, cycling and skating races); the field events seek to maximise distance – horizontal or vertical. In putting the shot and throwing the javelin, discus or hammer the object is to throw each of these implements the greatest distance, not to see who can throw them a given distance in the shortest time or to keep them in the air the longest time – though that could theoretically be the aim, as it could be in the jumping events. Normally, however, distance is given priority over time in such events. In diving, the only swimming event requiring vertical movement, neither time nor distance is of any significance and as in gymnastics, good style remains the principal objective, though quantified by the awarding of points. In racing sports between human or other animals, the object is to minimise time and not to maximise distance, though some 'races' on land and in water have involved trying to cover the greatest distance in a given time. For example, the last world record distance for the one hour run (an event not recognised by the International Amateur [sic] Athletic Federation for record purposes since the mid 1980s) was 20,944 metres, set in 1976 by Jos Hermans of the Netherlands. Analogous water-sports existed in which competitions also involved a race against distance rather than time. In the 1870s and '1880s plunging events were held in which each competitor dived from the side of a swimming pool with the object of travelling as far as possible, face downwards in the water, body motionless and 'no progressive action to be imparted to it other than by the impetus of the dive' (Sinclair and Henry, 1893: 110). The plunge ended when the competitor's face was raised above the water. Its sportised character is shown by the fact that in 1890 the record was claimed to be 75 feet 7 inches by G. A. Blake, set at Lambeth Baths, London, in 1880 (Sinclair and Henry, 1893: 111). Plunging competitions decreased in popularity during the 1890s, as did the one hour track run in the 1980s, and now hardly exist as competitive sporting events. In the case of indoor cycling, however, the one hour event has been retained.

Why are virtually all races today those which seek to reduce time rather than increase the distance covered? It has been suggested that it may be because time is felt to be in short supply whereas space, despite its finitude, seems to go on for ever. Also, 'speed and its stresses seem to interest most spectators more basically than endurance' (Weiss, 1969: 101) reflecting, perhaps, the modern tendency for instant gratification. In the case of the plunge, spectators apparently became bored with the extreme slowness of progression through the water. Elsewhere in sport speed (time) has increased in significance as, for example, in the case of the dribbling game giving way to passing in soccer and the development of the fast break in basketball (Penz, 1990). In track and field, the sprints have become more popular/glamorous than the long distance track races, the latter events now often missing from major track meets – especially those which are televised. Perhaps it is speed which provides the spectacle and the danger. After all, 'it is speed which transforms the hand into a dangerous fist' (Virilio, 1983: 115).

While spatial finitude is a major theme of this chapter I feel that it is also appropriate to allude briefly to temporal finitude. Time limitations are most explicitly stated in the sports that also have explicit spatial limits. A soccer game is temporally confined to 90 minutes. Other sports also have exactly defined finitude but in many cases it is not governed by the clock – for example the cases of three set tennis or 18 hole golf. But a game of golf is only over when the 18 holes have been completed; a 100 metres race is only completed when all athletes have finished; it is not only a game of baseball or cricket which could, in theory, go on for ever. In such sports events which could, theoretically, go on for an infinitely long time (because no time limit is stated in the rules) finitude is, nevertheless, invariably imposed. This has occurred progressively during the course of the twentieth century as time has become viewed as an economic resource, notably in the context of televised sport. Events likely to go on for too long have either died out through lack of interest – in the cases of plunging or running for distance – or have been 'artificially' terminated. In marathon races a time limit for finishing the race is now widely practiced; in tennis the sudden-death play-off put an end to very long games, an approach which is paralleled in soccer by the increasingly popular penalty shoot-out in the event of a draw. Similar comments could be applied to golf and ice hockey. In cricket the 'timeless' test matches of the 1930s came to an end when a game between South Africa and England remained unfinished after ten playing days; it remained unfinished because the England team had to return home (Brailsford, 1991: 27).

Several observers have noted the growing dominance of speed (time) over space (distance) leading to the observation that there has been a shift from geography to chronography or that pace has triumphed over space (Penz, 1990), sport reflecting a similar trend to that found in broader society (Der Derian, 1990; Virilio, 1983: 115). Hence, there are far fewer sports records in centimetres than in seconds, and even the few 'spatial' records (as in jumping and throwing) are part of 'a dynamic time configuration, trangressing the established horizon into an open future. The hierarchy of modern movement culture is: producing results – accelerating time – standardising space' (Eichberg, 1993c: 4). But I would aver that because all sport is not (yet?) reduced to an isotropic plane, landscape does still matter (see Chapter 6), even if its distinctiveness is being (literally) eroded (not only by time but also) by the ideologies of place destruction.

STRAIGHT LINES AND TERRITORIALITY

Even without the high degree of spatial measurement in sport, it is necessarily a highly quantified phenomenon. A quick perusal through the pages of any sports almanac or yearbook will reveal the minutely recorded statistical details of results and records, dates of birth and career statistics, averages and totals. Quantification is regarded by Guttmann (1978) as one of the defining characteristics of modern sports, distinguishing them from their folk-game antecedents. Quantification has, however, been interpreted in different ways by historians with a degree of resulting confusion. Eichberg (1982) and Guttmann (1978), two of the prime participants in the 'sport and quantification debate' (Carter and Krüger, 1990), take quantification to mean the recording and ranking of performance inherent in the centimetre-gram-second (c-g-s) ethic of achievement sport. They do not put very much emphasis on the basic concern of the present chapter, that is quantification meaning the geometric patterns and arithmetic details which define the spatial limits of play and the segmentation of playing and spectating space into sectors, zones and divisions. Indeed, it could be argued that the segmentation and geometry of space is more characteristic of sport *per se* than is the c-g-s orientation, simply because spatial confinement and separation from other uses is common to all sports whereas the c-g-s record orientation is significant in some (for example, and notably, track and field, swimming) but absent in many others (for example, golf, tennis, badminton, squash). And many of the much-loved statistics of sporting performance would be non-existent were it not for the spatial regularity of the fields, pools and tracks upon which records were set. Let me illustrate this point from the sport of cricket.

In the early days of modern cricket, without any specially prepared strip of grass on which to play, the teams agreed among themselves where the wickets should be pitched. Even after 1823 the pitch could technically be selected anywhere by the umpire and not until 1947 did the laws of the game explicitly ascribe the selection of the pitch to the ground authorities. However, the instant that the 1744 laws decreed that the cricket pitch should be 20.12 metres (in fact, 22 yards – one chain or four times one goad, a traditional English land measure) the first seeds of placelessness were sown on the cricket landscape. If the distance between the wickets on all cricket pitches was not 22 yards, or if the three stumps were not always $4^3/_8$ inches (11.11 cm.) tall, or if the crease was not always 4 feet (1.23 metres) from the wickets, all the batting and bowling statistics collected in Wisden's *Cricketers' Almanac* over the years would be meaningless. But the spatial limits of the boundary of the field of play in cricket were not included in the rules until 1885.

It could be argued that it was such boundaries, unambiguously marked with a visible line and defined in the rule books, and hence creating a more segmented landscape than hitherto, that are crucial in the defining of modern sport. Truly modern sport could be said to have commenced with the imposition of such visible forms of *territoriality*. This word has been used in several ways and in order to clarify my interpretation of it I need to describe the work of Robert David Sack (1983; 1986) whose examinations of territoriality have attracted considerable interest in human geography in recent years (Johnston, 1991). In one of the major reviews of human territoriality it has been noted that the word refers to the propensity for human beings to occupy 'spaces to which individuals or groups of human beings are bound emotionally' (Malmberg, 1980: 10). I will return to the emotional relationship between people and sport places in Chapter 6 and prefer here to apply a somewhat different approach to territoriality, viewing it more as a means of physical restraint, 'a primary geographical expression of social power' (Sack, 1986: 5); it is 'the device through which people construct and maintain spatial organisations .... a complex strategy to affect, influence, and control access to people, things and relationships' (Sack, 1986: 216); it views 'territory as emptiable space' (Sack, 1986: 88). Sack's interpretation, which has clear political overtones, is similar to that of Michel Foucault (1980: 68) who notes that 'territory is no doubt a geographical notion, but it's first of all a juridico-political one: the area controlled by a certain kind of power', and as I have demonstrated elsewhere (Bale, 1992b; 1993) Foucauldian notions of spatial segmentation as a form of power and control, as described in his history of the prison (Foucault, 1979), have clear parallels in the geography of the stadium (a subject to which I will return later in this chapter). Territoriality and segmentation are so pervasive that we barely notice them; they are something with which we grow up, literally from cradle to grave (Figure 4.1).

Figure 4.1 'As I understand it, we progress through play spaces and adventure playgrounds to leisure centres' (Source: Hewison, 1988)

Sack's 'theory of territoriality' has three bases, each of which is clearly evident in the sports landscape. The first is *classification* which refers to the categorisation of people in space, and in sports is typified by the spatial separation of players-spectators or home fans-away fans. The second is *communication*, namely the means of transmitting the clasification which 'requires only one kind of marker or sign – the boundary' (Sack, 1986: 32) which is invariably displayed with considerable clarity in sports landscapes, both on the field, court or course, and in the spectators' areas. The third basic element of his theory is *enforcement* which refers to the efficiency of using location, rather than alternative strategies, as a criterion for the exercise of power over people. As I showed in Chapter 2, resistance to territorial solutions of 'street football', for example, were not uncommon and at the present time there is resistance to all seat stadiums in Britain. But as a general rule, territorialisation in sports has prevailed with the help of the referee on the field and of surveillance in the stands. Resistance, while persistent, tends to be muted and arguments for the abandonment of territorialisation in sports have not been pursuasive.

The term 'territoriality' as used by Sack is not quite synonymous as the term 'segmentation' used by Tuan in *Segmented Worlds and Self* (1982). Whereas Sack clearly recognises the territorialisation of space as a manifestation of power relationships (as shown above), Tuan (1982: 11) sees an increasingly segmented world resulting from people's growing awareness of, and confidence in, self-detachment and their growing self-perception of greater individuality and need for privacy. Johnston (1991: 211) argues that segmentation is one of the outcomes of territoriality, though Tuan plays down the political dimensions, implying almost, that as society becomes more complex, segmentation results from psychology as much as from politics. Territoriality and segmentation are related in the development of modern sport but an untangling of the skein which binds them would need a separate book.

In the context of sport, territoriality seems to have assumed three broad forms or stages following a pre-sportive stage of integrated use of space with permeable barriers between players and spectators and the existence of mixed land use (see Chapter 2). The first stage of territorialisation was when playing space was separated from spectating space so that a segmented but monocultural sport-place was established. A second stage was characterised by segmentation within the crowd, though the sport place itself was still sited within mixed land use, often residential or at the edge of the existing urban area. The third stage occurred with not only the further individualisation of spectators within the sports place but also the separation of sport from non-sportive space by the establishment of 'sport estates' or specialised sport zones in particular parts of the city. In this way the landscape of sport came to mirror many other forms of separation in the broader society in which places are reserved for exclusive functions, the modern city having 'innumerable physical boundaries that keep people and activities in discrete areas (which) forcefully remind us of the city's delimited and segmented character' (Tuan, 1982: 7). Let me now explore each of the three stages of territorialisation outlined above.

ENCLOSING THE FIELD OF PLAY

In Chapter 2 I stressed that geometrical regularity was far from absent in the pre- and early-modern world of movement culture. It was found in the Greek stadium and in the straight lines of the gymnasium which mirrored the straight upright bodies of the non-sportive gymnasts in seventeenth century Europe. But the dimensions of the *stades* and gymnasia were not standardised; they did not all possess the same spatial specifications. It is possible, nevertheless, that forms of quantification such as measuring may have existed in the pre-modern period and the debate on this subject continues to attract the attention of sports historians (Carter and Krüger, 1990). There can be little doubt, however, that further forms of rationalisation and quantification have developed rapidly since the mid-nineteenth century. The spatialisation, specialisation and territorialisation of the modern sports landscape took place more or less contemporaneously.

The introduction of visible boundaries separating players from spectators was described in Chapter 2. I should stress, however, that the forms of spatial enclosure which have continued to be imposed to separate sportscape from other land uses have not always assumed such an unambiguous form as the straight white line enclosing the football pitch and it is to the variety of such spatial limits that I now turn.

Straight and curved lines and the forms of spatial limits

As noted earlier, the crucial importance of the kinds of straight lines separating the 'playing' space from that of the spectators was that they provided the final break with the pre-modern traditions and can therefore be seen as marking (literally) the emergence of sporting modernity. The straight lines and the large, powerful and solid stadium frequently enclosing them have been symbolically identified with masculinity and the curved line with femininity (Bondi, 1992: 159; Eichberg, 1993b) and, as noted earlier, it was men who formed the organisations which drew up the spatial rules of sports. But the straightness, angularity and hardness of the lines further symbolise modern sport's self-image and landscape – the streamlined body speeding in a straight line in a universe of right angles (Eichberg, 1993b). Contrast this environment with the softer, curved, rounded and ornamented shapes of the more natural pre-modern spaces of movement culture (the run along the winding paths through the forest contrasted with the *career* along the 100 metre straight). Curved lines would be dysfunctional, a waste of space, time and energy; the ornament is an expression of the pre-modern primitive – or even a crime against modernity (Eichberg, 1993b).

The spatial limits which serve to separate sportscape from landscape, though present in all sports, are not of equal 'hardness' and it is possible to categorise sports according to the permeability and standardisation of their spatial (and temporal) limits. These range from sports where the spatial limits are quite unambiguous to those where there is a considerable variation between the spatial extent of different fields or courses and sports might be classified according to the degree of rigidity or hardness of their spatial limits.

At one end of the spectrum there are a number of sports possessing very 'soft' limits where little attempt is made either to restrict participants to precisely the same geographic area or to attempt to replicate exactly the dimensions or playing surfaces of different places where the sport is practiced.

Indeed, part of the attraction of many sports is to experience the quite different sportscapes on which a particular sport takes place, a point which was made earlier with regard to golf courses.

Where explicit geographic limits are not formally specified the sport could, in theory, take place over infinite space. These sports are typified by races of various kinds where the emphasis is placed on spatial limits at the beginning and the end of the activity (that is, the start and finish line) but where lateral limits are rather vague. For example, in the cases of cross country skiing or running, orienteering, long distance swimming, especially in the sea, golf and sailing, arbitrary limits are invariably applied. Of course, physical barriers like walls, rivers, hedges or fences may restrict many lateral movements and most participants would in normal events take the shortest distance between start and finish. Nevertheless, the spatial finitude of such sports is much more opaque – and hence more like 'real life' – than in the two other groups of sports. Such sports are also undertaken in environments which are much more like the 'real world' – i.e. nature – than those with hard spatial limits.

A second group of team sports is played on demarcated areas which possess limits involving a range of permissible sizes. In football (soccer), for example, the playing area may be between 120 and 90 metres in length and 90 and 45 metres in width, though it must always be longer than it is wide; in bandy the length of the pitch must be between 90 and 110 metres and its breadth between 45 and 65 metres; in ice hockey the respective permissible ranges are 56 and 61 metres and 26 and 30 metres.

A third group is found at the other end of the spectrum and is composed of sports where the spatial limits should be exactly the same wherever the sport takes place. These are the sports which most encourage placelessness and are most removed from nature, though it must be stressed that even the most place-less of places may be surrounded by various kinds of elements which makes the overall landscape ensemble different from its neighbour in the next city. Two plastic football pitches might be exactly the same but the surrounding grandstands could be quite different, contributing therefore to a totally different sense of place. I will return to this theme in Chapter 6 and for the moment con-centrate on the spatial character of the 'field of play'.

Sports which have hard, precise spatial limits are of two broad types. First there are those whose spatial fixation is matched by a temporal fixation. They include a number of sports involving racing on land and in water where records play a particularly important role. There is little point in maintaining records for running, swimming, skating or cycling unless the spatial limits of races are rigorously standardised. If a 100 metres race produces a world record it cannot be allowed if the track or course turns out to be only 98 metres. The same applies to intra-course measurements. In a hurdles race the spaces between the hurdles must be the same for each runner in each event of a specified distance. Although it might be more fun for spectators (and, possibly, athletes) if this were not the case, the event only becomes meaningful in terms of serious achievement if the spatial parameters within which each and every athlete par-ticipates are the same all over the world.

But hard limits create certain problems, especially when the spatial limits appear to slow down temporal progress. For example, if the 100 metres world record becomes apparently unbeatable, will the 100 metres race be discontinued? If the javelin record exceeds the size of the field inside the spatially specified 400 metre track, will that mean the end of javelin throwing? To these questions the answer is an emphatic 'no'. If the 100 metres world record gets stuck at, say, 10.35 seconds, with several women equalling it but none bettering it, the stopwatch will start timing races to one-thousandth (rather than to one-hundredth) of a second so that a performance of 10.249 seconds will constitute a new record. And in the case of the javelin throw the weight or centre of gravity of the implement can be (and already has been) changed in order to retain the event within the confines of the stadium.

The second group of sports with hard and unambiguous spatial limits is what are broadly called 'court games' (e.g. tennis, squash, badminton). For example a basketball court must be 26 by 14 metres, a tennis court 23.77 by 10.97 metres and a netball court 30.48 by 15.24 metres. It is these kinds of hard limits which again provide great potential for extreme forms of rationalism and the tendency for one sport place to become exactly the same as any other, hence displaying 'sameness' or 'placelessness'. The imposition of such spatial limits as those outlined above can certainly be interpreted as a form of power, implemented by the spatial act of territoriality as described by Sack, and producing a world of spatial segmentation. The segments of sports space are frequently regular in shape – rectangles, squares, halves, circles, semi-circles. The sports landscape is, therefore, clearly one of geometry as well as geography.

A NOTE ON SPACE AND FLOW

The segmentation or territorialisation of space in the interests of more rationalized performance may have a negative effect on the state of mind known to psychologists as 'flow' – that is, a range of experiences found to be intrinsically rewarding and motivating in which self-consciousness is eliminated (Csikszentmihalyi, 1988: 6). Studies of flow (or 'autotelic experiences') have mushroomed in recent years and the concept's relevance to sport has not gone un-noticed (Mitchell, 1988). By implication, the changing nature of the sports landscape may in some way be involved in reducing the flow potential in sports. This is because modern, rationalised sports are 'eminently self-conscious and fraught with potential deviance' (Mitchell, 1988: 55), many sources of deviance being found in the numerous spatial infractions which so characterise modern sports. With so many spatial parameters, the potential for sport to – literally – flow is reduced. As Brohm (1978: 74) noted, the 'reduction of nature to geometry is the root cause of *the removal of play from sport*', the many spatial rules and regulations often inhibiting spontaneity and the spatial boundaries and segmentation of sports space encouraging deviance (cheating). Being caught cheating or making a spatial error creates a stigma or a sense of failure. As each player assumes a specific role, participants are expected to behave in a predetermined way. Each position in playing space limits the individual's field of operation (Vinnai, 1973: 51). While some sports have the potential for more spontaneity and flow than others, it seems logical that the more rule bound they become – and let me re-emphasise the spatiality of so many of the rules – the less spontaneous, play-like and flow-like they are.

GROWING SPATIAL STANDARDISATION; THE CASE OF BASEBALL

Some sports, such as batinton (a game based on badminton with table tennis scoring) and hockey, have a range of limits on their widths but not on their lengths (Arlott, 1977: 61, 422) while baseball can theoretically be played in infinite space, having no firmly prescribed outer spatial limits. Wherever different degrees of tolerance exist in the size of a sports area, true standardisation – and hence pure modernity – cannot be said to have really arrived. Nevertheless, the increasing spatial rationalisation (and standardisation) of such sports over time can be well illustrated by baseball, despite its idiosyncrasies. In recent years it has been averred that, in the belief that form should follow function, builders have erected 'huge concrete circles and called them baseball parks. Everywhere the emphasis has been on symmetry, uniformity, and keeping everything in balance' (Dickinson and Dickinson, 1991: 27). In 1976 it was noted that 21 out of 24 baseball stadiums were similarly symmetrical (Oriard, 1976: 39). The distinction between the traditional and modern baseball ground has been well described in these terms:

> Modern stadiums have become as standardized as modern players. The Polo Grounds and Ebbets Fields of past decades had as much real personality as any of the heroes or zanies who played in them. The Polo Grounds was the oddest-shaped park of them all – 258 and 280 feet down the foul lines, but stretching away abruptly to 475 feet in dead center. Each team had to play the park as well as the opponent. The few remaining Fenway Parks and Wrigley Fields with their short left-field foul lines and rustic beauty are being replaced by symmetrical structures glistening with bright colors and flashy ornamentation. They all somehow look alike . ... the modern ballpark is typified by Cincinnati's Riverfront Stadium: exactly 330 feet down each foul line, 375 feet in the power alleys, and 404 feet to center. (Oriard, 1973: 37-9)

An even more quantitative assessment of the geometric standardisation of the modern American baseball park compared with its classic predecessor is stressed by Lowry (1992: 3) when he notes that:

> ... unfortunately, ballpark asymmetry has decreased over the last three-quarters of a century, eliminating many of the peculiarities that make the ballpark a large part of the game's fascination. Specifically, asymmetry to the foul poles has decreased by 92 percent compared to what it used to be. The distance to the two foul poles differed by 36 feet on average in the 16 classic North American ballparks, whereas the distance to the two poles differs by only 3 feet today in the 26 current North American ballparks. Fourteen of the 16 classic ballparks, or 88 per cent, were asymmetrical, whereas today only 6 of the 26 current ballparks, or 23 per cent, are asymmetrical. Only 2 of the 16 classic ballparks were symmetrical, whereas today 20 of the 26 current ones are.

The changes in park geometry over the last half-century or more are clearly summarised in Figures 4.2 and 4.3. It has been suggested in rather élitist terms that the oval or circular 'all purpose' ballpark is mainly publicly financed and constructed this way in order to justify large public expenditures. As a result, while theoretically catering for all the outdoor sporting needs of the community 'it generally caters to (sic) none well and to all with mediocrity. Public-financed activity has given us ball parks without personalities' (Shannon and Kalinsky, 1975: ix).

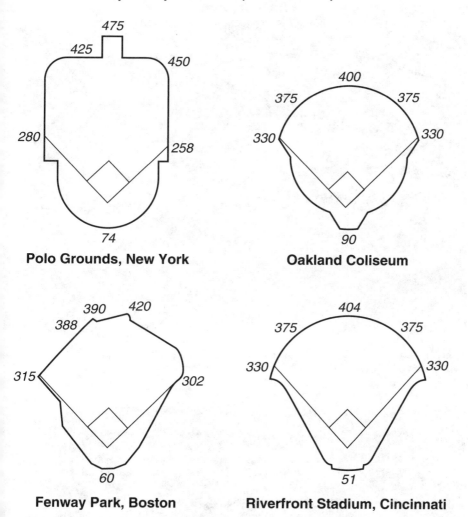

Figure 4.2 Traditional (Polo Grounds and Fenway Park) and modern baseball stadiums
(After Oriard, 1976: 39)

SEGMENTATION AND SPACE ON THE FIELD OF PLAY

On the field of play itself a number of spatial subdivisions exist, many of a visible nature but also a number which are invisible. Many lines drawn in sport-space delimit boundaries between participants (for example, lanes on a running track or in a swimming pool, the half-way line in team games). Such boundaries are further indications of modernising tendencies and have increased in number over time; witness, for example, the incremental increase in the number of spatial divisions on the football field (Figure 4.4) and those on the running track (see Chapter 6). Such spatial segmentation on the playing area shows little sign of abating. In the case of cricket, for example, a proposal designed to

Figure 4.3 The 'classical' and 'concrete saucer' landscapes of baseball; Fenway Park, Boston (above) and Atlanta Stadium (below). (Source: National Baseball Library, Cooperstown, NY)

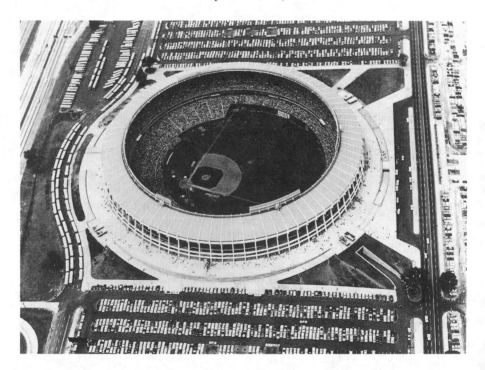

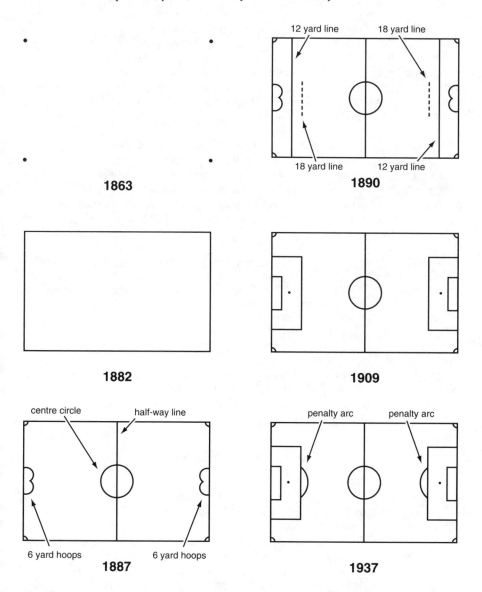

Figure 4.4 From points to rectangles and circles: the segmentation of the football pitch

encourage more attacking bowling has been for a series of concentric zones, centred on the wicket, to be marked on the field with only a specified number of fielders allowed in each zone (Lester, 1980). This may be the sign of things to come. Sport space also possesses a series of vertical limits. The cross bar, introduced in 1875, limited the vertical goal in football. Baskets, diving boards, hurdles, wickets, and gymnastic equipment all add a vertical dimension to what is sometimes perceived as two-dimensional space.

Other limits which, for most of the time, separate some players from others (for example, the goalkeeper from the striker or the bowler from the fielder) are not physically enforced; they are invisible boundaries, enforced by 'procedural' rather than 'constitutive' rules (Shore, 1993: 2), yet unwritten insistence on such invisible boundaries is a further indication of modernity in sport's spatial organisation. In the case of many ball games the early stages of their 'development' were typified by the notion of football's 'kick and rush' – a lack of any clearly defined division of labour among the players. As various forms of the 'passing game' developed, players assumed positions (or procedures) on the field, each position being separated by an invisible boundary but at the same time being linked by an invisible bond. In this sense, the space of the game, while at one level the 'legal' space of the field with its 'distinctive geometry' could also be interpreted as the team's space. As the philosopher, Paul Weiss (1969: 159) further notes:

> ... the space of a team is the space which the members together constitute by their attitudes, expectations, actions, and reactions. The members of a basketball team are interrelated in a continuously modified space which relates them intimately to one another, even when they are at different parts of the court. They constitute a spatiotemporal group in which the members are more closely together than they are to members of the other team, who may in fact be physically closer to them.

From time to time these invisible boundaries become liminal as modernist assumptions about strict positioning in space are questioned. The 'total football' – or post-modern football – of the Dutch teams of the 1970s, in which every attacker was also a defender and every defender also an attacker, might be cited as a case in point.

SEGMENTATION IN THE STANDS

In modern sport, it is not just players who have been separated from spectators but some spectators from others. Indeed, the strongest and most visible barriers in many modern sports landscapes are those separating one kind of fan from another. Having isolated the field of play from spectators, why should further segmentation have occurred among the spectators? Broadly speaking the reasons have been economic and what might also appear to be social and political reasons can be argued to be subsumed within the broader economic imperative. Although fences were erected around some sports grounds to keep undesirables out, it was much more common for enclosure to be undertaken in order to charge admission for spectators to be allowed in. Throughout the twentieth century there has been an increasing territorialisation of the spectating areas of sports grounds with individuals being gradually separated from each other and also confined individually in particular spaces. Such segregation of fans should be seen as an example of one of Michel Foucault's 'substantive geographies', that is, the geometries of Foucault's texts are not de-personalised 'spatial laws' but are best understood as fully-peopled geographies (Philo, 1992a: 156-7).

Hence, all seat stadiums in England are not simply 'plans' but containers of the frustrations, resentment and sometimes resistance of human beings reacting to control in a small but important part of modern life. Opposition to the 'containment' of fans is frequently voiced in the pages of the numerous football fanzines (Bale, 1992: 48-9). Hence, it is possible to find allusions to stadiums as 'prisons' (Eichberg, 1988) but, at the same time, as sites for resistance and 'carnival' (Giulianotti, 1991). And to state, as Lord Justice Taylor (1990: 12) did, that 'sitting for the duration of the match is more comfortable than standing' is far from 'obvious' (as he also put it); what is known is that what may be more comfortable (some prisons, for example), may not always be enjoyable – a paradox shared by many over-humanised landscapes (Relph, 1981).

I do not want to repeat the detail of the various stages of spatial confinement of the stadium which I have examined elsewhere (Bale, 1992; 1993) but if 'it is common knowledge that the seventeenth century created enormous houses of [medical] confinement' in the form of 'lunatic asylums' (Foucault, 1965: 38), it should also be common knowledge that the twentieth created equally large 'houses of confinement' in the shape of urban sports stadiums – the major foci of confinement of modern urban crowds. Reading Foucault's history of the prison, *Discipline and Punish* (1979), I was struck by the great similarity between the transition of punishment on the one hand, and of sport on the other, each being transformed from activities undertaken in corporal/public space to those found in carceral/private space. In pre-modern times punishment, madness and sickness were, like the antecedents of sports, public events found in public spaces. They were subsequently confined in spaces which became increasingly segmented. For example, spectating space in the stadium was initially unsegmented and fans, having paid for admission, were able to wander around the ground at will. In Britain it subsequently became segmented on the basis of rich and poor, seating and standing, and later on the basis of home and away 'ends', though this latter place-based segmentation was not found in many sports nor in all countries. Later still, the stadium space was fully segmented by placing each individual in a seat. It was also subjected to sophisticated methods of surveillance with closed circuit television becoming the stadium analogue of Foucault's panopticon – 'this enclosed, segmented space, observed at every point, in which the individuals are inserted in a fixed place, in which the slightest movements are supervised, in which all events are recorded' (Foucault, 1988: 197) – to such an extent that the stadium might be viewed as 'as the new "ideal type" of good socio-spatial engineering' (Philo, 1992b) and sport as 'perhaps the social practice which best exemplifies the "disciplinary society", analysed by M. Foucault' (Brohm, 1978: 18n). Indeed, the stadium is regarded as such a secure form of containment that it is, in fact, actually used as a prison in times of national security or repression. It was the Paris cycling stadium, the Vélodrome d'Hiver, which was used to incarcerate the 13,000 Jews who were rounded up by the Paris police in 1942 (Webster, 1993: 15). In the Chilean fascist revolution in 1973 internees were held by armed guards in the stadium in Santiago (Eichberg, 1988: 35). More recently, there have been moves from the Metropolitan Police in London to 'relocate' the famous Notting Hill street carnival, which the organisers want to be a quasi-Rabelaisian form of 'organised chaos', to 'a variety of sports stadia',

Figure 4.5 Football at Borås, Sweden, 1912 (Source: Moen, 1990: 97)

these being seen by the police as being 'more controlled conditions' (Jackson, 1988: 221). The sports place, therefore, has changed from being one of open, public space to one of segmented and panopticised confinement. The word 'enclosure' has traditionally been used to define particular spaces within stadiums and, like the house, the school, the prison, the hospital and the theatre, the story of the sports landscape has been 'one of enlargement and of progressive partitioning' (Tuan, 1982: 52; see also Eichberg, 1986). Such transition can be summarised by contrasting the crowd scene at an early twentieth century football match with the equivalent in the modern, all seat stadium. Figure 4.5 shows a game of football being played in 1912 in the Swedish town of Borås with the spectators scattered on the banks around the ground, unsegregated and mingling freely with each other. In the modern stadium spectators have been individualised in numbered seats, each being fully identifiable through their computerised ticket and from knowledge gained from the pervasive forms of surveillance which characterises the modern sports environment. This view is perfectly summarised by the comments of a police officer on the freedom of movement of football fans at the Maine Road ground of Manchester City: 'if you're going to segregate it's got to be pure segregation' (Murray, 1992: 28).

I might point out that the stadium-as-prison might be complemented with the analogy of the stadium-as-clinic. Today the application of physiological, as well as mathematical, science to sportscape is obvious at almost any serious sports event and the links between science and sports were clearly drawn in the physical landscape with the emergence of the stadium-laboratory which unified the demands of competitive sports with those of data-oriented science. In early twentieth century Germany medical research in sports became popular and sports laboratories were most rationally located in sports stadiums themselves. The first of these was established in Dresden before the First World War (Quanz, 1992: 5).

All seat stadiums, clinically and scientifically organised, are now common throughout the world of sport. Most, but not all, spectators have come to fully accept them and no longer seriously question the desirability or otherwise of terracing for those who wish to stand and mix with friends and colleagues and it is often argued that such modern spatial arrangements mirror those of the world of theatre and that sport has today become theatricalised.

THEATRE OF SPORT OR SPORT AS THEATRE?

The first chapter of Gerhard Vinnai's (1973) *Football Mania* is titled 'The football machine' and in the early part of this chapter I similarly used metaphors whose sources were science and technology. I now want to undertake an alternative reading of the spatiality of sportscape by adopting a 'softer' metaphor, that of 'theatre', borrowed from the humanities, in order to illustrate the ambiguous and liminal nature of many of the spatial margins or boundaries I have been discussing so far. This change in the use of metaphor parallels the recent tendency of a number of writers to reject 'hard' analogues of landscape such as 'system' and adopt 'softer' metaphors, one of which is 'theatre' (Cosgrove, 1990a: 345; Cosgrove and Domosh, 1993). The theatre can also used, not only as a metaphor for the wider world, but also for sport. In the theatrical metaphor, therefore, sport, theatre and landscape come together. My basic point in what follows is that rather than seeing the *modern* sport archetype as theatre, it is sport *per se*, in all its forms, which is theatrical.

Sport is frequently alluded to as theatre. Welsh rugby is termed the 'people's theatre' (Smith, 1981) while the arts critic of *The Guardian* noted that 'good sport is pure theatre' (Billington, 1992), combining as it does, narrative tension with aesthetic skill. Theatres and sports arenas are both *representational* spaces (in more ways than one) and, in the past at least, have been visually similar. The Roman theatre was, in design, an attenuated version of the stadium. Like sport, the theatre has spatial arrangements which are 'exercises in applied geometry' (Cosgrove, 1985: 52); indeed, it is often used for 'staging' sports events such as wrestling, boxing or weightlifting. Theatre also shares the characteristic of hosting 'spectacles', at least in the sense the word is used by MacCannell (1992: 238), that is, when the audience transmits an attitude towards a performance. Total passivity on the part of the audience, excluding even the politest of applause, would encourage the use of the word 'sight' rather than 'spectacle'.[2] Numerous other analogies between sport and theatre have been drawn. Sport events can be 'planned for and staged just as in the theatre' (Rigauer, 1993: 291); 'the drama of a good game of football as it unfolds itself has something in common with a good theatrical play' each possessing mimetic tension, perhaps excitement, a climax and then a resolution of the tension (Elias and Dunning, 1986: 51); sport and theatre invariably involve a team performance (Kuntz, 1973: 307; Mangham and Overington, 1987: 27;

Table 4.1 Types of performance

	Play	Sports	Theatre	Ritual
Special ordering of time	Usually	Yes	Yes	Yes
Special value of objects	Yes	Yes	Yes	Yes
Non-productive	Yes	Yes	Yes	Yes
Rules	Inner	Frame	Frame	Outer
Special place	No	Yes	Yes	Usually
Appeal to other	No	Yes	Yes	Yes
Audience	Perhaps	Usually	Yes	Usually
Self-assertive	Yes	Partly	Partly	No
Self-transcendent	No	Partly	Partly	Yes
Completed	Perhaps	Yes	Yes	Yes
Performed by group	Perhaps	Usually	Usually	Yes
Symbolic reality	Often	No	Yes	Often
Scripted	No	Partly	Yes	Usually

(After: Schechner, 1988: 12)

Schnecher, 1988); events are 'staged', each may have 'clowns'; the terms 'play', 'drama', 'players', 'upstage' and 'spectators' are used in each, though in theatre the word 'audience' is also, but not invariably, applied. 'Act' forms the root of both *acting* and *action*.

Sport and theatre are both regarded by Callois (1962) as forms of *ludus*, that is, although they may be play-like they each have conventions imposed upon them with only limited amounts of 'carefree gaity' (*paidia*). It has also been argued that among 'performance spaces', those of sports have more in common with theatre than with ritual or play (Schechner, 1988: 12-3). According to this view, theatre is more a sport analogue than a metaphor. The relations between four kinds of 'performance' (Table 4.1) shows sports and theatre as 'middle terms' where rules exist as 'frames'. Ritual is strictly programmed and play is free activity but theatre and sport, in a sense, combine play and ritual with rules saying what can and cannot be done and existing as frames. Between the frames there is freedom and the better the player the more this freedom will be exploited (Schechner, 1988: 14).

Sport and theatre are often said to differ fundamentally in that the former has an uncertain outcome whereas the latter is scripted and hence predictable. Cashmore (1990: 77), for example, is quite clear about this when he writes that 'as soon as the unpredictable element of competition is gone ... [sport] ... becomes pure theatre'. Likewise, it has been argued that because sports are not rehearsed or simulated, they cannot be regarded as theatrical (Oates, 1987: 106). But most sports are carefully planned (as the American term 'game plan' implies) and in some sports individuals' performances are choreographed – gymnastics, synchronised swimming and ice dance come to mind – and hence predictable, though the individual ranks in the competition are not and the uncertainty of the final result is always there. The case of professional wrestling falls between sport and theatre: 'the matches are known to be fixed but a certain willing suspension of disbelief is practiced' (Schechner, 1988: 10).

At the same time it could be added that the 'outcome' of a scripted play may seem to be different each time it is seen, according to an individual's 'reading' of it.

Sport as theatre is often used more specifically as a metaphor for *modern* sport. It is also used to imply that the modernisation (or the implied theatricalisation) of sports has negative characteristics. For example, it has been suggested that by moving sports indoors, the new, often domed, environment reduces 'heroic myth to *theatrical* spectacle' (Oriard, 1976: 37, emphasis added) and that in huge stadiums sport becomes 'a spectacle presented on a *remote* stage' (Kilburn, 1980, emphasis added). However, not only 'sport as theatre' but 'theatricality' itself has been projected in a hostile way with words like 'stagey', 'play-acting', 'making a spectacle of oneself' and 'making a scene' each having negative connotations, reflecting vestiges of long-standing prejudice against the theatre (Barish, 1966: 329; Daniels and Cosgrove, 1993: 66). The map of the modern stadium with spectators today confined to seats does increasingly appear to look like a plan of the theatre and perhaps sport is becoming more theatrical (if, for the moment, this is interpreted as an increasing physical and emotional 'distance' between players and spectators).

The rationalisation of the body in civilised society has traditionally involved the careful deployment of passions and can be argued to include the 'ordered, mediated, cerebral and relatively passive pleasures of spectating' (Shilling, 1993: 165) while sports 'as theatrical representations, with a clear differentiation in space between different types of players (the ground, the seating and stand) are undoubtedly *a creation of modernity*' (Archetti, 1992: 214). With modernity the discriminating spectator represents a move from ritual to theatre, the participating audience fragmenting 'into a collection of people who attend because the show is advertized, who pay admission, who evaluate what they are going to see before, during and after seeing it' (Schechner, 1988: 142). But what is often forgotten in the negative application of 'theatre' to sports is that the spatial histories of theatre and sport have each displayed the tendency towards segmentation and that the 'modern' form of theatre is only one of several which (even currently) exist.

Certainly, much early theatre was like early sport; in medieval streets actors sought active involvement from their audiences but after the mid-seventeenth century a growing distancing occurred between them (Tuan, 1982: 103), exactly the same situation having developed in street football a century or more later (see Chapter 2). In the eighteenth century theatre, however, the distancing of a 'civilised' audience from the performers was far from complete and there was no shortage of crowd disorders inside theatres involving fighting and the destruction of theatre property, often as a response to an unsatisfying performance (Lawrence, 1933: 178) – not unlike 'football hooliganism'. The 'intrusion of the audience into the actors' precinct persisted until the middle of the eighteenth century' (Burns, 1972: 74) and the convention of audience as voyeur, resulting from the dominance of the lighted stage over an audience in a darkened auditorium, has been dated from as late as 1880 (Burns, 1972: 77), more or less the same time as football, cricket and rugby spaces were likewise being unambiguously separated from their audiences (page 28). By the twentieth century the theatre had assumed a rather different social setting with its more

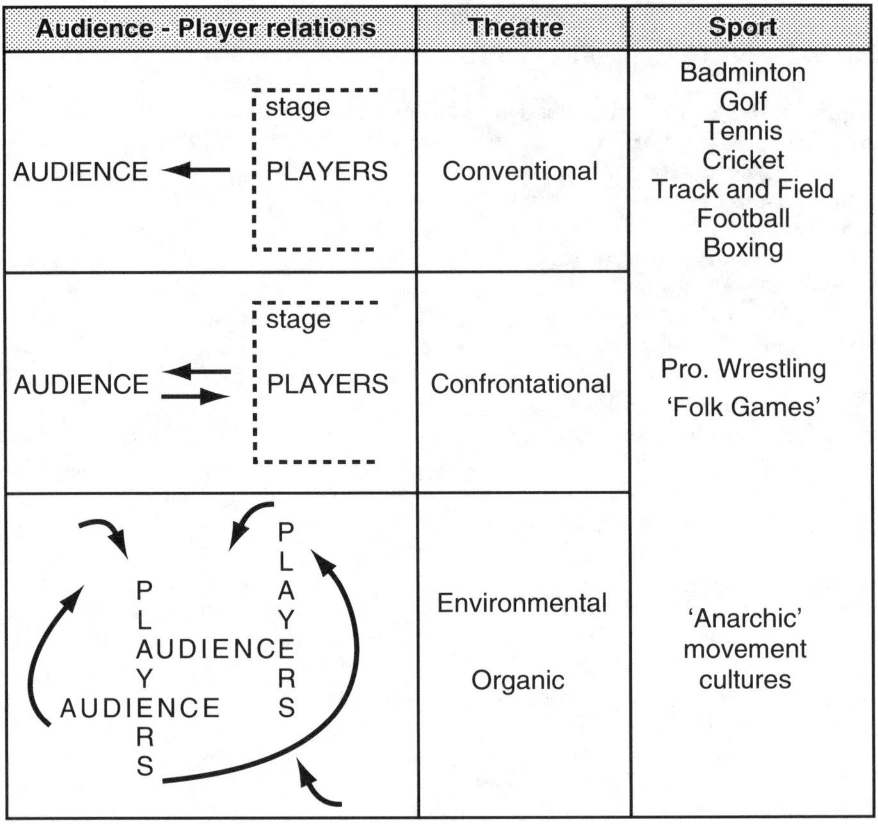

Audience - Player relations	Theatre	Sport
AUDIENCE ◄— ┆stage / PLAYERS	Conventional	Badminton Golf Tennis Cricket Track and Field Football Boxing
AUDIENCE ⇄ ┆stage / PLAYERS	Confrontational	Pro. Wrestling 'Folk Games'
PLAYERS AUDIENCE PLAYERS AUDIENCE	Environmental Organic	'Anarchic' movement cultures

Figure 4.6 The segmented and unsegmented worlds of theatre (left) and sport (right) (After Tuan, 1982: 191)

restrained audience, emotionally distanced *and spatially* separated from the performance with excitement being restricted to a 'feeling level' (Elias and Dunning, 1986: 84). The more dialogical and spatially interactive forms of 'theatre' were now reserved for melodrama and later for the more 'common' pantomime, music hall, circus, and cabaret, though in cinema the more unruly tradition of nineteenth century threatre continued well into the 1950s, exemplified in that decade by the rough behaviour in cinemas by the British 'Teddy Boys', often associated with their rowdy response to Bill Haley's 'Rock around the Clock', the theme tune of the movie, *Blackboard Jungle*.

Individual sports vary considerably in their 'theatricality' but so too do various dramatic genres. But the spatial relationships between players and audience are, in drama and sports, always of significance. It could be argued, therefore, that it is in the changing (and present day) spatiality of sport and theatre that the similarities between the two are greatest. Modernisation implies the clear definition and spatial separation between players and spectators and this might logically lead to a situation where the fan becomes totally passive. In the ortho-

dox ('modern') theatre, which I view as analogous to the modern sports environment, spectators have an 'almost private experience', sitting in the dark in
their separate chairs, contemplating scenes 'out there' and putting an increasing
stress on the eye, rather than on other senses (Tuan 1982: 189); in other words,
reflection rather than corporeal participation (Bourdieu, 1984) where the spectator's contribution becomes that of an outsider's gaze.

Many would agree that the Thatcherite dream for British football, already
achieved in some sports, was that of an 'image of a stadium full of spectators
silently watching the performance and not taking part in the drama, who conse-
quently cannot change the result' (Archetti, 1992: 214). This ideal type can be
seen increasingly in sports, but has existed for many years in the theatre, cinema, and in its extreme form, in television. The notion of a 'critical distance',
imposed by a bourgeois economy of the body (Bourdieu, 1984; Shields, 1991:
96) and applied to players and spectators is helpful here and can be interpreted
as the emotional or physical distance which is reached between them when the
spectators become so passive as to no longer influence the outcome of play,
becoming merely 'imaginary participants' (Archetti, 1992: 215), as in middle
class theatre and in total contrast to, say, working class football or boxing.

It is clear, however, that the degree of theatricalisation, defined here as the
fundamental distancing (emotionally as well as physically) and separation
(essentially, a form of territorialisation) of the various participants (that is, the
reaching of the 'critical distance' between players and spectators) varies considerably between sports, and between different periods of time in particular
sports. Consider, for example, professional wrestling which is virtually a theatrical performance masquerading as sport or, more accurately, perhaps, a pre-
modern theatrical performance where the audience is regularly engaged in the
action while the wrestlers themselves often engage one another outside the
ring. The spatial boundaries are constantly and deliberately violated while the
referee's 'authority' is always being upstaged by wrestlers and spectators
(Shore, 1993: 7). Less dramatic examples of the liminal nature of sport's
boundaries may be found in, for example, football (Figure 4.7), though such
liminality was not always favoured. For example, in a football programme for a
Sheffield United game in 1907, polite, non-dialogical behaviour was encouraged among spectators, when it was noted that 'continued bellowing at the top
of your voice ... gets on people's nerves and takes away a lot of the enjoyment
of the game' (quoted in Mason, 1980: 232). Such advocacy of polite behaviour
in early modern football can be compared with the traditional attitude in tennis,
for example, where the umpire often calls for silence. In such situations the
(middle class) tennis audience concurs and applause is polite and at specific
times, as in the theatre. The audience and the players engage in 'turn-taking'.
Traditionally, tennis spectators have not shouted or urged on a player; they do
not engage in singing or beating drums or in rhythmic chanting or clapping.
Such behaviour could be regarded as assisting the competitors in some cases or
putting them off or interrupting the performance in others. While acceptable in
many sports – and indeed, contributing to the enjoyment of the game, rather
than detracting from it as the 1907 football programme suggested – it is clearly
unacceptable in others.

The involved attitude and behaviour of spectators at football or boxing

matches contrasts with the more polite ('theatrical') applause traditionally displayed at cricket and tennis matches. In football there are strong aural and visual links between spectators and players, including banners, flags, music, drums,
chants and insults. Should the same crowd involvement occur in tennis as
occurs in football it would have exceeded the critical distance demarcating
modern from pre-/post-modern spectating behaviour. The distinction between
the different kinds of 'distance' between fans and performers in sports is graphically illustrated by Zurcher and Meadow (1970: 190) in a paper on bullfights
and baseball:

> Unlike the *matador* who constantly communicates with the crowd, the baseball players
> are seen to remain distinctly aloof from them. The player's allegience is to the team, and
> he who performs ostentatiously for the crowd is ostracised as a 'grandstander'. Contrast,
> for example, the baseball player's downcast eye and turf-kicking toe after an outstanding
> move with the *matador's* haughty glance and proud posture following a good series of
> passes .... It might be said that in baseball the crowd is expected to observe, in a relative-
> ly detached way, the spectacle being performed for them on the field. At the bullfight,
> however, the crowd is expected to be one with the *matador*, to participate, fully, in the
> emotions of the fight.

In recent years there does appear to have been a tendency towards the imposition of a critical distance as the modernist project would wish. All seat stadiums and greater constraints on crowd behaviour reflect this trend and create
milieux where loitering and aimless strolling are discouraged. The restrictions
on where people can and cannot go in sports environments, when fans should
and should not chant, as in the musically orchestrated singing in north
American ice hockey, what they can, and cannot bring with them to a game as
in the example of police confiscation of flags and banners at some English
football matches, or when they can or cannot talk as in tennis, are further exem-
plifications of control over socio-spatial interaction.

Paradoxically, however, in view of the modernisation thesis, there are also
signs that the critical distance between players and spectators is actually being
reduced in sports which have traditionally been more 'theatrical' in this respect.
The noise and excitement now found in English cricket has created a more carnivalistic atmosphere at some of the 'stately homes' of the game. In tennis and
badminton crowd involvement is also more evident than ever before while in
track and field the triple jumper, Willie Banks, started the idea of rhythmically
orchestrating the chanting and clapping of the crowd in unison with the rhythm
of his athletic performance. Traditionally, the crowd had been hushed while
athletes in jumping events took their approach run with applause being restricted to the completion of the jump. Players and spectators are increasingly dedif-
ferentiated.

In football and other sports, 'gesturing' or 'display' has become common
among carnivalistic (or 'clown-like') characters such as the post-modern footballer Paul Gascoigne (Figure 4.7) or the tennis player John McEnroe. Indeed,
in such relatively bourgeois sports as tennis, badminton or cricket, the growing
liminality of boundaries suggests that they are merging with – or being appro-
priated by – the more working class sporting behaviours associated with foot-

Figure 4.7 Gary Lineker (left), the modern footballer and Paul Gascoigne (right), his post-modern equivalent. They are analogous to modern and confrontational forms of theatrical performance respectively

ball and boxing. Attempts to bourgeiosify football (all seat stadiums, family enclosures, executive suites) have therefore been paralleled by the proletariani-sation of tennis (crowds shouting, players gesturing) revealing, perhaps, a polarisation of sporting milieu.

In football, an increasing number of dialogical antics directed at spectators rather than other players include various acrobatic feats, somersaults and brief spells of dancing, following the scoring of a goal. In this respect, it is interest-ing to note that just as some dance has become more sport-like (Banes, 1987), some sport seems to be coming more dance-like. In sports, more unrestricted kinds of body movements can be interpreted as forms of resistance to the 'mod-ern' traditions of self-discipline, lack of ostentation, and the suppression of emotional display. In these ways the 'clown' or 'fool', far from 'inhabiting the edges of staged and "real life" ' as normally occurs, is able to assume a centre-stage position – an inversion, perhaps even a perversion – of modern hierachi-cal society (Mangham and Overington, 1987: 121). In post-modern sport fools can and do assume a centrality denied them in other areas of life.

Such boundary violations, therefore, appear more frequently than the appar-ently neat and tidy world of modern sport might lead us to believe. They exem-plify the liminal nature of its boundaries, often appearing to be worlds of betwixt and between, or marginal play (Shore, 1993: 3-4):

In liminal or marginal play sport overflows the normal boundaries of the game. For instance play may spill over from the official players to encompass pseudo-players like spectators, managers, players on the bench or technical support teams. Play can become spatially marginal when the playing field's boundaries are temporarily breached to include the spectator stands or other peripheral areas as part of the play. In relation to time, play becomes marginal when it flows into periods before or after official play. Or when 'time out' periods become an important part of the play itself.

The effects of the audience clearly spill over on to the field of play and appear to be crucial in influencing the outcome of sporting contests, clearly transcending the boundary between spectators and players in some of the most apparently 'theatrical' of sports. Basketball and ice-hockey, for example, may appear 'theatrical' in the sense that they take place indoors, 'in the round', on more or less identical plane surfaces in brightly lit environments with the seated and individualised audience in relative darkness. Yet it is in these sports, in their 'theatrical' milieux, rather than in those played outdoors in more varied environments, that the 'home field advantage' is found to be greatest.[3] In the absence of physical variables with which the home team might be more familiar, this has been attributed to the presence of the audience whose participation is regarded as crucial in contributing to the home advantage (Edwards, 1979; Bale, 1989: 29-33). In such cases as these the audience is returning/going to pre-/post-modern traditions, becoming (or, perhaps, having always been) much 'closer' than the 'theatricalisation thesis' might suggest.

Liminality is important in sports because, as elsewhere, it 'represents a liberation from the regimes of normative practices and performance codes' (Shields, 1991: 84). That is, the strictly ordered world of rigidly defined geometrical and ordered cells which sport ought to be according to its spatial rules and regulations, is often found to be a shifting interstice, widening and narrowing over time and between sports.

It is now appropriate to return to the theatre and to stress that, in addition to the orthodox (or 'modern') theatre, other forms exist, notably the confrontational and 'environmental' (or 'organic') theatre. In confrontational theatre the players make gestures to the spectators and *vice versa* (as in the case of the bullfight, and of the footballers, discussed earlier). In the case of environmental theatre the spaces 'occupied by the audience are a kind of sea through which the performers swim ... there is one whole space rather than two opposing spaces' (Schechner, 1973: 39). The spectator and the performer share the same space and sometimes exchange spaces. The analogy here with pre-/post-modern sport is obvious (Figure 4.6).

THEATRE AS SPORT

Paralleling the tendency for sport to use theatre as a metaphor and, at the same time, to theatricalise and territorialise itself, the world of theatre has, implicitly and explicitly, used sporting practice as 'a metaphor, a structuring principle and an exemplary model for theatre practice and in doing so has continually provoked questions about spectatorship and identification' (Cosgrove, 1982: 125).

In the period of revolutionary activity in post-1917 Russia and 1920s Germany, when contemporary theatre was concerned with breaking down boundaries between players and spectators as part the transformation of established modes of representation and production (Kern, 1983: 201-2), radical or 'organic' theatre used sport as its model. 'The organic theatre tradition has always insisted that spectacle, sport and theatre are by their very nature public discourses but differ at the point of their social extension' (Cosgrove, 1982: 126) – the polite bourgoise theatre with its traditionally passive audience contrasting with football or boxing with their working class traditions and greater sense of crowd involvement. Hence, the radical and controversial Russian actor-director, V. E. Meyerhold, saw the spectator as a fourth creator of a play, together with the author, director and actor, being 'compelled to employ his [sic] imagination creatively in order to fill in those details suggested by the stage action' (Braun, 1969: 63). Vladimir Mayakovsky, the Soviet playwright, believed that readers and performers of his plays 'should alter the contents in order to make it modern, of the day, up to the minute' (Braun, 1969: 165). Meyerhold argued that:

> ... we must remove the boxes and abolish seating in tiers. The only design suitable for a performance created by the combined efforts of actors and spectators is the amphitheatre, where there are no divisions of the audience into separate classes dependent on social standing and financial resources .... Also we must destroy the box-stage once and for all, for only then can we hope to achieve a truly dynamic spectacle. ... the new stage will have no proscenium arch ... . (quoted in Braun, 1969: 257)

Conventional theatrical space was most emphatically 'destroyed' in the 1920s and 1930s with theatrical festivals for the masses, notably the workers' Olympics and the Nazi *Thingspiel* (Eichberg, 1977). In such 'events' actual sports stadiums were used to host massive displays, often involving the audience. The introduction of stadium plays at sports events really did lead to the proscenium arch being replaced by an open air theatre in the round. Hence, 'the spatial arrangement of the amphitheatre or arena became a structural principle of the *Thingspiel* theaters. The action – without background or curtains – was visible from all sides' (Eichberg, 1977: 139). The zenith of such mass events was reached in 1936 at the Nazi Olympics. Indeed, the theatricality of the Olympic Games has continued with the elaborate, sometimes Disney-inspired, performances of the opening and closing ceremonies (though since 1936 the theatricalisation of politics in this form seems to have declined).

The German producer, Melchoir Vischer, claimed to 'see sport as the central rallying point of the theatre – the new theatre' (quoted in Willett, 1977: 147) while Bertold Brecht[4] took boxing rings and stadiums as his models, describing the latter as 'those huge concrete pans ... with ... the fairest and shrewdest audience in the world', adding that 'there seems to be nothing to stop the theatre having its own form of 'sport' and increasing its contact with the public, providing them with more involvement and fun' (quoted in Cosgrove, 1982: 138). But this meant the opposite of being 'seduced' by a 'performance' and in the interests of encouraging placelessness he modelled some of his theatrical productions on the milieu of boxing and 'ruling out all but a minimum of make-up, costume or setting, Brecht...made the concert or lecture platform as unemotional and unhypnotic as the boxing ring; it became impossible for the actors to do more than demonstrate and illustrate; the audience could no longer be "carried away" (Willett, 1977: 148). Brecht's view was that the audience in the sports arena knows; that is, 'it is not afraid to make demands, is critical, unequivocating' (Bathrick, 1990: 132). He even went so far as to present his play *Im Dickicht de Städte* as a wrestling match and in the foreword he advised the reader to 'judge the competitors' form impartially and concentrate on the finish' (Bathrick, 1990: 71). The sporting environment would, Brecht assumed, create 'a critical but dispassionate audience, which would regard the actor in the same wide-awake spirit as it judged a sporting event' (Bathrick, 1990: 144), alive to the performer's technique in the same way a sports crowd was appreciative of physical skills (Bradby and McCormack, 1978: 112). The parallels with a truly modern (segmented) sports event seem obvious though it should be equally clear that Brecht failed to appreciate the extent of partisan attitudes and behaviour among crowds, especially at team sports (Needle and Thomson, 1991: 29). This is not to say, however, that the average football crowd is anything but much more informed and much more analytically talented about the performances and the performers they are watching than is, respectively, the average theatre audience (Emslie, 1990: 165).

These scenarios, particularly those of Meyerhold and Brecht, for a democratised geography of the theatre provided the stimulus for experimental theatre in the 1960s and 1970s which 'involved audience participation, creation of new kinds of spaces for theater, a widespread interest in shamanism: performances that heal, transport, transform' (Schechner, 1985: 148). Here can be seen a 'move from theater to ritual ... when the audience is transformed from a collection of separate individuals into a group or congregation of participants' (Schechner, 1988: 143), more typical of twentieth century football. In so-called 'theatre-sport' the audience suggest a theme and the actors improvise on it. These tendencies in theatre sound strange when placed against the recommendations of the British government's Taylor Report (1990) for all seat football stadiums, taking as it does the modern, fully segmented theatre with its passive and polite audience as its implicit model. The fact that 'distance' between players and spectators may be breaking down at the same time as barriers are being set up reflects, in fact, the ambiguity of modernity itself.

The barriers between players and spectators assume a different form if electronic mass media are viewed as an extension of threatricalisation. Some aspects of television sport are explored in more detail in Chapter 8. When spectating takes place in the home in front of a television receiver, the house itself can be interpreted as a 'closed-off cell' (Baudrillard, 1988: 18) where 'emotional feedback' is impossible (Schechner, 1988: 173) – a domestic extension of the the already highly segmented and panopticised stadium. I should note, however, that watching sport on television can be interpreted as 'a way of joining the crowd' - television as a 'gathering place' where spectators can relate to other people and imagine being in the places they see (Adams, 1992: 123). Although television sport has tended to focus on élite performers and teams, the rapid growth of local TV, cable and satellite stations has meant that even supporters of 'lower division' clubs do not have to travel to the stadium to watch a game.

There is one final point I want to make in exploring the parallels between sport and theatre. This relates to the significance of 'place' (even landscape) as much as 'space' in each genre. The modern sports landscape can be described as tending towards 'placelessness' in its geographical sense of places looking and feeling alike with 'dictated and standardised values' (Relph, 1976: 120; see the following chapter). When used in theatre, however, the word 'placeless-ness' describes the post-modern – or at least the avant-garde theatre (typified by Ionesco, Becket and Genet) – and refers to the result of the minimal atten-tion paid to the spatial setting and the lack of spatial distinction between actors and audience (Burns, 1972: 86-8). Yet the amorphous nature of the post-mod-ern stage/auditorium and the modernity of the isotropic sports field each in their own way serve to focus the attention of the various 'actors' on the basic message of respective 'performances'. In sports, place is rejected in order to focus fully on victory and achievement and in theatre in order to focus on the identities and relationships imposed by society. In each case, the objectives are facilitated by 'space'. 'Place' and 'scenery' would simply distract 'players' from their 'performance'.

From mingling with the players, to being separated from them by a white line, to being segregated in seats, to watching sports from the armchairs of their own homes, sports spectating has indeed been an example of a 'great confine-ment'. I have tried to show, however, that it is far from lacking in counter-ten-dencies. Spatial confinement is the basic framework for modern sports – but an over emphasis on the marked out artificial boundaries and segments, while being the constitutive rules of sport, ignores the possibility of empathetic engagement between spectators and players (Shore, 1993: 6-7). I believe that theatre in all its forms is, therefore, a good analogy of sports at different times and in different places – certainly better than representing only modern sport as a theatrical representation. The softer sport-theatre analogy becomes not one of increasing order but one of ambiguity; indeed, the theatre analogue allows us to see ambiguity as the name of the game.

SPORT LANDSCAPES AS URBAN ZONES

I have been looking at the increased spatialisation of sport, from the level of the playing field to that of the stadium. But how should the segmentation of sports space be viewed at the scale of the city? The modern city, just like the modern stadium, is characterised by 'fragmentation, break-up and separation' resulting from the application of 'technological and technocratic rationality' (Lefebvre, 1991: 317) with its carefully zoned land uses, either resulting from the 'forces' of social ecology or, these days, from the edicts of land use planning systems. Sport has long featured in this homogenisation of urban land uses.

Perhaps the most detailed and systematic study of change in sporting land use in urban areas has been undertaken by the Swedish sports geographer, Olof Moen (1990; 1992) who focussed his attention on the changing location of sports facilities during the twentieth century in the Swedish towns of Borås and Uppsala. The essence of Moen's study was that during the twentieth century sporting land use has not only become more suburban but has also become much more segmented with distinct agglomerations or zones of specialised sporting land use characterising each city (Figure 4.8). Such zonation reflects, of course, the neat and tidy world of the planner, a replication at a different

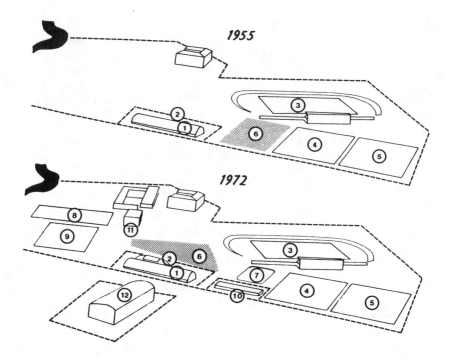

Figure 4.8 The growth of the main sports park in Borås, Sweden, 1955–72 (Source: Moen, 1990: 181)

level of scale of the increasingly neat and tidy world of the football field (from kick and rush to well-defined 'positions'), the running track (from unstandardised sizes and absence of lanes to the regular 400 metre track with regulation lanes – see Chapter 6), and the stadium itself (segmentation in the stands). The first such urban sports zones were developing in mainland Europe in the 1920s and 1930s (Lyngsgård, 1990). They were functional responses to the wishes of urban planners, viewing the city as a series of segmented spaces where different land uses could be neatly and tidily compartmentalised. The typical sports park would contain a stadium, velodrome, football fields, training areas, indoor badminton and ice hockey facilities, and tennis courts, and would be geographically isolated from the rest of the city, contributing to the 'planned obliteration of variety in the urban arena' (Philo, 1986: 26) – mirroring at a different scale the planned obliteration of variety in the sports arena.

The enclosure of sport in the city is a parallel of enclosure in the countryside since it reflects a loss of disorder in the landscape (Figure 4.9). Putting sports together like this makes a certain amount of sense, just like putting people together in seats in segregated sections of the stadium may seem to make sense. It may make urban life, like stadium life, more comfortable but it is contestable whether it makes it more 'enjoyable'; there are such things as comfortable prisons. It certainly improves the well-being of those local residents who often view the sports stadium in the same way as they view any other 'noxious facili-

Figure 4.9 The neat and tidy world of urban sports; golf to the left, handball to the right in the sports zone of the Copenhagen suburb of Ballerup. You don't need to find your way around with such efficient communication of territoriality (Photo by Laila Ottesen)

ties' but at the same time it removes that facility from its community and places it in a placeless 'zone'. In such a place it is easier for it to become a space to enter and leave – to fill and empty – rather than a place to relate to. And the possibility of residents sorting conflict out for themselves is denied by the simple expedient of territorialisation – "a consensual" embrace of the rational' (Lefebvre, 1991: 317). In a segmented world of sport the mixing of differences at various levels of scale, from the stadium to the city, disappears; hence the landscape becomes predictable.

Folk residuals

This chapter has charted the spatial nature of modern sport, emphasising its geometry, its increased segmentation and its tendency towards sameness. The combination of artifice and territorialisation defines the modern landscape of sports. It is a rationalisation of the physical environment which mirrors the rationalisation of physical movements and of social relations and their orientation towards competition, inherent in the value system of modern sports (Rigauer, 1992: 63-4). But is it as simple as that? Do other ambiguities exist (in addition to those such as the ambiguous nature of sport as theatre) in what are generally thought of a modern sports?

Residual elements, reminding us of the folk-game traditions, do still exist within modern sports with their international governing bodies, meticulously organised bureaucracies and regular spatial parameters, and also in the form of continuing folk games exemplifying pre-modern conditions. But consider first, the sport of women's lacrosse. Just as baseball could theoretically go on for ever in time, so women's lacrosse could theoretically take place on a field as large as the players wished for there are no defined spatial limits in the rules of this game. In men's lacrosse, the rules prescribe quite explicit limits, namely 100 metres in length and 64 metres in width. In the women's game, however, the two team captains agree between themselves where the spatial limits should be before the game starts. The arbitrary division of space in the men's games is replaced by a more 'negotiated' method of division in the women's, an interesting example in view of the fact that arbitrary confinement has been found to be a recurring image in many women's lives (Rose, 1993: 144).

A hint of ambiguity in modern sportscapes lies in horse racing. Tracks (courses) are not of standardised size or composition and timed records, though of some significance in the United States, are relatively unimportant in comparison with records in track and field or swimming. The lack of interest in 'the record' in horse racing is likely to result from the intense interest in gambling, the importance of which rests on the order of finishing, but not on the timed performance, of the horses. In other equestrian events, such as show jumping, timing is important in determining the ranking but these events are not undertaken on standardised courses either; hence the lack of significance of the record.

In other cases relict activities exist, less formalised than the internationally governed (but minor) sports such as lacrosse, and played on non-sportised land. A good example is the English game of knur-and-spell, a game played in the north of England (mainly in Lancashire and Yorkshire), and regarded as 'perhaps one of the most remarkable examples of survival' of old games still existing in an economically advanced area (Holt, 1989: 68). A case study of the game as played at Colne in Lancashire reveals that it involves a small ball ('knur'), suspended from a gallows-like frame ('spell') so that it can be struck with a kind of golf club. The winner is the player who can hit it furthest on the basis of the highest aggregate distance after a series of 'strikes' or 'knocks' (Tomlinson, 1992: 196). A different style of game is played in Yorkshire. The significant point here is that it is played on the moors and commons around the towns under 'spatially unconfined' conditions, being 'regionally varied' and 'self administered'. In the 1970s, at least, 'no consultants were needed to lay out the playing area; no further specialisation complicated the sport' (Tomlinson, 1992: 203), even though several thousands would watch sponsored 'championship' events (Holt, 1989: 69). The game had not become sportised, in contrast to the relatively late 'survivals' such as hurling and curling, ancient games which in order to survive 'had to take on the organisational forms of modern sports' (Holt, 1989: 70). But knur-and-spell is not unique. In parts of Tuscany a game known as Palla, which appears to have been descended from medieval tennis, is played in an organized form in small village squares (Morgan, 1985). Rules are adapted to suit local conditions and hence no regulation spatial parameters can be used.

Many traditional games became sportised, others died out, and others reappear in what might be termed 'museumised' form. Street football in

Ashbourne, Derbyshire, the Eton wall game, Florentine *calcio* and Siena's *pallio* are more self-conscious representations of activities which were once rooted in folk-culture but are today part of the 'heritage industry'. Their non-standardised appearance is simply cosmetic. It is also possible that sports are continuing to develop with the clandestine colonisation of non-sportised space and hence reverting to pre-modern spatial characteristics but this is a subject I will leave until in Chapter 8.

CONCLUSION

The last two chapters have focused on two basic characteristics of the sports landscape, its 'improvement' on nature by moulding its shape, and its territorialisation through the application of geometry. The landscape paradigm for sport is one of straight lines and land use specialisation. Such characteristics apply to both the 'field' of 'play' (note the increasing inappropriateness of conventional language to describe what I am talking about) and to the areas for spectators. A crucial point to bear in mind, however, is that within such modernisation, ambiguities remain. The world of sport is not yet as neat and tidy as might be expected, given the plethora of guidelines (literally) and statistics, rules and regulations, by which the spaces of sport are governed. Boundaries are rarely as impermeable as they appear on maps and plans; resistance to sporting confinement has assumed many forms and zombie-like passivity and predictability, on the part of players and spectators, is not yet with us. And the folk-culture of sport has not quite 'been attenuated into a few last souvenirs' (Horne, 1986: 184) as its museumised versions might suggest.

Yet it would be foolish to deny the broad tendency towards a predictable world of sportscape. Some sports require identical spaces where competitions may take place but even in these sports placelessness contains elements of ambiguity.

NOTES

1. Tuan includes 'athletes' as well as 'children' in the sentence from which this quote is taken but he is surely wrong to do so, given the seriousness of sporting participation con noted (at least in Amerian usage) by the word 'athlete'.
2. All 'performances' would not be regarded as 'spectacles' by, for example, MacAloon (1984).
3. The 'home field advantage' is the widely observed phenomenon of a team (or individual) achieving better results when playing at home than away (see Bale, 1989: 29-33).
4. In 1929 Brecht published a paper on 'the crisis of sports' in which he argued against their commodification and in favour of 'un-cultivated (and, thus, not respectable)' sport as an end in itself (see Rigauer, 1992: 69n). Note also, his article in the Berliner Börsen-Courier, 6 February, 1926, titled 'Mehr guten sport' (Brecht, 1964: 6). The iconographic significance of sport (especially boxing) in Weimar Germany is well described by Bathrick (1990) and the sport-theatre analogy is explored further by Hoberman (1984: 7-12).

5

A ONE WAY STREET? PLACELESSNESS AND MODERN SPORT

In one of several papers on what is arguably the world's major sport, Henning Eichberg has described the history of track and field athletics[1] since the late nineteenth century as a 'pure history of records' (1990b: 123; see also Eichberg, 1990c; 1990d). He could just as easily have been describing sports such as swimming, speed skating, track cycling or, with minor changes of emphasis, football, tennis, boxing or many other sports. His essential point is that since the end of the nineteenth century nothing has happened to change the fundamental direction taken by sport in general and track and field in particular, its basic trajectory towards its *citius-altius-fortius* goal being metaphorically termed a 'one way street'. It is not my intention in this chapter to contest that highly appropriate metaphor but to examine it in the context of the changing landscape of track and field athletics, taking it as a paradigm example of modernity in a sporting context. While retaining the one way street metaphor I will emphasise its twists and turns (that is, its contradictions and paradoxes) and, maintaining the metaphor, the occasions when we may have stepped off it or run along side it, even though continuing to follow its general direction. I will also note how among the things we encounter along the street, some are rather surprising with many residuals of pre-modernity remaining well into the twentieth century. I will suggest, furthermore, that we still have a long way to go before we reach the street's end which, when it is reached, will lead those concerned with its administration to decide whether to make a U-turn or treat it as a cul-de-sac.

PLACELESSNESS AND SPORT

Many modern landscapes are characterised by what Edward Relph (1976) called placelessness which refers to both a form of, and an attitude towards, the cultural landscape. Placelessness is in many ways the ultimate form of modernity, mass produced and international in style. As Kenneth Frampton (1985: 26) put it, 'the bulldozing of an irregular topography into a flat site is clearly a technocratic gesture which aspires to a condition of absolute *placelessness*' which would result in 'the weakening of distinct and diverse experiences and identities of places' (Relph, 1986: 6) and their replacement by 'commonplace and mediocre experiences' (Relph, 1986: 78). Many modern landscapes are characterised by placelessness or sameness in which 'different locations both look and feel alike, and in which distinctive places are experienced only through superficial and stereotyped images' (Relph, 1986: 118). We can buy Coca Cola Lite, eat pizza, chicken curry biriani or moussaka, buy Shell oil, and watch Brazil play football on video, in virtually any place in the world. It is often felt that we live in an increasingly de-differentiated global village. Suburbia, shopping malls, international airports, high rise flats, office blocks, factory farms and fast food outlets often exhibit standardised designs which result in one place looking virtually the same as any other. The adoption of international styles where the same company logo (for example, the 'Golden M') is replicated from Kansas to Korea is today a commonplace occurrence. Standardised McNuggets are sold throughout the world in standardised restaurant designs.

But it is not necessary for the functioning of McDonald's restaurants for each to be the same; for suburbia to operate, houses do not have to be identical; for apartment dwellers to dwell it is not vital for tower blocks to be standardised. We do not need Coke, imitation foreign foods or videoed football to survive. Indeed, in the world of business and retailing it remains possible to include forms of 'regional inflection', resulting in geographical differentiation which counteracts and interacts with the contemporaneous process of homogenisation. So while the food is the same the external appearance of McDonald's in Salzburg is different from that in Stoke-on-Trent.

In the case of so many sports, however, it is necessary for the spatial parameters of the immediate physical environment to be as identical as is humanly possible, irrespective of local or global location. As Eichberg (1986: 14) notes, 'interest in being in a position to compare performances led to technical conditions of competition being 'equalised', and to the homogenisation of space and its monofunctionalism'. Running tracks and swimming pools are milieux which 'are not judged primarily by their capacity for giving visual pleasure but for providing the opportunity for cultivating excellence in particular skills' (Appleton, 1975: 178) and sports like swimming and track and field could not exist as we know them unless their immediate landscapes – the pools and tracks – were internationally standardised. The space of such sports is close to abstract space – 'formal and quantitative, it erases distinctions' (Lefebvre, 1991: 49). These are the most placeless of sports and in few, if any, other areas of modern life are there such pressures for one place to be the same – exactly the same – as any other of its kind. As shown in the previous chapter, the stadiums surrounding the tracks have also displayed a tendency towards sameness in recent decades. These pressures reflect the environmental and spatial fixations of sports, outlined in chapters 3 and 4, which combine to encourage a homotopian dimension in much of the modern sporting landscape.

RUNNING TOWARDS MODERNITY: ON THE RIGHT TRACK?

The modern culture of racing (as opposed to running) 'requires unilinear move-ment in a straight-ahead direction, with progress or a career, with results mea-sured in temporal units' (Eichberg, 1990b: 251). Sportised running gradually emerged during the late nineteenth century and can be exemplified by the start of the 100 metres race in the 1896 Olympics in which technique and spatial segregation were already evident. Thomas Burke, the winner of this event, was wearing spiked shoes which had been introduced almost 30 years earlier (Quercetani, 1964: 2) and was using a crouch start which had been first adopted by the coach Michael Murphy of Yale University in 1884 (Quercetani, 1964: 2). If one is to judge from a photograph (Lovesey, 1979: 50) of the start of the 1896 (English) AAA 100 yards championships in which all four competitors appear to be using variations of the modern technique, it was almost certainly more widespread than the styles adopted in the Olympic event suggest. In the Athens event, the runners were segregated in separate lanes, hence avoiding the bunching, tripping and stumbling of pre-sportive, more carnivalesque, running. The race was run along a straight cinder (not natural grass) track measured at exactly 100 metres; it was timed to one-tenth of a second, again differing from the pre-sportive tradition where timing was not necessary to find a winner – only the comparing of what was happening at the moment was important (Eichberg, l990d: 118). In subsequent years the race was rationalised further with more precise measurement of both space and time, a more rational track surface which neutralised the vagaries of weather, more rational styles of run-ning, the perfection of the bullet start assisted by starting blocks, the more rational forms of body-moulded running costume so that wind resistance could be minimised, and the more rational dietary and medical provisions to aid the maximisation of performance. Even in 1896 racing appeared to be a very seri-ous business and it was to become more serious as it became more like a busi-ness. With all the advantages of *fin de siècle* athletics, however, something was lost. The link with the popular culture of carnival disintegrated and no laughter was left in the new world of track and field, especially in the 100 metres which, because of its limited time span and its 'tunnel vision' became the paradigm of modern sportisation (Eichberg, 1990b: 130).

Such rationalisation or modernisation was characterised by various forms of specialisation, spatialisation and standardisation, the same kinds of things hap-pening in similar centimetre-gram-second sports such as swimming, track cycling and speed skating, and required a growing rationalisation of each sport's land use. Such rationalisation assumed a number of forms and in explor-ing those I will exemplify the somewhat ambiguous nature of Eichberg's 'one way street'. The first five forms of rationalisation exemplify sport's fixation with space and time; two others illustrate its environmental fixation.

The specialisation of events

Early track meetings included events like the three-legged race or the sack race, undertaken in stadiums in front of amused crowds (Eichberg, 1993a). These were to disappear as racing became a serious affair with no time for apparent frivolity. Several of the track and field events of the first modern Olympics no longer exist except as curios of a bygone age. Formerly, the jumping events on the track and field programme were divided not only into the high, long and triple jump but also into each of these events (a) using a running approach and (b) from a standing position. The standing jumps existed in parallel in the early Olympic programmes but were discontinued after 1912, the standing triple jump after 1904. Jumping events have undergone specialisation into their modern forms and the standing versions have been marginalised in terms of serious competition, though national records for the standing high and long jumps were still listed as official records in Sweden and Norway until the mid 1960s. The number of events recognised as world records by the International Amateur (sic) Athletics Federation (IAAF) has also been reduced, from a figure of 64 (including 15 track walking events) in 1952 to 25 (two track walks) in 1991. Major casualties of such specialisation have been those events measured in imperial rather than metric units. The mile is now the only remaining imperial distance over which official world records are ratified.

A related development was the increased specialisation of roles, or division of labour, among athletes. A feature of much early sport was the diverse number of events (indeed, in some cases, the diverse number of sports) in which athletes could not only take part but also excel at the highest levels of prevailing competition. The polymath nineteenth century sportsman, C. B. Fry, is a case in point, being the world long jump record holder, English international cricketer and top-class footballer. As late as the 1930s Patrick O'Callaghan was the world's greatest hammer thrower as well as being Irish high jump champion. Such a diversification of performance was to be replaced by the specialisation of athletic roles, a true characteristic of modernity.

The specialisation of land use

As I emphasised in Chapter 3, modernisation is typified not only by the separation of roles but, concomitantly, by the compartmentalisation or segmentation of space. This was, however, a very gradual development. For many years of the early modern period athletics, like other sports, had to share with other land uses. This could sometimes have alarming results as during a quarter mile race in 1868 when the English champion, Edward Colbeck, collided with a sheep which had wandered on to the track; Colbeck nevertheless won the race in just outside 50 seconds (Haley, 1978: 130). Although the 1896 Olympics were held in a stadium designed with sport (albeit, ancient Greek) in mind, the games of 1900 were not, the track and field events being held in the Bois de Boulogne in Paris, 'constructed for lovers strolling hand in hand rather than for runners racing neck and neck. Races were held on grass because the French did not wish to disfigure the park with a cinder track. A slightly off-course discus was likely to land in a tree' (Guttmann, 1992: 22). These Olympic track and field events were not held in a stadium – reflecting the low-key status of the event – but all subsequent ones were. Increasingly there was to be a place for everything with everything in its place.

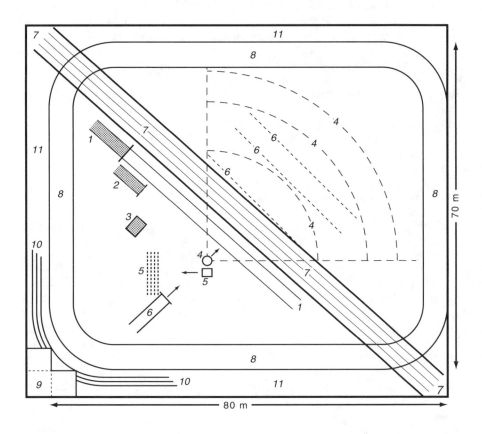

Figure 5.1 Plans of track and field areas of the early twentieth century, such as this Swedish example from 1907, were displaying an increased sense of order. 1: long jump; 2: triple jump; 3: high jump; 4: discus throw; 5: shot putt; 6: javelin throw; 7: 100m straight; 8: running track; 9: pavilion; 10: seating area; 11: standing area (Source: *Årsbok med styre-berättebe öfuer verksamheta under årt 1907*, Tryckeri-Aktielbolaget, Stockholm, 1908: 79)

The area shown in Figure 5.1 reveals track (100m) and field events taking place in the same space but the temporal pressure to complete a full track and field programme necessitated spatial expansion. Track and field required an arena within which specialisation could be accommodated, rather than simply an area. Early sprint races of more than 100 metres were not segmented (that is, they were not run in lanes), illustrating the less strongly defined spatial character of sport in the early days. Lane markings on highways seem to have been introduced in the second decade of the present century (Relph, 1987: 81) and although analogous lanes in track racing were first used during the same period – in the 400 metres in the Olympics of 1912 – they were far from universally adopted in this event even in the 1950s. Particular spaces were not yet reserved for particular athletes.

The mixing of different traditions of body culture also existed. Consider, for example, the period between the demise of traditional folk-games and the full adoption of modern sports in East Africa. During the 1930s when the first modern track and field events were being adopted in Kenya, traditional African folk games and dances took place alongside the imported English sportised forms of running and jumping. As late as the mid-1940s Kenyan athletics meetings featured spear throwing, using an unstandardised and indigenous implement rather than the regulation javelin. This mixing of folk and sportised events illustrated the character of a transitional period in the evolution of modern track and field, pre-modern and modern activities being carried on side by side during the period of adoption of modern sport (Sang, 1993).

But such a lack of clarity in the definition of athletic events was not restricted to African colonies undergoing the process of sport-adoption (or sport-imposition). An advertisement for an 1879 athletic meeting in Wolverhampton listed both running and cycling events; it was a sports' event rather than a sport event (Brailsford, 1991: 109). In the English AAA championships in 1931 the sprint hurdle race was held on the field in the middle of the arena. Was it a track or field event? From 1932 the ambiguity was removed and it became a track race. Running races would, thereafter be held on the track, field events on the field. But which field events were to occupy such a space, and from which sports should they come? In Leni Reifenstahl's film of the 1936 Olympics, gymnastic equipment can be seen inside the running track while track events were taking place but such mixed land use had disappeared by the time of the 1948 Games. Into the 1960s in Britain, however, the annual AAA championships continued to hold tug-of-war events, an activity much more in keeping with the strength tradition of folk-games, until 1977 when the Tug-of-War Association started to hold its own separate championships. The space of the stadium was becoming purified, given over solely to a limited and prescribed number of track and field events from a single sport. Specialised land use is a dimension of territorialisation and can be argued to have led to increased efficiency in many areas of society (Sack, 1986). Track and field was no exception with land use specialisation becoming the norm.

The standardisation of distance

Certain Olympic track and field events have featured in regulated competitions since 1896 but have changed in terms of the distance run. The sprint hurdles race was over 100 metres in the first modern Olympics but since 1900 has been over 110 metres. The steeplechase was over a distance of 2,400 metres in the 1900 and 1904 Olympics while in 1908 it covered 3,200 metres, only thereafter being established as 3,000 metres. It continued to be an anomaly among the track and field events, reflecting pre-modern residuals in so far as it was not until 1954 that the IAAF introduced a set of rules (i.e. number of hurdles etc.) for the event, thereby inaugurating the basis for records (Quercetani, 1964: 176). But even today the geography of the steeplechase course displays a particular idiosyncracy and has not been completely standardised; tracks vary from place to place with respect to the positioning of the steeplechase water jump, this being inside some 400 metre circuits but outside in the case of others. In this event the route is not yet routine.

The standardisation of size and shape

The size and orientation of track and field space has also been standardised for purposes of validating athletic records. In 1900, for example, the circle from which the hammer was thrown was nine feet in diameter but since then it has been seven feet. Until 1904 the shot was putt from a seven foot square but since then from a seven foot circle.

Until relatively recently the size of running tracks varied considerably, ranging from 300 to 500 metres. The 1896 Olympic stadium at Athens was U-shaped, resembling a theatre extended at both sides. The track had a narrow radius with right angles at one end of the arena (Figure 5.2a). The grass oval in the park used for the Paris Olympics of 1900 was 500 metres; the track at London's White City Stadium (Figure 5.2b), home of the 1908 Games was a third of a mile or 536.45 metres while the 1912 games at Stockholm had a 383 metre track (Figure 5.2c). That at the 1920 Antwerp Olympics was 400 metres and in Paris in 1924 it was 500 metres. By 1928, when the Olympics were held in Amsterdam (Figure 5.2d), the 400 metre track had become the standard size on which track events were to be held at the Olympic Games (Wimmer, 1976: 39). But tracks of various sizes continued to be used for many serious competitions. In the 1920s the famous Bislett Stadium in Oslo had a 500 metre track with two right angled corners. In 1939 the world record for the 800 metres was set by Rudolf Harbig on a 500 metre track in Milan and international races were still being held on a 500 metre track in Cologne in the early 1950s. Some straight tracks of 400 metres existed at the start of the present century and 200 metre straights were quite common, especially in the USA but gradually disappeared during the 1960s as the 200 metre sprint became standardised as a race around a curve. In 1976 the IAAF Congress approved a recommendation by its Technical Committee to eliminate 200 metre and 220 yards performances on straight tracks from the world record schedule as part of the process of standardisation.

For many years the famous running track at Fenner's at Cambridge University measured three laps to the mile and events were run in a clockwise direction. It survived in this form, with serious competitions taking place there, until 1959. Indoor events are still held on tracks of variable length and circumference though these are increasingly becoming standardised as 200 metre ovals. For world records to be recognised by the IAAF, however, the limiting size of the track is 220 yards for indoor performances and 440 yards for those outdoors.

The standardisation of criteria for victory (or the triumph of quantification)

The stopwatch or the tape measure are not the only ways in which athletic performance may be judged. Early, non-sportised jumping events were judged

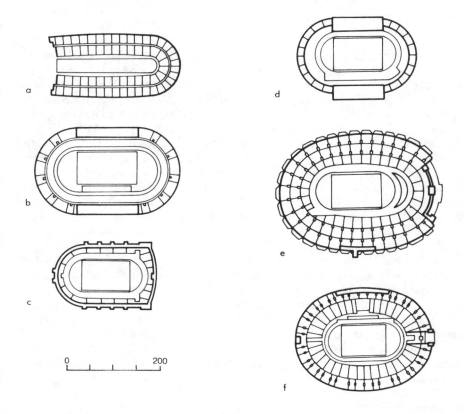

Figure 5.2 The changing size and shape of selected Olympic track and field spaces, 1896-1936. Plans show (a) Athens, (b) London, (c) Stockholm, (d) Amsterdam, (e) Los Angeles, and (f) Berlin. The Los Angeles Coliseum and the Berlin Olympic Stadium would be at least adequate for the hosting of future Olympic Games (Source: Wimmer, 1976: 40)

more by aesthetic criteria than by time or distance achieved. In contrast to the English emphasis on the quantified performance the early German gymnastic movement judged running on the basis of 'good form' as much as on winning while in Scandinavian gymnastics the movements of high jumpers were based on aesthetic and hygienic considerations rather than sportised achievement. An upright position – good posture – was judged superior to aggressive competition (Eichberg, 1990b: 130). The legacy of 'style' as a criterion by which sporting achievement could be judged in track and field continued in a residual form for a surprisingly long time as a reminder of the previous, and certainly non-English, body-cultural tradition. In Britain (somewhat paradoxically), for the greater part of the twentieth century, a style prize was awarded in the national track race walking championships. In this case 'style' was not measured on any quasi-scientific points basis as in ice-skating or gymnastics but by the collective impressions of the judges. The winner of the style prize was not necessarily the first across the finishing line but the ideology of achievement sport prevailed and in the mid-1970s the style prize was discontinued.

The standardisation of micro-topography

Replacing the pre-modern traditions of utilising existing land uses, the first running track in England was built at Lord's Cricket Ground in London in 1837 – 'a narrow path designed for two man races – but faced with gravel and measured by surveyors' (Lovesey, 1979: 15). Nearly 30 years later, however, the first Oxford-Cambridge athletics match in March 1867 was held 'on the spongy grass surface of a wet cricket field at Christ Church' (Haley, 1978: 130). In Britain and its Empire, many races continued to take place on grass, even after the Second World War. In 1950, for example, the Empire Games were held on a grass track in Auckland, New Zealand and some of the world's greatest performances occurred on similar tracks in Australia into the 1960s. For example, in 1962 the men's mile and the women's 800 metres world records were broken on grass tracks in Wanganui, New Zealand and Perth, Australia respectively. A good grass track, usually laid out and manicured on an immaculate cricket field, was often believed to be as 'fast' as, or 'faster' than, many cinder tracks.

By the late 1950s, however, the majority of important track meetings took place on cinder tracks, though the composition of such tracks had always varied considerably. The track for the 1908 White City (London) Olympics was composed of 6 inches of engine and house ashes on top of 12 inches of hard core and another six inches of ashes (Webster, 1940: 111). The more sophisticated 1912 Stockholm Olympic track, regarded for many years as the fastest and firmest in the world, was made up of a 15 centimetres surface layer of mixed (as in concrete) slag (from locomotives and a local electricity works), and mould mixed with sand, mortar and marl (Webster, 1940: 117). In Britain red marl was used in the composition of the track at Perry Barr, Birmingham while in Reykjavik, Iceland, the track was composed of volcanic lava. The result of such variation in track composition meant that the experience of running varied considerably from place to place, the groundsmen who nurtured the tracks being skilled artisans whose reputations were often highly regarded. The hand of a human being was still reflected on the surface of the track.

The introduction of starting blocks was a further rationalisation of the running track. Invented in 1927, these were first used in Chicago in 1929 and from 'experiments conducted on a large scale' it was concluded that from their use an average sprinter could gain 34/1000 of a second (that is, about 30 centimetres in distance) in a 100 yards race (Quercetani, 1991: 41). For several years, however, starting blocks were viewed as unfair artificial aids and were not widely used. George Simpson's world record 100 yards time of 9.4 seconds, achieved in 1929, was disallowed because of the use of blocks and even in the 1936 Olympics sprinters used small trowels to dig their own starting holes in the track. Blocks were not sanctioned by the IAAF until 1948 when they were used for first time in the Olympics. Today they are a compulsory part of the sprinters' micro-environment.

The last Olympic Games to be held on a cinder track were in Tokyo in 1964. Such tracks had been carefully prepared with running and racing in mind and were used for little else.[2] It was a classic example of sport monoculture and given the seriousness with which racing was taken tracks were tended scientifically, being given over to 'fallow' for a few days before a major meeting so that they could be perfected for races. During freezing or wet weather and periods of over use such tracks deteriorated rapidly; they were eventually to give way to surfaces made of synthetic materials in order to conquer the physical environment's natural interference with the regimen of running.

The first synthetic running track was constructed in the United States in 1950. Subsequent widespread adoption of this innovation can be illustrated by the fact that in Sweden the number of cinder tracks declined from a total of 556 in 1983 to 431 in 1990 whereas during the same period the number of synthetic tracks increased from 82 to 115 (Moen, 1993: 48). In the same country in 1991, no less than 91 per cent of all official athletics competitions were held on synthetic tracks (Moen, 1993: 48) and in recent decades all major championship events have been held on such surfaces.

The bodily experience of running on such surfaces does not vary significantly from place to place, though it is different from running on natural surfaces, grass and cinders. For major competitions IAAF Rule 137 states that, *inter alia*, competitions directly under IAAF control may only be held on synthetic surfaced tracks conforming to standards approved by the IAAF. These cover such aspects as thickness, hardness, tensile strength and ductile yield. Synthetic tracks, therefore, further contribute to the standardisation of the athletic landscape. But they also intensify athletic production. This is because they can be used much more frequently than tracks of other composition and texture and also enhance performance. It is widely believed that they are one second per lap faster than cinder tracks. Because they do not deteriorate in bad weather they also encourage an increased 'Taylorisation' of the training regimen and, because they can be used more intensively than more natural surfaces, can also be interpreted as further alienating the athlete. As Rigauer (1981: 72) notes, 'the indications of alienation begin to appear in top-level sports when the individual discipline declines into a highly specialized activity or when rationalized training methods are used, for example, interval running, which coerces the athlete into continual repetition of the same precisely fixed and isolated narrow tasks'. On the placeless synthetic 400 metre track we get closer and closer to the optimal performance. As a marxist observer noted, 'the ideal situation in sport is only reached when grass, which has already been reduced to its geometrical properties and so to speak artificialised, is actually abandoned for synthetic materials and the race track thereby loses all connexion with the earth' (Ziemilski, 1965: 9, quoted in Brohm, 1978: 74). We get, in reality, very close to the theoretical isotropic plane/plain.

The neutralisation of the environment

The physical environment, in its various forms, has always posed a problem for track and field. The insistence on 'fair play' between competitors implies fair play between competitions. Once the record becomes important, however, it seems unfair for one competition to be be held in an environment which favours record breaking. Hence, factors like wind assistance and altitude are judged to favour competitors in some competitions while their benefits are denied participants in others. One of the observations commonly made about modern sport is that it should be undertaken in environment-less conditions and since the mid-nineteenth century technology has been utilised in attempts to eliminate environmental influences on performances, rationalism having sought to validate athletic records without extraneous environmental assistance. Such assistance should logically include the architectural style of the surrounding stadium buildings (and the spectators themselves – see Chapter 4) and in recent years there has been a tendency to produce internationally standardised concrete saucers which shut out the city of which the stadium is part. Such architecture tends to make one stadium, as well as each track, much the same as any other. 'Sameness' becomes even closer to homotopia when athletic events are held indoors where temperature can be controlled and rainfall and wind eliminated.

Track and field sports have been held indoors since since 1861 when the first American indoor meet was held in Cincinnati, Ohio (Quercetani, 1991: vi). Gaslit events in an adapted hall were held in London in 1863 (Lovesey, 1979: 86) but in England – though not in North America where indoor athletic competitions were frequently held – such immurement was sporadic and the AAA indoor championships were not introduced until 1935 when they were held at the Empire Pool, Wembley. Today indoor track and field is widely found throughout the 'western' world, often in places such as southern California and Spain where the climate would permit performances out of doors.

Another way of eliminating the effect of certain meteorological variables would be to ignore any records set with assistance from such conditions. Wind, for example, can exert considerable influence on athletic performance in a large number of events. Since 1936, however, records set with wind assistance of more than 2 metres per second in the sprint and hurdle events up to, and including, 200 metres and the long and triple jumps, are not acceptable. Wind speed is measured by an anemometer placed halfway along the straight on the inside of the track. In other events athletes make adjustment to the meteorological landscape by adjusting their technique. In javelin throwing, for example, a headwind requires a decrease in the angle of release proportional to the velocity of the wind. A wind from behind dictates an increase in the angle (Terauds, 1985: 101).

CONTRADICTIONS OF THE SPATIAL FIX

The fetish of space which I have shown to characterise sport in general (Chapter 4) posesses a number of contradictions which suggest that while track and field has experienced many rationalistic tendencies along its 'one way street' from before the 1896 Olympics to the present day, it has not yet reached its cul-de-sac or its U-turn. Indeed, the rationalisation of the street may have hardly begun.

Despite sport's spatial fetish and the extremes to which chrono-technology goes to record individual performances, it is inevitable that the distance covered by athletes is always more than that that claimed for the event. Even in events such as the 100 metre sprint athletes rarely run in an exact straight line and as a result run further than they need to. In middle and long distance track running the distance covered exceeds that notionally attributed to the race because of the added distance involved in overtaking. Indeed, if the record has become the ultimate object of modern sport it could be argued that in sports like running, time-trials where individuals simply run against the clock (as in, say, certain cycling events where records are only ratified if a single person is participating at a time), would represent a more modern form of competition.

Despite the time-space fetish where performances are measured to one-hundredth of a second, track measurements are, in fact, permitted to vary. The track measurements are taken 30 centimetres outward from the kerb or, where no kerb exists, 20 centimetres from the line marking the inside of the track. Hence, running tracks do not measure exactly what they are claimed to be. In measuring a track, two independent measurements must be taken. These may not differ from each other by more than $0.0003 + L \times 0.01$ metres where L is the length of the track in metres. This formula gives the highest permitted difference between two measurements for 100 metres of 4 centimetres and for 400 metres of 13 centimetres. This has important implications for events which are timed to one-hundredth of a second since an improvement of a record by 0.01 of a second in say, a 10,000 metres event will be meaningless if tracks vary by as much as a centimetre per lap, which they are likely to do.

A somewhat curious paradox is that whereas starting blocks and electrical timing had been introduced at the 1948 Olympics and have become a integral parts of modern track and field, the notion of the mechanical starting gate, present in the Greek stadium, and designed to prevents false starts, never caught on in modern track and field, despite its widespread use in horse and dog racing. For some years an electronic starting gate where 'sprinters leaned against canvas belts which were released electronically by the gun trigger' was used at indoor track and field meetings at Madison Square Garden in New York but it never became popular (Harris, 1973: 264n).

Curved tracks, even if they are of identical distances, do not provide athletes with equal opportunity. The geometry of the 200 metres curve both enables and constrains. Athletes in the outer lanes run round more gentle curves than those on the inside. It has been shown that, as a result, in a 20 second 200 metre race the runner in the inside lane suffers a penalty of 0.07 seconds. For 400 metres the difference between just the two innermost lanes is 0.02 seconds (Jain, 1980: 435). There is, therefore, a further contradiction of the spatial fix, even more paradoxical in this case with the demise, since the mid 1960s, of the 200 metre straight. The flat 400 metre running track is yet another contradiction in a sport where the spatial dimensions of the milieu seek to maximise performances. The expedient of the banking of tracks, as in track cycling at velodromes, 'would increase speed for 200m., 400m. and 800m. races, and the closing stages of middle distance races' (Dwyer and Dyer, 1984: 142). It would be surprising if such a modest form of modernisation did not take place in the near future.

CONTRADICTIONS OF THE ENVIRONMENTAL FIX

The contradictions associated with the spatial fix in track and field can be matched by those related to the fixation with the natural environment, the effects of which track and field has sought to eliminate. First, consider which climatic elements might interfere with athletic performance and how many of them are taken into account when nullifying a 'record' performance. Wind, rain, temperature, relief, barometric pressure, humidity and air quality all have some effect on athletic performance but of these only one, wind, is considered as worth measuring in relation to potential record-setting. What is more, there is the further contradiction of the wind gauge being used for some events but not others. The pole vault, discus throw and the javelin are undoubtedly affected by the wind, each in different ways, but it is not taken into account for record purposes. There is also a statistical fallacy about eliminating records in sprint events achieved when a wind above the legal limit appears to be blowing behind the runners. This is because an association (between a favourable wind and a fast time) does not infer causation. In other words, the wind speed and the athlete's time may be independent of each other. Many athletes achieve their fastest time in non-wind assisted races. A fixation with environmental factors has diverted attention from the apparent contradictions of such inferences.

A further problem about wind in sports arenas is that it does not blow in straight lines. This means that if several measurements are taken at different points along the track, they will not be equal and it is possible to establish that an occasional positive reading will be found among a general negative wind flow (Lobozeiwicz, 1981: 122-6; Murrie, 1986: 392). Indeed, the general assumptions upon which the measurement of wind velocity is taken in track and field athletics are wrong. This is because it is assumed that the anemometer positioned at the 50 metre point of the track records the wind situation in each of the lanes for the entire 100 metre length. The presence of high grandstands, for example, cause the wind's strength and direction to vary over the area within which track events take place (Figure 5.3). The measurements taken at the standard position of the wind gauge do not coincide with with average of measurements taken along the track. As a result it is likely that many record performances should not have been ratified because of an invalid measurement.

Although fewer track meets take place indoors than outdoors, in some events the best indoor performance has been superior to that out of doors. A basic contradiction here is that superior indoor performances, achieved in the more rational milieu, are not acceptable as absolute records, though the contradiction has been lessened somewhat by the introduction of separately recognised world indoor records by the IAAF. With the growth of domed stadiums, however, the distinction between indoors and outdoors becomes blurred, especially if the roof is retractable as in the case of the Toronto Skydome (see Chapter 8). With the likely development of 400 metre synthetic tracks in environments where the landscape can become enclosed at the switch of a button, a track meet can be indoor one minute and outdoor the next.

The fixation with the physical environment is belied in relation to altitudinal effects on athletic performances which have become increasingly well known

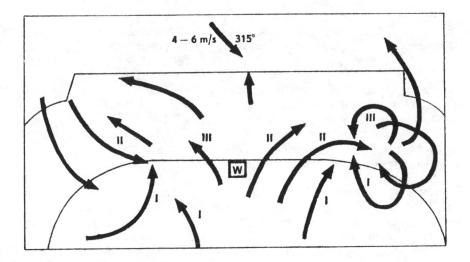

Figure 5.3 The wind, unlike the track, does not run in straight lines. Wind pattern for the 100 metre straight at Dziesieciolecia Stadium, Warsaw, from observations taken in 1966 (Lobozeiwicz, 1981: 124)

since the 1955 Pan-American Games and the 1968 Olympic Games were held at Mexico City. Whereas all wind assisted performances are invalidated for record purposes, those achieved with the assistance of altitude are not. It is well known that performances not requiring excessive aerobic involvement benefit from high altitudes. Aerobic events, such as long distance running, on the other hand, generally suffer from altitude. The results of the Mexico Olympics graphically demonstrated this. In an increasingly rationalised sport it was an irrational location at which to hold a major event (though the dangers of inferring causation from association, noted earlier, should not be ignored).

The philosopher, Paul Weiss (1969: 105), has argued that 'ideally a normal set of conditions for a race is one in which there are no turns, no wind, no interference, no interval between starting signal and start, and no irregularities to the track – in short, no deviations from a standard situation' and that with modern high-tech equipment it will be possible to come closer to making ideal measurements in which every factor, no matter how slight its influence, is given a weight in the final result. Should such a dismal prediction ever be realised, only then will a truly modern sport have been created and the end of the 'one way street' will have at last been reached.

FROM THE ZEN OF RUNNING TO THE MASS MARATHON

As part of achievement-oriented running, there has always been a strong school of thought which argued for training in natural surroundings. One of the reasons for such kinds of 'temporally and spatially looser kinds of training' (Rigauer, 1981: 39) is to avoid or reduce the boredom and monotony resulting from 'interval training' – 'continuous repetition of temporally, spatially, and quantitatively set training tasks, interrupted by controlled pauses for recovery' (Rigauer, 1981: 33). The Australian coach, Percy Cerutty, encouraged his runners to train among wild sand dune landscapes and bush and the Swedish tradition of *fartlek* (speed-play) training took place in meadows and forests. Such training in natural landscapes, as typified by *fartlek*, was not seen as an end in itself and was intended to be physically punishing. The Swedish world record holder for the mile during the late 1940s and early 1950s, Gunder Hägg was a well known user of the *fartlek* method and often finished his training in a state of extreme fatigue (Wilt, 1959: 27). This kind of running was a form of preparation for serious sport which would take place in the spatial confines of the running track and stadium.

Despite the spatial fixation with the 400 metre synthetic running surface, the late 1960s and 1970s seemed to signal a change in emphasis in the culture of running which might lead to the assumption that the end of the one way street of sportised athletics was in sight. This change, which hints at the equivocal nature of modernity itself, was characterised by an apparent shift from running on the artificial, standardised track to running in the countryside, woodland and on the beach. In cities runners started to claim back the public space of the street. More significantly, the emphasis was placed on running, not on training or racing.[3] Popularly known as 'fun running' or the 'jogging revolution', running now seemed to de-emphasise competition and the record and instead emphasise a kind of communion with nature and the freedom of bodily experience. The opening pages of *The Zen of Running* by Fred Rohé (1974) captured the spirit of the times:

> This experience is a newly discovered form of meditation or one more way for you to discover you. So I suggest that you joyfully, exuberantly, take a short run (short may be 10 yards or 10 blocks – that's your own private affair). Do your run in the cleanest air you can find. Be as undressed as possible so that you get well bathed by sun and air. If there's a beach or park without a lot of broken glass, do your run barefoot. This gives you a foot massage which stimulates all the nerve reflex points in the soles of your feet, which in turn stimulate all the organs of your body. By being barefoot you also get grounded, this direct contact with Great Mother Earth meaning that electrical equilibrium is established between you and the planet.

It is not clear whether this was zen, asceticism, mysticism, metaphysics or simply another variant of late 1960s West Coast hippydom, but it was certainly a quite different form of movement culture from that of the centimetre-gram-second ethos of achievement sport. You ran where you liked, as far as you liked and as fast as you liked, seeking nature, not victory or the record. According to Rigauer (1993: 298) this represented an 'uneconomic' (in contrast to the 'economised') form of movement culture seeking to overcome the industrial socialisation of the human body and replace it with 'meaningful bodily capacities'. In some cases such running could even be interpreted as being mildly subversive. In the United States, home of autopolis, such an act may have been a mild, though sanctioned, form of rebellion and it has been noted that running may mean that your ego will be bolstered by getting somewhere under your own power (Winters, 1980: 19). In surveillant totalitarian states, running as a form of spatial freedom may have clashed with prohibited parts of the city or region which, through running, could be opened up and observed at close quarters.

But things seemed to happen to the running revolution; the 'joy through running' syndrome did not last for long and I believe that Rigauer (1993: 298) overstates the significance of the more experiential 'running revolution'. For a start, it is doubtful if many serious, achievement-oriented runners, actually made a conscious decision to convert themselves from racers to joggers. How many star athletes 'revolted' and became ideologically converted into joggers? Indeed, as many stars got older, they simply carried on in the same body cultural mold, apeing their younger colleagues in achievement oriented sport in the burgeoning 'veterans' age categories. Witness, for example, the quest for the first four minute mile by a 40 year old and the statistical recording of a 'world marathon record' for over 70 year olds. And far from an alternative economy of running made up of a 'sport praxis that included various possibilities of appropriating and developing physical movements, perceptions of the body, and bodily knowledge' (Rigauer, 1993: 298), what limited 'revolution' did exist was soon incorporated into mainstream sporting ideology in two ways. First, the jogging movement itself all too often became, like aerobics (Stam, 1988: 137), a form of 'grim duty' as joggers became slaves to the stop watch and the styles of the sports goods industry. It could be argued that the joy of movement became a new form of 'voluntary servitude' (Baudrillard, 1988: 38) or 'flagellantist delusion' (Berking and Neckel, 1993: 68), overly planned, lacking in spontenaiety, an operation rather than an action, and 'the pleasure not of pure physical exertion but of ... an endless functioning' (Baudrillard, 1993: 46-7). In short, the whole thing was taken too seriously with the contradictions of organised fun runs, training schedules and jogging trails reducing, if not eliminating, any mystical potential which might have existed in experiential running. Running, therefore, became rationalised, though in different ways from racing. Jogging served to reduce medical costs – a rationalisation of the body in the interests of the state; and jogging also serves to increase sexual attractiveness in the interests of consumer culture (Turner, 1984: 199). The notion of running in bare feet became replaced with the idea of running in Adidas, Puma, Nike, Reebok, Brooks or Asics and other forms of 'leisure wear'.

Perhaps more significantly a second form of incorporation resulted in the jogging movement being co-opted by the mass marathon, or more accurately by the mass road race phenomenon. Running in 'free space' gave way to the marked line on the ashphalt road of the stopwatched marathon route and during the late 1960s, 1970s and 1980s the number of road races grew rapidly. It has been recorded, for example, that 5 marathon races were held in the USA in 1959; by 1969 the respective figure was 44 (Martin and Gynn, 1979: 205) and by 1977 it had reached almost 200 with the number of starters in the New York Marathon increasing from 126 in 1970 to 16,005 a decade later (Cooper, 1992: 244). At the same time the number of 10 kilometre track races declined. On occasions pole vault events were held in shopping malls, showing that it was not just running events which could break out of the stadium. And it was not just the marathon and the 10 kilometre races that took to the roads; races over a

wide range of distances, from the mile upwards, showed that the spatial confines of the track were not prerequisites for serious racing. In this way the
running revolution became sportised. It became a racing revolution born of
innovations which 'served the purpose of managerial capitalism' which used
'capital and technology to meet a demand that was as much created by road
racing administrators and sponsors as determined by the market' (Cooper,
1992). Races like the New York and London marathons became business enter-
prises.

The shift of running from track to road, with training taking place in a wide
range of other environments, might at first sight appear to reflect a further
contradiction, even a step away from Eichberg's 'one way street' or a more
fundamental change hinting at a shift to post modernity in sport with runners
breaking out of the stadium and claiming back the street from the motor vehi-
cle. The old seemed to be new again with racing being taken to the people and
back to ordinary environments, in the tradition of nineteenth century pedestrianism. The music and carnival atmosphere associated with many such events
also hinted at less serious running. I have made clear in the previous paragraph,
however, that the interpretation that modernity is in any way in question would
be misleading. Indeed, the urban marathon has been said to bear 'all the signs
of the most modern modernity with its 'staging of individuality as a collective
event' (Berking and Neckel, 1993: 67–8). Post-modern it may be in some
respects, with the incongruous juxtapositionings' of whole grain food being
taken together with isotonic sports drinks, raw bodies carried by high-tech
shoes, and spiritual tendencies coexisting with the results of modern
research (Berking and Nickel, 1993: 71), but it nowhere makes a break with
achievement ideology and hence the underlying modernist ethic. Any carnivalistic elements in such events are essentially of an ersatz nature – mass-mediated
and compromised (Stam, 1988: 137). Runners may have stepped off the one
way street but they were still running along side it.

One interpretation of the road racing phenomenon, as deadly serious as any
track event and where the prize money runs into millions of dollars, is that it is
an alternative form of athletic 'production'. What I am hinting at here is an
analogy (but only an analogy) of two models of production, one 'Fordist' mass
production and the other 'post-Fordist' flexible accumulation (Harvey, 1989:
141 *et seq*). Fordist production is typified by rigid capital equipment, mass production, uniformity, centralisation and bureaucratic regulation, among many
other characteristics; its ideology is modernism. Post-Fordist production, on the
other hand, includes 'small batch production', flexibility, decentralisation and
deregulation; its ideology is post-modern (Harvey, 1989: 177-9). Fordism has
its analogies in running. It refers to the production (of races) being geared to
rigid capital equipment (the standardised dimension of the arena); the routinisa-
tion of processes (standardised training, interval running); a growing division
of labour and standardisation of outputs (the limited number of events); its centralisation (a few Grand Prix spectacles). Post-Fordist flexible accumulation, on
the other hand, is characterised by the ability to switch from one system of production to another with 'non-dedicated' machinery (from track to road, from
one place to any other – roads being available everywhere). For sport read
Fordism; for street sport read post-Fordism. Track racing is analogous to mass

production, street racing to 'small batch production', able to meet the whims of the most recent athletic fad. Track races are uniform; road races are varied, up hill and down dale. Considerable investment is found in stadiums and tracks whereas in street racing no special investment is required. Such developments reflect progressive but superficial changes, not fundamental shifts in ideology.

Contemporaneous with the post-modern trend for serious running to take to the streets has been the development and widespread adoption of the synthetic surface so that fun running – and indeed other forms of body-cultural activities – can take to the track. Like the synthetic turf of the football field and the modern roofed stadium like the SkyDome, the synthetic running track is an ambiguous sportscape; it is not quite what it seems to be. While giving the appearance of having been designed for faster performances and improved records, wheelchair races for the local handicapped community can take place on it in the same meeting as a world record attempt for the 100 metre sprint. Hence, modern sportscapes return sport space to its pre-modern traditions of the multifunctional use of land, from sport events to sports' events. Modernity, therefore, is again shown to be double edged.

CONCLUSION

Inherent in the nature of modern achievement sports are great pressures to produce homotopian spaces or placeless landscapes; in the modern stadium 'nothing gratuitous is allowed to exist; everything must be useful and come up to technical expectations' (Ellul, 1965: 384). But the contradictions of the track and field landscape force me to stop short of suggesting that the 'ritual of the record' has fully embraced the 'sacred seriousness' to which Eichberg (1990b: 132) refers. It is still possible that in some places the environmental fixation in sports and the provision of unusual visual pleasures in the natural landscape can come together in apparently contradictory situations. The best example I know of occurred in 1968, the year the Olympic Games were held in Mexico. The environmental fix predicated that the US Olympic track and field trials should be held at an altitude approximating to that of Mexico City, about 2,500 metres above sea level. But the site chosen for the trials was at the virtually uninhabited South Lake Tahoe in the Californian sierras. A synthetic 400 metre track was constructed in the middle of a natural forest with pleasant meadows and snow-capped peaks in the background. A number of athletic meetings, including the high profile Olympic Trials, were held there, despite very little provision being available for spectators (Figure 5.4).

Although modernist forms are often likened to the machine – and the running track might be so metaphorically described in its function as a production line for records – I have tried to show that there are still too many contradictions for the notion of the running track as machine to be anything more than a somewhat crude metaphor. World records cannot yet be choreographed for TV spectaculars; world records can still be set in villages with very few people (or even TV crews) present. This is not to say that as we move along the 'one way street', much more rational landscapes of sport will not be produced; indeed, the signs are that this is exactly what is happening despite superficial appearances, such as the road running boom, to the contrary.

Will the placeless running track, identical to all others of its kind, reduce the gratification gained from the sporting experience? If it is indoors and surrounded by bland container architecture the answer is likely to be that it will. If it is a concrete bowl of a stadium with a retractable or permanent roof which shuts out the surrounding landscape it will, like the prefabricated box, become a placeless blandscape. On the other hand, if track and field meetings continue to be held in humanised stadiums, the surroundings in which the placeless track is set will convert the broader space into a place. And as with all allegedly 'placeless' environments, many would agree that 'the nature of a building's soul,

Figure 5.4 From forest glade to synthetic track; South Lake Tahoe, California, scene of the 1968 US Olympic track and field trials (Source: *Track and Field News* 21 (12), 1968: 1)

after all, isn't dictated by its shape but by its significance', sport being able to endow even the most cumbersome stadiums with dignity (Weil *et al*, 1991: 28). Hence, the stadium may be able to retain a sense of place or *genius loci*. This, of course, exists at the moment as many athletes confirm when they have run at such places as the Bislett Stadium in Oslo or at the Olympic Stadium in Stockholm. These places are not just anywhere; in these cases – and in others – place still matters and it is the sport landscape and a sense of place which forms the content of the next chapter.

NOTES

1. I use the American term 'track and field' synonymously with the British equivalent, 'athletics'.
2. In some countries, notably in Scandinavia, cinder tracks were also used for speedway racing and, in winter, ice skating.
3. Eichberg (1993c) suggests that such changes are reflected in the broader awareness of the socio-economic notion of 'limits to growth' during this period.

6

Sportscapes and a Sense of Place

In 1988 the football (soccer) club, Charlton Athletic, was forced by local government edicts to leave its home ground, The Valley, and engage in ground-sharing with another London club, Crystal Palace. Charlton fans were outraged and demanded that their club return 'home'. To the fans The Valley was more than a football ground; it seemed to possess an almost quasi-religious or spiritual significance. It was an example of 'felicitous space ... the sort of space that may be grasped, that may be defended against adverse forces, the space we love ... eulogized space' (Bachelard, 1969: xxxi), investigations into which could be termed topophilia. Tuan (1974: 4) applies this word to an intense sense of place or to situations where sentiment is coupled with place – 'the affective bond between people and place or setting'. Like many British football grounds, The Valley was a much-loved place (Bale, 1992b); it was also an authentic place, fans possessing an unselfconscious sense of place, 'that of being inside and belonging to *your* place both as an individual and as a member of a community, and to know this without reflecting on it' (Relph, 1976: 65).

In contrast, residents of the historic area of Brumleby in the Osterbro district of Copenhagen were distressed to discover in 1990 that the Danish national football stadium, *Parken*, was to be reconstructed and enlarged and in doing so turned through 90° so that it abutted much closer than previously to their precious yellow and brown painted mid-nineteenth century cottages. In particular, the shadows cast by the giant stands would now destroy the idyllic summer evenings which the residents traditionally spent eating and drinking in the sunlight. The soft, broken shadows cast by the mature trees between the houses would be replaced by the new shadows which (like the spatial parameters of the football pitch) would be straight and hard, covering a wider expanse of the residential area, and earlier in the evening, than had hitherto been the case (Nagbøl, 1993). *Parken* had become a landscape of fear (Tuan, 1979), a sort of 'hostile space' (Bachelard, 1969: xxxii), or a source of topophobia.

These two stories reflect two senses of place which landscapes, including those of sports, may generate. Topophilia – literally a love of place – assumes many forms, varying in intensity and strength of emotional response.

Topophilia may involve 'fleeting visual pleasure; the sensual delight of physical contact; the fondness for place because it is familiar, because it is home and incarnates the past, because it evokes pride in ownership or of creation; joy in things because of animal health and vitality' (Tuan, 1974: 247). Topophobia involves the opposites of these; it is an attitude which produces resentment and fear towards disliked places and landscapes. It seems reasonable to argue that sports landscapes which act as sources for topophilia are 'good landscapes' while those which cause 'topophobia' are 'bad'. Rather more explicit criteria could be applied in order to identify good and bad landscapes. For example, a good sports landscape would have involved local people in its making and maintenance; if it had been developed by mindlessly following some planning formula it would be, at best, mediocre. It would be good if it contained elements which were of no technical use but nevertheless provided people with pleasure – flower beds, trees, incrementally developed architecture, asymmetry, etc., but bad if it was regimented, straight edged and forbade small pleasures like walking on the grass. It would be good if it reflected human weaknesses, perhaps an absence of coordination; bad if it had somehow sought perfection but failed to achieve it (Relph, 1989: 286). The relationship between local people and the sports place should not be merely a connection between two groups (for example, residents and stadium developers) but two worlds becoming one. Such a relationship would produce mutual understanding and caring (Seamon, 1993a)[1]. The bad sports landscape does not necessarily infer a bad game; but a bad game can be compensated for, to an extent, by an attractive and varied landscape ensemble from which the spectator or player can obtain gratification (Raitz, 1987b).

The central purpose of this chapter is to explore, in rather more detail than that outlined above, the characteristics of sports landscapes which people find attractive, create fond memories, or provide a sense of place. Such sources of topophilia, resulting from sensory pleasures, might intuitively be thought to be solely visual but the other senses – aural, olfactory and tactile – also create topophilic sentiments linking sport and place. Nostalgia and myth further foster and evoke such feeling.

Before proceeding I must briefly digress in order to examine the apparent contradiction which may lie in the 'prison-like' representation made of some sports places (for example, the stadium) in Chapter 4 and the present suggestion that those who occupy them may hold them in great affection. Am I being inconsistent? The answer is no, on several grounds. First, all places accommodating a given sport are not (yet) the same, so experiences will obviously differ. Secondly, it could be argued that the affection people hold for even highly territorialised places results from a form of 'false consciousness', that is, they think that they are enjoying themselves whereas they are, in fact, being duped by the provision of a modern day version of 'bread and circuses'. Such a view is a form of marxism, and while thought by some observers to be patronising, is not without appeal to writers both in sports (Brohm, 1978; Vinnai, 1973) and in geography (Harvey, 1989), though approached from quite different perspectives and levels of sophistication. Thirdly, it is possible that no single image summarises the popular view of a given place. Ordinary, humdrum places may appear crude and even ugly to the outsider but to those who regularly occupy particular spaces – for example, on football terraces – they become redolent of fond and vivid memories. Fourthly, it can be argued that a love of place can be generated by the experiences people have there, rather than the character of the place itself; 'places become specific as we give them meaning in relation to our actions as individuals and as members of groups. Places are significant, not because of their inherent value, but rather because we assign value to them in relation to our projects' (Entrikin, 1991: 16). This digression clears the ground for the major part of this chapter – a consideration of the sensory pleasures which the landscapes of sports provide for those who occupy them.

I will adopt two broad approaches to an exploration of the gratification provided by sports landscapes. The first approach is less well developed and somewhat speculative (some would say far-fetched), drawing mainly on 'prospect-refuge theory' – an 'unashamedly Darwinian framework' in the words of its proposer, the geographer, Jay Appleton (1990: 12; see also 1975; 1984). He views the symbolism of certain landscapes as having opportunities for thrills and satisfaction. The second is a more humanistic approach and bases gratification on morphological elements, the pleasing sensory experiences of which are culturally derived. This approach employs ideas from a large number of scholars but notably Tuan (1974) and Relph (1976). The relevance of each approach to the sports landscape may be explored in turn.

SPORTS, PROSPECTS AND REFUGES

Although Appleton's major works, *The Experience of Landscape* (1975) and *The Symbolism of Habitat* (1990), have nothing explicitly to do with sports,[2] several allusions are made to movement in the landscape in the context of various recreational activities which often possess sportised versions. As a result, his broad argument that the aesthetics of landscape may be interpreted by means of its functional as opposed to its morphological characteristics, and that social, cultural and economic influences on perceptual response to environment have not fully eradicated bio-physiological bases, are certainly worthy of examination in a sports landscape context. In short, Appleton would view a meadowland vista with a distant forest as a symbolic or subliminal means of escape or source of refuge, rather than merely a nice looking place to go for a run. The forest edge has indeed been shown to be one of the most attractive of recreational environments though it must be stressed that the 'forest refuge may not be literal to have an effect on preference' (Ruddell and Hammitt, 1987: 251).

In essence, Appleton's arguments are that feelings for, and the aesthetic properties of, landscape may be interpreted by means of prospects, refuges and hazards which combine to constitute prospect-refuge theory. Prospects refer to views, or environmental conditions conducive to obtaining a view, while refuges are conditions conducive to hiding or sheltering. Hazards are interpreted as sources of danger which need to be avoided in order to attain comfort or safety. In brief, the theory states that 'the ability to see without being seen is conducive to the exploitation of environmental conditions favourable to biological survival and is therefore a source of pleasure' (Appleton, 1975: 270). Crucially, 'the ability to see without being seen becomes a source of satisfaction in itself *even when isolated from any ulterior questions of survival,* [just as] the ability to run fast ... persists as a source of satisfaction when it is no longer needed as a prerequisite for survival' (Appleton, 1975: 177-8, emphasis added). In effect, therefore, sport can be interpreted as an environmental experience. What concerns me here is the role of the landscape in enhancing that experience. Of course, in placeless environments, like the standardised boxing ring in a darkened hall or the synthetic running track inside the concrete saucer, 'techniques of body movement are developed for the satisfaction which they afford for their own sake' (Appleton, 1975: 178) but other sports involve the fitting of body movements into a context where they can more effectively evoke the satisfaction which comes from the successful strategic participation in the landscape with its symbolic prospects, refuges and hazards.

Consider, for example, downhill skiing with the prospect of the start, the 'gates' and natural topography as hazards and the refuge of the finish. 'The run begins in an environment whose features pertain strongly to the symbolism of prospect: the elevation of the site, the distant view with the clear, refuge-free horizons, the surface devoid of hiding-places, the brightness and whiteness of the gleaming snow. If the sun is shining through a clear sky the imagery is further strengthened. Finally, there is that hallmark of the prospect sensation, falling ground' (Appleton, 1975: 179). All of the refuge symbols – the valley, the trees, buildings, the finishing line – lie below and the run itself transfers the athlete from the world of prospect to that of refuge. There is also, of course, a strong sense of hazard *en route*. Symbolic prospects, refuges and hazards can be conceptualised for a large number of sports. Indeed, the inherent spatial character of sport – the conquest of distance – is an invitation to conceptualise it as a basic form of progression from prospect to refuge, the landscape being symbolically represented by various elements of the sport in question. In golf, argues Appleton (1975: 189), 'the ball becomes the representative of the player, almost a symbolic extension of his personality, so much so that he uses the personal pronoun to refer indiscriminately to the ball and to the player who struck it. "It's all right for you; you're on the green, but I'm in the rough" '. And golf, like the other sports noted above, reveals parallels between the game and the language of prospect-refuge theory, the shot from the tee representing prospect, the various impediments (rough, sand traps, trees, etc.) representing obvious hazards, and the hole being 'the most fundamental of refuges' (Appleton, 1975: 189). In team sports the field of play could be interpreted as providing the prospect, the opponents' goal the symbolic refuge, the opposition being the hazard. In races on land and water, the course and the finishing lines represent prospect and refuge respectively with elements like hurdles and water jumps (in track races) or waves and currents (in open water swimming, canoeing and boating) being hazards.

Sports, with their finite spaces, may be interpreted as symbolic representations of the broader landscape with its horizon, the view of which directs attention to 'speculation to what lies beyond it, and the horizon itself seems to be the key which can provide the answer to such speculation' (Appleton, 1975: 90). The horizon seems to have assumed particular significance since the late eighteenth century when it began to be viewed as possessing the same qualities previously possessed by heaven, but instead of looking upward the eyes now sought a horizontal goal. Religiousness became horizontalised, based on the incipient secularisation of the presence of God (Kayser Nielsen, 1993b: 9). The 'never-ending' swimming events (noted on page 31) take on a new light when viewed through a new appreciation of the horizon – a yearning for infinity combined with the fear of emptiness, creating a need for mediation between the two extremes. In sports, movement and yearning for the frontier are conjoined by the the 'cultivation' of the infinitely receding horizon. In this way, sport is viewed as the aim to exceed oneself yet stay within a given spatial framework. The 'cultivated horizon' therefore becomes one of the characteristics which make sports attractive. Horizontally arranged space provides 'possibilities and a sense of confinement, a space of extraction and excess on the one hand, and enclosure on the other' (Kayser Nielsen, 1993b: 21). In a sense, the horizon is also similar to the sports record in that it is something to be striven for, but on reaching it another immediately appears – as with record-breaking. In many sports the finishing line, or other boundaries indicating the finitude of sport space, provide ways of coping with infinity. The fact that sports make infinite space finite could be argued to serve as one of their attractions.

The general notion of prospect-refuge theory can be invoked to explain the attraction of sports through the landscape *functions* (not features) of prospects (including the horizon), hazards and refuges (Appleton, 1990: 26). It is clear, however, that some kinds of people prefer some sports landscapes – indeed, some sports – rather than others. This is not the place to discuss such considerations on the basis of physiology but the work of the psycho-analyst, Michael Balint (1959), is full of ideas which implicitly relate sport, space, landscape and psychology, using terms not unlike those used by Appleton. The essence of Balint's approach recognises a condition common in sports, namely, the voluntary and intentional self-exposure to fear 'and the confident hope that all will turn out well in the end' (Balint, 1959: 24). The notion of 'fear' in sports reminds me immediately of Appleton's model. Balint comes close to describing what amounts to prospect and refuge when he describes, for example, 'cricket, where on the whole runs may be scored only by leaving *the safe zone*' (Balint, 1959: 24, emphasis added), and, I should add, returning safely to it. Many other games and sports such as rounders and baseball also have a 'zone of security' or 'home' (or refuge), reached only after 'accepting exposure to danger (or hazard) more or less voluntarily' (Balint, 1959: 24, brackets added). The home plate has been regarded as the main spatial symbol in baseball, providing as it does both a starting point and a safe haven. Giamatti (1989: 87) sees baseball as a narrative plot where the object of both teams is to return to home after a daring exploration in open space while Springwood (1992: 290) believes that this metaphor is even more successful for Japanese baseball in the 1990s in capturing the particular cultural significance of personal space and a home to which one can return. In jumping events in track and field, gymnastics, trampolining or diving the thrill to the spectators increases with the distance of the athlete from the safe 'earth' (Balint, 1959: 25). The extent of the *thrill* derived from such events is, therefore, not simply the result of the symbolic landscape configuration but also of the distance from, or nearness to, the security of home. In effect, it can be argued that these basic (Freudian) components, may, through the media of space and landscape, contribute to the attraction of sports. Balint goes on to define one who enjoys such thrills 'away from the safe earth' as being 'philobatic' while those who dislike such thrills and prefer 'to clutch at something firm when his (sic) security is in danger' are termed 'ocnophilic' (Balint, 1959: 25).

The implication of these two types is that representatives of each may be attracted to different sports and, as a result, different sports landscapes. It might intuitively be felt that philobats would prefer sports like long distance running, cross country skiing or road cycling, where most of the body is away from the security of the earth and 'the thrill is the greater the farther we dare get away from safety – in distance, in speed, or in exposure; that is to say, the more we can prove our independence' (Balint, 1959: 29). Likewise, it might be assumed that ocnophils need objects to cling on to, and are not so spatially adventurous, staying in empty spaces as short as possible. Sprint events, wrestling, squash, badminton, and table tennis (clinging on to rackets) might be termed ocnophilic. But things are not simple as this dualism suggests and it is evident that ocnophilic tendencies appear in what would seem to be philobatic situations. The pole-vaulter may represent a paradigm example with the immense thrill of the speed and fear of take-off combining with the ocnophilic grasp of the pole to provide seemingly 'magic powers' which enable him to brave the philobatic state (Balint, 1959: 29).[3] It is even possible to interpret football as possessing, on the one hand, a philobatic sense of open space and on the other an ocnophilic joy of the ball, the safe corners and lines of the playing field; that is, freedom and constraint (Kayser Nielsen, 1993a). The landscape and its spatial characteristics are clearly implicated in the thrill or satisfaction derived from sports events, on the part of athlete or spectator.

Before concluding this section it is worth refering to the landscape implications of training (something rather ignored in the serious social scientific study of sport), as opposed to competition. Appleton's allusions to the experience of landscape in movement culture basically involves 'recreational sport' which I take to be nearer recreation than to my interpretation of sport. In the context of achievement sport the role of the broader landscape in the sporting experience is somewhat reduced, though not in training which approximates somewhat more to the recreationists' experience. This is not to deny, of course, the possible *symbolic* significance of landscape elements to the serious athlete but it is much more concrete in the case of the recreationist or athlete in training simply because time can be taken to enjoy the landscape rather than focus solely on victory and achievement as one would tend to do during serious competition.

ELEMENTS AND ENSEMBLES

The second approach is rather less controversial and is derived from the work of American geographer Karl Raitz (1987b). This applies Relph's (1976) concepts of place and placelessness to the sports landscape and basically argues that the more complex the landscape ensemble and the more varied the places at which the sport is played, the higher the level of gratification gained from the sport experience. The significance of place to the sports experience is introduced by Raitz by asking why people should go to sports stadiums at all when (a) many of them know little about the finer points of play, (b) many have poor seats and can see little of what is going on, and (c) most could be at home watching the game on television where the fine detail could be better observed by the camera's zoom lenses with replays constantly being employed to remind them of the action or to pick out detail which they may have missed. The answer that Raitz proposes is that there is more to the sports event than the game itself.

Studies, known under the general headings of landscape evaluation and environmental psychology, constantly emphasise that landscapes with a variety of elements in them are more attractive than those possessing few or no variations. Variety is the spice of life, in the landscape as elsewhere. Elements in a landscape may therefore be considered as analogous to words in a book (Unwin, 1992: 191). This is indicated in Figure 6.1 by the contrast between complex and simple landscape ensembles being related to high and low levels of gratification respectively, though it should be noted that over-complex environments can lead to 'sensory overload' and hence, displeasure (Smith, 1979: 175).

Visual pleasures

'Sight is without doubt our dominant sense, yielding nine-tenths of our knowledge of the external world' (Pocock, 1981: 385). An 'emphasis on scenes' is important for an understanding of the aesthetic appeals of sports (Lipsky, 1981: 18) and the sports 'spectacle is about seeing, sight and oversight' (MacAloon, 1984: 270). The landscape of sport is made up of a varied collection of elements which combine to make an ensemble encountered by the sports participant. Whereas Appleton's 'prospects' and 'refuges' are explored

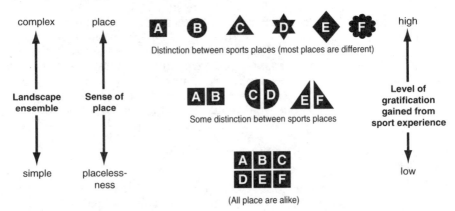

Figure 6.1 Perceived differences between sport place ensembles, senses of place and level of gratification. Places are indicated by letters (after Raitz, 1987b: 17)

Figure 6.2 The stadium at Siena, Italy

from a functional perspective, the 'elements' in the overall landscape ensemble are more usually regarded morphologically. The ensemble for a downhill skiing event will include the surrounding hills, the snow itself, the neighbouring forests, ski-lifts, hotels and practice slopes. The views of them are part of the skiing experience. If downhill skiing were to take place indoors with imported snow and air conditioning units, skiing would be a different experience; the exhilaration would be missing. Gratification is increased when the site elements come together to create a pleasurable experience – 'proper sport takes place in a proper environment' (Raitz, 1987b: 7).

I have stressed in the previous chapter that many placeless sports milieu (for example, the synthetic running track or the rectangular plane of the basketball court) may be surrounded by an equally placeless element such as a concrete bowl or a containerised sports hall, lacking variety and often appearing totally sterile. As I showed for the example of American baseball (pages 78–79), recent decades were widely felt to have witnessed an increasing 'sameness' in a new generation of stadium designs (page 80). Similar criticisms have been made of some recent British football stadiums (Bale, 1992). On the other hand, the synthetic 400 metre track may be surrounded by architecture or elements in the landscape which are able to turn the sterile space of sportscape into a place; as Norberg-Schultz (1979: 5) put it, 'a place is a space which has a distinct character', possessing a spirit of place or *genius loci*. The stadium in Siena, shown in Figure 6.2, has a synthetic running track and the standardised, rectangular football pitch for the Italian Division 2 club which plays there. It is not one of Italy's grand stadiums like the San Siro in Milan, the Stadio Olympico

(Rome), the Stadio Luigi Ferraris (Genoa) or the Stadio Communale in Florence (Inglis, 1990), but surrounded by trees and residences in its natural bowl it is a pretty place, clearly part of the city. It could not be anywhere; for me it has a sense of place. Such landscapes, within which even the most rational and quantified activities may take place, are often (though not invariably as previous chapters have shown) composed of many individual elements which together combine to produce a visually pleasing, and hence topophilic, landscape ensemble.

Cricket and baseball are much-loved sports. Their attraction in large derives from the perception of much-loved elements in the landscape ensembles, although it can be argued that the landscapes of such sports are often mythical (Chapter 7). The same is true of many other sports and a varied ensemble is only likely to be lacking in indoor sports such as basketball, squash and badminton, with their predictable spatial parameters and played in highly confined spaces; but even here banners and pennants can turn a plain grey wall into a glorious splash of colour. In some cases ingenious and amusing ways are found of symbolically and visually countering the drabness of the modern 'stadium as prison'. This was exemplified in the late 1980s by the introduction into England's football 'enclosures' of a variety of zany, inflatable objects ranging from dinosaurs to fried eggs and from Frankenstein's monsters to bananas (Figure 6.3). Surveillance and control often have a shadow in the form of such displays. Nevertheless, where sports events are played in spaces which are not particularly distinctive (for example, swimming pools, high school gymnasiums, sports halls), attention is necessarily focused on the the game itself. There is often little else from which to gain visual gratification. In other cases, however, the landscape surroundings can be of considerable importance.

Cricket is regarded by many as one of the most 'scenic' of sports (see Chapter 7). It has been suggested that 'in no other sport does winning so little affect the aesthetic, spectacular and entertainment values' (Arlott and Cardus, 1969: 62) and it could be added that in cricket the landscape elements are of greater significance to the potential level of participant gratification than in any other sport. This is because of cricket's relatively slow and frequently interrupted pace which allows (even encourages) the spectator's (and the player's) attention to wander from the physical activity of the game itself and hence gain enjoyment from the milieu beyond the actual game. When waiting for players to take the field, during the run up to bowl, between overs, while recovering the ball from 'fours' and 'sixes' and at lunch or tea, spectators have time, which is an essential part of the game, in which to absorb the elements and ensemble of which the play itself is but part. The legendary cricket writer, Neville Cardus, noted that 'cricket as a combat and as a display of skill could be fascinating in the Sahara, no doubt, ... but you have never even wooed cricket, let alone won it, if you have looked on the game *merely* as a clever matter of bat and ball' (Cardus, 1929: 34). Another observer implies that the ensemble contributes a *major* component of the overall cricket experience when he notes that 'it is the ground as much as the game which makes cricket ... [and] ... cricket needs an appropriate setting as much as worship needs a good church'; almost as an aside it is added that 'if the game becomes exciting so much the better' (Heald, 1986: 7). The poet and keen observer of the English cricket scene, Edmund

Figure 6.3 Inflatable bananas in the 'football prison' (Source: Stoke *Evening Sentinel*)

Blunden, was fully aware that the variety within the ensemble contributed to the level of gratification obtained from participating in cricket. While playing he noted lyrically that 'the game itself grew dim, the action lost its precision and importance, and only the sweet-breathing, singing, shining, swaying, rejoicing universe of nature had any existence for me' (Blunden, 1985: 137). Without such surroundings, attention would be solely focused on the game itself and as a result enjoyment for many spectators would lapse unless the quality of the game was of a high standard. Blunden (1985) also perceptively points out how the grounds of first class cricket clubs, where achievement-orientation among players is greater than in the more humble village game, has led to more 'austere cricket grounds, untouched with mysticism', where the élite player cannot be 'distracted from his function' by peripheral, distractive elements. A diminution of difference and an increasing sameness in the ensemble is implied in the ethos of achievement sport since the landscape ensemble should not interfere with the sporting (like the theatrical – see page 95) performance. And as noted earlier, the visual elements of the sports landscape will be of less significance to the élite athlete in competition than in training.

The sports landscape is often integral, and not merely incidental, to the sport experience. To the untutored visitor, the spectators at an English football match may appear to be a homogeneous mass. The hardened fans, however, will gain gratification from the sport experience by seeking out certain 'neighbourhoods' of fans with whom they particularly relate and share common interests (Raitz, 1987b: 9). The places in the stadium which such fans occupy are their territories, defended against intruders and jealously guarded. Meeting with friends on a regular basis in these traditionally defined places is a major element of the sport experience. One well documented example of an intra-stadium space which has particular significance for those who occupied it is 'The Hill', an area of raised ground in the south east corner of Sydney Cricket Ground (Lynch, 1992). Its blue collar, masculine wit contrasted with the politeness of the traditional English game and, in a small way, represented the Australianisation of the English game of cricket, gradually coming to accommodate a much-loved place in Australian popular culture.

> The Hill, as part of the sacred turf of the SCG had forged a place of cultural endearment in Australia's popular imagination, albeit a place of considerable notoriety. While the SCG is the grand old lady of Australian sports stadia, The Hill is her larrikin son, prone to stray into the seamier side of life, to push the collective to its limits, to imbibe, to carouse and transgress. (Lynch, 1992: 16)

By the 1960s The Hill had developed a very strong sense of place. It was the 'place to go to rub shoulders with the mob, to live and feel the roar of the crowd, to move with it, and rise and fall in its collective upheavals' (Lynch: 25). It was, until relatively recently, a 'hallowed and rowdy cultural icon' where crowds 'played with the margins of acceptable behaviour' (Lynch: 44-5) but its associations with 'hooliganism' at a time when cricket was undergoing an image change and becoming an increasingly bourgoise form of entertainment, led to progressive attempts to sanitise and territorialise the site. As a result, a grandstand and individualised seating now exist where once was found a 'symbolic piece of grass'.

SPORTS LANDSCAPES AS SPECTACLES

The term 'spectacle' addresses 'precisely the values embedded in the idea of landscape ensemble as a source of attraction and gratification in sports events' (Raitz, 1987b: 9) and the notion of sports as spectacle has been explored by John MacAloon (1981; 1984), particularly in the context of the Olympic Games. Spectacles are attractive because all we are expected to do is to watch; unlike the case of festival, we do not have to take part (MacAloon, 1984: 269-70). But spectacle implies something more than simply a sporting event; it is an extraordinary event, spectacular, and going beyond the more modest expectations of day to day sports. Sports events like the Olympics or the World Cup – veritable worlds-as-exhibitions – contain a huge collection of landscape elements, human and physical, for the spectator to absorb and to subsequently remember as a once in a lifetime experience. Sports events such as the Olympics are sporting spectacles which take 'the "realities" of life and defuses them by converting them into appearances to be played with like toys, then cast away, (but) it simultaneously rescues "reality" from "mere appearance" and re-presents it in evocative form' (MacAloon, 1984: 275). This 'double dynamic' may be one of their major sources of attraction. A further source, certainly in former times, may have been that the athletes who inhabit the Olympic land-scape are not simply athletes; they 'represent' places far and wide, the Games providing a source of 'cross-cultural voyeurism' or 'popular ethnography' (MacAloon, 1981: 262) for spectators as they see athletes from far away places in the flesh.

This positive view of sport as spectacle is countered, of course, by one which sees its increasing spectacularisation as simply one dimension of a society of the spectacle (Debord, 1987). In such a society, images permeate everyday life. The notion of sport as 'bread and circuses' is summarised by Alt (1983: 98) who sees sports spectacles as fostering a world of 'atomised' individuals who become dependent on the gratification provided by such spectacles.

Whether the choreographed opening and closing ceremonies of the modern Olympics are religious rituals or merely choreographed kitsch is irrelevant to the present discussion. The point is that people, many of whom have no interest in sports, are attracted to them, in the stadium itself or more likely, on televi-sion. In large part, the attraction is simply visual.

Sports places as home

Open space signifies freedom while enclosed space signifies security (Tuan, 1974: 27-8) and various sports landscapes may seem attractive because of their open vistas (for example, golf) or enclosed spaces (for example, stadiums or arena-based sports). Entering enclosed spaces may create a sense of 'hereness' (Cullen, 1970) and permits 'rapid visual exploration from a static position with space appearing to be efficiently bounded' (Jakle, 1987: 55). Such enclosures can also be viewed as a subset of Appleton's refuges and Balint's 'zones of security'. The sports stadium appears to satisfy both the attractions of security associated with enclosure and those of freedom associated with openness.

Refuge and home are almost synonymous and in the case of the stadium, fans, literally, have their 'home turf'. Their team is said to play 'at home' and in some countries a condition for a football club to be affiliated to its national association is that it has a home ground. For more modest clubs, the focal points in their histories are the football field and the club *house* (Ottesen, 1990: 34; 1993: 3). One football fan stated that his home ground 'may be plain, lack-ing in architectural distinction and historical glamour, yet we resent an out-sider's criticism of it. Its ugliness does not matter ... ' (Bennett, 1988). After a temporary but lengthy absence in a neighbouring stadium, the fanzine[5] of the football club, Charlton, announced that they were finally going home. The fans had fought to return their club to its home, The Valley (Figure 6.4). Their strength lay in their sense of place. Indeed, it was stated by the major fan activist in the return to The Valley campaign, that 'For those who grew up on its terraces and shared its greatest celebrations with family and friends, it has the comfortable, familiar feel that more properly belongs to home' (Everitt, 1991: v). Of course, it must be recognised that those who view such a place as 'home' may be relatively small in number and gender-specific. What is signifi-cant is the metaphorical use of the word 'home'.

For some the home ground is more important than the team. One football fan

Voice of The Valley
The DELIRIOUS Charlton mag

No 37	November 1992	£1

After 2,611 days and 182 matches in the wilderness, we can finally say it again

LET'S GO HOME!

UPTON PARK FINAL

Figure 6.4 The front cover of the Charlton Athletic fanzine, published to coincide with the return of the south-east London club to The Valley, following a lengthy period of ground sharing with other London clubs

wrote to me of his affection for Manchester City's Maine Road ground in these words:

> I have been a supporter since birth, well, since my parents first took me when I was around two years old. Since that time my interest has revolved more around the stadium than the team. Of course, I support the team through and through, but to me the club is Maine Road as that is the only part of the club that rarely changes. Managers, players, directors, and even supporters come and go but the stadium never disappears.

When an English minor league club Wealdstone (in north London), left its traditional home ground (Lower Mead) and started ground-sharing with a neighbouring club, a lifelong fan noted, 'I am almost indifferent. To me, Wealdstone was Lower Mead and Lower Mead was Wealdstone. The club I loved is dead'. (Lacey, 1992: 92)

While retaining the notion of sports landscapes as homes, and, as a result, sources of intense topophilia, I now want to take a quite different landscape and stress its sporting attractiveness also from the perspective of it being a kind of home or sanctuary (Skolimowski, 1987). The landscape of the forest is perhaps the classic non-urban example of a symbolic refuge (Appleton: 1975: 241); it has also been viewed as the home of early humanity, 'the warm nurturing womb out of which the hominids were to emerge' (Tuan, 1974: 115). Today the forest remains an attractive milieu for recreationists and is given considerable attention as a source of topophilia by both Bachelard (1969) and Tuan (1974).

The forest is not an unfamiliar place for sporting activity but while woodland is preserved for amenity use, none, to my knowledge, has been nurtured solely with sport in mind. More usually, as in the construction of skiing pistes, they are destroyed (see pages 60-61). Yet in cross country skiing, biathlon, cross country running and most notably in the sport of the forest, orienteering, the arboreal landscape plays an integral and important part in the sport, and in making it attractive to participants. What is more, the forest is an immensely attractive landscape for *training* for many sports, especially those involving a large amount of running. Many athletes testify to the attractiveness of woodlands for training, numerous senses being aroused including those of smell, sound and tactility, impressions of nature and environment being important elements of the runner's experience. For male athletes a forest provides a kind of home or safe haven where they can run and gambol away from the concrete of the city and in an environment where it is easy to get lost, yet claim it as their own. As one runner commented, 'I've really discovered this forest for myself ... there's nobody knows it better than I do ... this is my forest' (Lutz, 1991: 161).

Yet the forest and other 'remote' places are more likely to be patronised by men than by women athletes unless large numbers of competitors or groups are involved. The joy of running in the forest for some might be replaced, for others, by fear. Women athletes might not fit into 'wild' spaces where the attraction for men may reflect, for some, the desire to conquer nature but for others a kind of 'ecomasculinism' – a masculine challenge to the 'emphatic relationship with nature that some environmental feminists hold' (Nesmith and Radcliffe, 1993: 390). Such a 'challenge' might assume the simple enjoyment of strength, power or speed without acting them out physically in the form of a contest, carrying the man out of machismo into a state of beauty and expressiveness (Bly, 1993; 195-6).

Sports landscapes as landscapes of religion

Close contact with nature, which may be through sports, is also regarded as similar to a religious experience (Telema, 1991: 609) and some of the home-like qualities attributed to some sports places verge on the religious. Indeed, to state that sport is a modern, secular form of religion is something of a cliché. It is, nevertheless, a serious claim made by a number of scholars. Sport has been presented as a practice of religion, a ritual of protestantism (Korsgaard, 1990: 118), while Von Korsfleisch (1970) has seen the Olympics as a religious cere-mony, as did de Coubertin himself. Novak (1988) has written an entire book on the subject of sport as religion, observing that going to the stadium 'is half like going to a political rally, half like going to a church' (Novak, 1988: 19). He continues in more emphatic terms by adding that sport is radically religious: an impulse of freedom, respect for ritual limits, a zest for symbolic meaning, a longing for perfection and many other characteristics of religion can be applied, with a good degree of conviction, to sports (Novak, 1988: 29-31). Associated with all religions are sacred places and, if Tuan (1974: 99) is correct in averring that a sacred space is one possessing 'overpowering significance', then it is dif-ficult to deny the inclusion of particular stadiums and sports landscapes among them. Indeed, sacred places have been defined as those buildings and land-scapes which reinforce and even extol everyday patterns and special rituals of community life. These places, 'essential to the lives of the residents because of community use or symbolism' (Hester, 1993: 279) seem well typified by those of sport.

The affection fans have for particular sports places comes very close in strength to the affection shown by those with an obsessive religious adherence to religious places or 'sacred soil' (Tuan, 1975: 24-5). The term 'sacred turf' is, of course, widely used in a sports context and is a form of sporting 'geopiety' (Wright, 1966; Tuan, 1975). 'Arenas', writes Novak (1988: 126), 'are like monastries; individual games imprint on memory single images blazing as if from an illuminated text. Awesome places, a familiar, quiet sort of awe. Our cathedrals'. Likewise, Lipsky (1981: 18-9) regards the ball park as a 'sacred space, made sacred by the pious attitude of the fans who enter it'.

The fact that people seem to treat sports places like religious places helps explain their sense of topophilia. The strength of feeling (as 'irrational' as the reli-gious) towards some English football grounds, has secured them in their place in the face of more rational locational alternatives (Bale, 1992b). Just as the links binding people to their cities have, in the past at least, been of a religious nature (Tuan, 1975: 24), so appear the links that bind the British football fan especially, and (possibly) those of other cultures and sports, to their sports p(a)laces. The sports arena represents an example of a place-based community which continues to exert an influence on people in a world where modern individualism seems to be triumphing over more traditional forms of communal life (Entrikin, 1991: 67).

ENSEMBLE AS ICON

The landscapes of sports possess many elements, often rather small features which are taken for granted by those who daily pass them by, which are as much icons for the sports fan as the classical religious symbols of the Renaissance are for pilgrims or tourists. The secularised icons of sportscape are images which both record and carry a heavy conceptual and emotional weight (Horne, 1986: 67), creating in the observer a sense of topophilia. 'When we designate certain images and objects as "icons", we are really asserting that (they) are extraordinary in that they embody particularly important values, or even some residue of the sacred' (Goethals, 1978: 24, quoted in Slowikowski, 1991). They may be the much loved or permanent landscape elements in and around stadiums – the Wembley Towers, the Shankley Gate, the clock at Old

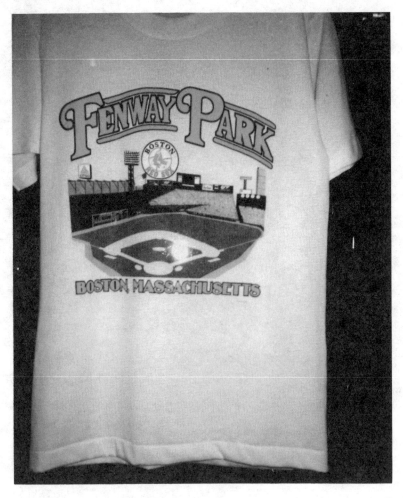

Figure 6.5 Fenway Park, Boston, photographed on a T-shirt in the souvenir shop at the Boston Park Plaza Hotel

Trafford with the reminder of the 1958 Munich air disaster, or the 'Green Monster' at Fenway Park (Figure 6.5). The statue of Arthur Wint in Kingston, Jamaica, that of Gareth Edwards in a shopping precinct in Cardiff and that of Paavo Nurmi at the Olympic Stadium in Helsinki (and elsewhere in Finland, and his head on the ten mark bank note), contribute to a sense of national identity through sport. That of Stanley Matthews in the centre of Stoke-on-Trent does more for local identity. Sporting iconography can assume more humble forms than the statues of sports heroes. Outside many small American towns, welcoming signs, painted on large billboards as a form of place-boosting, most frequently include allusions to the sporting prowess of local teams or individu-

Figure 6.6 The achievements of the local high school sports teams (the 'Millers') are projected to passers-by at Yukon, Oklahoma

als (Zelinsky, 1988: 4). Sometimes claims to sporting fame (however humble) are painted on more substantial features, adding greater dominance to the place of sport in the cultural landscape (Figure 6.6).

Sports iconography in the form of welcoming signs along the highways of America are institutionalised forms of image projection, usually erected by civic boosters. Less official forms of sporting iconography are the modern equivalents of medieval religious graffiti which take the sports landscape into the streets. Crudely daubed phrases praise the power of local football teams and denigrate their opponents, though little systematic research has been done on sports graffiti *per se*. By wearing badges and T-shirts with sporting allegiances emblazoned on them individuals are turned into walking representations of their teams. A sports stadium can be truly said to have become a much-loved place when it appears, recreated, on a tourist's T-shirt (Figure 6.5).

SPORTS ENSEMBLES AS HERITAGE

Religion and nostalgia are closely aligned in the sense that each creates a yearning for something better than the present. Each also provides a potent source for topophilia. Sport has its place among the sources for nostalgia, its sporting legends being the most obvious, be they people or places. Many stadiums are officially designated as national monuments while in others instant history and the invention of tradition guarantee that tourists regularly visit them.

Nostalgia for the countryside is reflected in the ways cricket and baseball are symbolised as rural/idyllic (see Chapter 7). Indeed, in the case of baseball, the myth that the sport was 'invented' in a cow-pasture in Cooperstown in up-state New York has led to Cooperstown itself becoming a simulacrum where no distinction can be made between the real and the model. The place where baseball was (re)created is a town founded and flourishing on myth, the result of the wish to invent and 'nostalgise' baseball. Today in Cooperstown the Baseball Hall of Fame, and seemingly every other retail outlet, is in some way related to the 'national pastime'. Another example of sporting hyper-reality can be found at Dyersville, Iowa, the film setting for the highly successful baseball movie, *Field of Dreams*. Here, the baseball field used for the film, set on a farm in quintessential middle America, has been retained as a shrine for pilgrims wishing to 'field their dreams' in the nearest thing to the baseball myth (see Chapter 7) that actually exists (Lowry, 1992: 44-6; Mosher, 1991). The landscape is not taken from history but, like villages which specialise in restoring fantasies, it is played back from the movie (Figure 6.7). It is a reflexion, not a reflection, of sporting experience (Schnechner, 1985: 91).

In Britain, the best example of a town which is intimately identified with sport, and owes its *raison d'être* and visual character to it, is, in my view, Newmarket, home of British horse racing. It is impossible to visit Newmarket and fail to identify it with racing. Not only does it have the headquarters of the Jockey Club but also the museum of horse racing, a huge number of stud farms, numerous training grounds, its own famous racecourse, and a large collection of retail outlets relating centrally and marginally to horse racing. My own impressions are that it is somewhat more 'horsey' than Saratoga, New York.

In the United States (and gradually in other nations) a frequent source of

Is This Heaven?

Where Dreams Come True

"Field of Dreams" Movie Site

We invite you to step up to bat at the world renowned "Field of Dreams". This baseball diamond carved from a cornfield is where the Academy Award nominated movie was filmed in the summer of 1988. The "Field of Dreams" is located on two farms 3.3 miles northeast of Dyersville. Open daily 10 a.m. to 6 p.m. - April thru November.

Figure 6.7 Where dreams come true? Promotional leaflet from Dyersville, Iowa (Source: Dyersville Area Chamber of Commerce)

topophilia is the nostalgia reflected in and generated by the large number of Halls of Fame (Snyder, 1991). These couple nostalgia with religion, being a combination of museum and shrine, dedicated to praising sporting heroes and displaying various quasi-religious relics (or memorabilia) of the past. They recreate memories of famous deeds of days gone by and it has been observed that 'the ultimate *raison d'être* for a sports hall of fame, like the ancient Greek sanctuary, is the glorification of sporting heritage' (Redmond, 1973: 2).

Although sport does not monopolise the US hall of fame scene, it certainly dominates it. The daily hoardes that descend on Cooperstown are engaged in nothing less than a secular pilgrimage.

The heritage industry has a voracious appetite. Some stadiums are recognised as heritage but sports heritage has the potential to break out and expand away from stadiums and halls of fame. There is every reason for 'sports trails' and sports tours to develop (they already exist) as places seek to capitalise on, and create, an affection for sports landscapes and places. Sports heritage does not only try to prevent the destruction of 'meaningful' sports places; it also tries to invent tradition and write 'instant history'. Within a few months of opening the new national stadium in Copenhagen, the authorities were organising guided tours of the ground and its newly established hall of fame. There are few major stadiums in the world which have failed to provide such tours while cities also anchor themselves to their sporting traditions as part of their tourist industry. Liverpool is no Newmarket or Cooperstown but it does advertise itself as the soccer capital of the world and encourages 'soccer city weekends' (Bale, 1992b: 75-6).

Auditory and olfactory elements of the sports landscape experience

So far I have implied that affection for sports places derives mainly from the dominant sense of sight. But other senses frequently contribute to the enjoyment of a visit to a sports event and in milieux where landscape elements are few in number, noises and smells may serve to compensate for the lack of visual pleasures. Noises and smells associated with sports places have been recounted by fans on several occasions as creating a sense of place. Although not as important as the sense of sight in recording the landscape elements which contribute to a sense of place, sports would not be the same without their sounds and smells.

THE SOUND OF SPORT

Sports events obviously create islands of noise in an otherwise relatively quiet part of the city, generated not only by the crowds responding to the events of the game itself but also by traffic generated by it. Often, the sound of sport greets the fan before the sight of it, adding to the pleasant sense of anticipation – the sound of leather against willow, the ripple of applause, the roar of the crowd – these are the sounds of sports geography. In the United States 'cheering was originally an integral part of [American] football that linked the fans intimately to the players' (Oriard, 1981: 38-9). In the late 1860s footballers at Princeton University trained some of their classmates to shout for them in order to intimidate their opponents from Rutgers and 'organized cheering at football games was born' (Oriard, 1981: 39). Such intimate involvement is common in various football codes throughout the world.

For Novak (1988: xv) 'there is no substitute for the squeak of sneakers on the court and the sound of the ball slipping through the cords' at a game of basketball. For the cricket writer, John Arlott (1984: 57), the game played at Taunton evoked the sound 'of lowing cows in the cattle market punctuating the applause of the crowd'. To football fans, the auditory landscape of sport is a major part of the experience, and the character of stadium sound has been excellently described by Nick Hornby (1992) in *Fever Pitch*, his brilliant book about a life-long obsession with Arsenal football club. In it he identified various categories of football noise:

> ...the formal, ritual noise when the players emerged (each player's name called in turn, starting with the favourite, until he responded with a wave); the spontaneous shapeless roar when something exciting was happening on the pitch; the renewed vigour of the chanting after a goal or a sustained period of attacking. (And ... among younger, less alienated men, that football grumble when things are going badly). (Hornby, 1992: 75)

Music forms a distinctive element of the overall sound of sport, Snyder (1993: 176) going so far as to suggest that it 'is one of the primary phenomena associated with a sports event'. The sound of music in sport can assume several forms. One basic division might be between formal and informal sports music. The former could be (a) integral or (b) incidental to the sport itself. Music is integral to the activity in the case of gymnastics, figure skating or synchronised swimming. These sports require music for them to take place. Music is important, but incidental to the sporting action, in the case of national anthems which serve to generate feelings of patriotism and place-pride and are played before the start of international events. Music which preceeds events or takes place at half-time is simply additional crowd entertainment. Sounds which fall into Snyder's category of 'background and motivational' sports music may be the formally organised encouragement, as in the case of cheerleaders in much US sport, or the more disorganised (though far from non-orchestrated) music made up of songs and chants from the fans themselves. In the case of football (soccer), such songs may also involve a variety of musical instruments – trumpets, drums, klaxons, etc.

The lyrics of terrace songs are often patriotic, savage, unkind and obscene – but also humourous and in Britain and Latin America they are nowhere near as sanitised as those of the 'cheerleaders' at American football. They often mock the opposition and praise the home team and are part of the attraction of going to a football match, creating memories to be savoured. Such songs may be illustrated by one from Argentina and one from Britain. The San Lorenzo fans love their club, even when languishing in the lower division without a ground of their own:

> We are the great San Lorenzo fans
> that don't have a ground
> that put up with relegation
> despite the years
> the moments we've lived through
> I will always be by your side
> beloved San Lorenzo

> (Archetti, 1992: 231)

If this affirms the loyalty of fans in difficult times, the following example draws humourously on masculinity, working class culture and local pride in support of the English football club, Sheffield United. It is rendered to the tune of John Denver's *Annie's Song* and is extracted from a lovingly self-published anthology of British football songs (Bulmer and Merrills, 1992).

> You light up my senses,
> Like a gallon of Magnet,
> Like a packet of Woodbines,
> Like a good pinch of snuff,
> Like a night out in Sheffield,
> Like a greasy chip butty,
> Oh Sheffield United,
> Come thrill me again ...
>
> (Bulmer and Merrills, 1992: 92)

Alternatively, the denigration of the opposition is a frequent feature of such songs. Consider, for example, the following Manchester City song about their local rivals, United and its home ground, Old Trafford. It is one of many crude (and virtually incomprehensible) English terrace songs performed to the tune of Wild Rover.

> Old Trafford they say is a wonderful place,
> But I know it's really a fucking disgrace,
> And as for United I know they should be,
> Shovelling shit on the Isle of Capri.
>
> (Bulmer and Merrills, 1992: 119)

Like it or not, would an English football match be the same without such songs? Would ice hockey be the same without the sound of the traditional organ? Or north American basketball without the rock music? Who would make the noise if the British football stadium was filled with executive boxes? Would an embourgoisified 'audience' respond in the same way? Would polite applause replace the 'rolling roar' throughout the match (Hornby, 1992: 76)? Would sports events be the same without their various soundscapes? If noise is regarded as unwanted sound, it is probably the wrong word to use in the present context since for sports fans the presence of sport-induced sounds contribute to the process whereby environments become places with a particular ambience (Pocock, 1988: 64). The sound of sport is a major medium for the enhancement of the sport landscape experience.

Fully modernised sport will alter the nature of the soundscape of stadiums and arenas. The showgirl 'cheerleaders' of American football have been viewed as catering for 'television-football, not spectator football', taking the place of announcers with their 'inane prattling' during parts of the game. Such people 'fear silence' whereas the true fan does not require constant noise and can use breaks between plays by 'resolving strategy and agonising over his team's predicament' (Oriard, 1981: 39). Electronically amplified sound will also increase and hence reduce the sponteneity of the crowd's songs and chants. This has already happened at Manchester United's ground at Old Trafford.

Landscapes of Modern Sport

Smell can also conjure up images of place and contribute to the overall experience. Smell is an important emotional sense and certain smells are therefore
deeply important to individuals (Porteous, 1985). The smells of sports are more
than the commonly sensed odour of liniments emanating from the changing
rooms. For Michael Benson (1989: xxv) the early memories of baseball were
'the smell of rust and cigars' while 'industrial' smells and stale cigarette smoke
often evoke nostalgic reminiscences of particular English football places (Bale,
1992b: 71). As one gets close to the English football stadium the smell of the
food vendors' products, while not exactly pleasant, certainly evokes an
impending sense of sport. Cricket at Tunbridge Wells is linked to the pleasant
odour of rhododendrums while in downhill skiing events 'the scent of ever-
green forest and cold, dry air mingles with the blue wood smoke wafted from
the valley' (Dunleavey, 1981: 82). Approaching the gates of the Oakland-
Almeda County Coliseum in California in time for a big football game, the
gratification from the experience must be enhanced by the large number of
olfactory stimuli: air smelling of 'soaked grass and warming sun, of shiny slick
programs fresh with ink, new angora sweaters, popcorn, beer, cigars, plastic
raincoats, coffee, peanut shells, mustard, hot dogs, the alkaline of new concrete' (Novak, 1988: 4). To what extent would these be denied the fan in a
world of antiseptic sports places where, like motel bathrooms, all seem to smell
the same? And there is one point here which relates to my earlier discussion of
modernisation and sport; modernised sport, particularly when driven indoors,
seems likely to drive out sensory quality (Porteous, 1985: 368).

The smells of sports are likely to be highly idiosyncratic; while running
through the woods in springtime, I find that the smell of bluebells enhances the
athletic experience. In summer the sweet smell of honeysuckle has the same
effect, as does the smell of the pine forest at any time of the year. The idea of
placelessness may be expressed mainly in visual terms but while not as significant as sights and sounds in conjuring images of place, smells should not be
ignored in any assessment of the senses and the role they play in the overall
sport experience.

Motion provides us with a direct experience of space, a sense of possibility and
of freedom (Tuan, 1986: 100). But as I have stressed earlier (Chapter 4), the
spatially confined character of sports constrains the freedom and flow that
might otherwise exist. To an extent, therefore, athletes increase their freedom to
experience the vitality of abandonment in space during their training which,
while often scientific and regulated, does not possess the same degree of spatial
confinement as the competitive event (though if one was to subscribe to the
psycho-analytic view, it is the very security of confinement which may be a
source of attraction). In training, the athlete may be able to encounter landscapes which might be otherwise avoided, environments in which movement
and the sense of touch can be more varied than in the more clinical environment of competition. Again, however, I should stress that significant gender
differences may exist in athletes' willingness to venture into certain places for
training.

The sense of tactility brings the body, literally, 'in touch' with the landscape but the feeling of vitality derived from movement varies according on the nature of the surface over which the athlete is moving. The white concrete of a road or pavement or the sanitised surrounds of the weight-training room are unlikely to compare with the ambience of the forest where pine needles combine with soil to provide a perfect cushion on which to run (Figure 6.8). Despite the increased rationality of running one form of training ideally incorporates the forest environment. This is known by the Swedish word *fartlek*, which translates as 'speed-play'. It was initially advocated by the Swedish coach Gösta Holmer and was specifically related to the forests and meadows of his native landscape. In such training the athletes should 'play with speed', sprinting for certain periods, walking and jogging for others. While exhausting (see page 114), it was less strictly regimented than 'interval running' on an artificial track.

Figure 6.8 Running in the forest near Eksjö, Sweden; a masculine sense of place?

Another environment fondly recalled by athletes is that of the beach. The oft-quoted description by Roger Bannister (1957: 11), of the joy of running bare-foot and freely on firm sand and the sensory experiences derived therefrom, is worth repeating:

> I stood barefoot on firm dry sand by the sea. The air has a special quality as if it had a life of its own. The sound of breakers on the shore shut out all others. I looked up at the clouds, like great white-sailed galleons, chasing proudly inland. I looked down at the reg-ular ripples in the sand, and could not absorb so much beauty .... In this supreme moment I leapt in sheer joy. I was startled, and frightened, by the tremendous excitement that so few steps could create. I glanced round uneasily to see if anyone was watching. A few more steps – self-consciously now and firmly gripping the original excitement. The earth seemed almost to move with me. I was running now, and a fresh rhythm entered my body. No longer conscious of my movement I discovered a new unity with nature. I had found a new source of power and beauty, a source I never knew existed.

'Most runners would admit an esthetic, sensual component in their running as well. Long distance running induces intermittent but sometimes extraordinarily intense and pleasurable awareness of the environment' (Winters, 1980: 22) sometimes resulting in an apparent blending of body, nature and landscape. Dunleavey (1981: 81) notes that experienced skiers 'become part of the envi-ronment, moving in response to gravity, to undulating terrain, to shifts in the depth and quality of the snow'. To the downhill skier, 'the outside world is an objective correlative for the unity of being, the harmony of nature, experienced within' (Dunleavey, 1981: 81). On cross-country skis 'the human animal becomes a creature of wood and plain, kin to the deer, ruffed goose, the otter, the snowshoe hare and other creatures who share the winter landscape'(Dunleavey, 1981: 82). When other human beings are indoors, in the depths of winter, the skier emerges, 'rejoicing in the rhythmic coordination of arms and legs, the spontaneous generation of ever-increasing energy, the exhilaration of breathing deeply in well-oxygenated air, ... the sense of physical well-being with no hint of exhaustion ... that is the skier's bounty' (Dunleavey, 1981: 82). Studies in humanistic psychology point to 'altered states' in which awareness is heightened through sport. Space and landscape, in such situations, appear in altered states themselves, some athletes claiming that they are able to perceive many more details, and in sharper form, than usual (Murphy and White, 1978: 41).

Some athletes evaluate races by the landscapes through which they are run, Winters (1980) citing two of his favourites as the Avenue of the Giants Marathon in California which offers miles of redwood trees and Washington's Cherry Blossom Classic, held among ornamental cherry trees in the spring. The wide variety of urban landscapes experienced by runners in the London and New York marathons is often claimed as a major attraction of such events. The marathon in a placeless environment is possible but it is unlikely to be popular.

A sense of power and abandon can come, of course, from speed and move-ment in automated sports, which despite their conflict with nature, enable the participant to experience the environment in a new way. The techno-sports par-ticipant experiences new relatioships with nature and landscape. As the great landscape interpreter, J. B. Jackson (1957-8: 25) put it, such experiences may be of:

> ...an abstract nature, as it were; a nature shorn of its gentler, more human traits, of all memory and sentiment. The new landscape, seen at a rapid, sometimes even a terrifying pace, is composed of rushing air, shifting lights, clouds, waves, a constantly moving, changing horizon, a constantly changing surface beneath the ski, the wheel, the rudder, the wing. The view is no longer static, it is a revolving, uninterrupted panorama of 360 degrees. In short the traditional perspective, the traditional way of seeing and experiencing the world is abandoned; in its stead we become active participants, the shifting focus of a moving abstract world; our nerves and muscles are all brought into play. To the perceptive individual there can be an almost mystical quality to the experience; his identity for the moment seems to be transmuted.

SPORTS AND TOPOPHOBIA

In his introduction to *The Poetics of Space*, Gaston Bachelard (1969: xxxii) stressed that he is concerned with topophilia, and that 'hostile space' is barely dealt with. Tuan (1979), on the other hand, has devoted an entire book to *Landscapes of Fear*, a counterpoint to his *Topophilia*. Sports landscapes can, of course, project images of fear and discontent as well as love and affection. To an extent, this has already been noted in the dissatisfaction sports fans have with some modern sports landscapes. In such cases technical efficiency turns against itself, taking something away from the potential sport landscape experience. In rational sports landscapes the sports participant may feel more comfortable or more safe but in small ways the enjoyment of the experience is reduced. This is essentially what Relph (1981) termed the paradox of rational landscapes.

Two other sorts of hostility or even fear can be found to characterise some landscapes of sports. The first results from certain sportscapes which possess negative connotations in the sense that they are viewed by certain members of society as akin to 'noxious facilities'. The sounds and smells of sport which might create affection in some create hostility in others. In Britain a good example is the football stadium which, among members of the general public, tend to possess negative imagery (Bale, 1990). When new stadium developments are mooted in suburban areas, local residents frequently oppose such landscape change and engage in political activism to prevent stadium construction. The same applies to the proposed development of sports landscapes such as speedway or car-racing tracks (Bale, 1989: 245).

A second situation when sports landscapes may become fearsome is when the spillover effects which they generate may create fear in passers by or local residents. The classic example here is again, the traditional and rather stereotypical view of the British football stadium and the over-amplified 'hooligan' image which has become associated with it. In this case, some sections of the community are literally afraid to journey in the proximity of the stadium before and immediately after a game. This is not a new, nor peculiarly British phenomenon, however, and other well-documented examples include the deadly spillovers from motor cycle and car racing events where it has been shown that deaths from imitative dangerous driving tend to increase locally during the periods of such events. In 1992 nearly 60 motor cyclists were injured in unofficial races (labelled as 'delinquent competition') between 50,000 bikers who flocked to Le Mans during the weekend of the 24 hour event held there (Katz, 1992: 3).

As noted earlier, landscapes which may appear highly desirable for sporting activity (especially training) for some people may be landscapes of fear for others. When I talk about the freedom of running on the urban common or in the forest (Figure 6.8) I may be mainly talking about the sporting experience of white, heterosexual males. To other groups such spaces may be a constraint. 'Sexual attacks warn women [athletes] every day that their bodies are not meant to be in certain spaces, and racist and homophobic violence delimits the spaces of black, lesbian and gay' sportspeople (Rose, 1993: 34). Referring to the use of urban space for sports by women in the Ruhr, it has been noted that the types of free green areas favoured for sporting use by women are difficult for them to reach and 'women seldom use these places alone or after dark because of fear of sexual harrassment and attacks' (Klein, 1993: 150). So while it is sometimes felt that women have a more sympathetic attitude than men towards nature, they appear less free to experience that nature through training for sports. More women than men might be expected to gain pleasurable sporting experiences in natural landscapes but more might also be expected to have bad experiences in the very same kind of landscapes. This is confirmed by the results of research undertaken into top-class sportsmen and women in Finland (Lyytinen, 1993).[6]

CONCLUSION

In this chapter I have tried to show that despite the rationalisation of modern sports, many sports landscapes are, for a variety of reasons, much loved places. People may be attracted to particular sports because of their own psychological make up; others because they feel the landscapes of sports symbolise deeply held needs, and other because such places generate affection through sentiment. It is possible, of course, that such affection is the result of what radicals might call 'false consciousness'. It may well be within the interests of the powerful in society to dupe the masses with the spectacle and the 'bread and circuses' which modern sport and their landscapes may be said to represent. At the same time, however, the landscapes of sports continue to provide many genuine pleasures. As with other landscapes of spectacle (Ley and Olds, 1988) it is possible to 'engage with' the sport place, using it to nurture friendships, and to 'commune' with landscape and nature. This is not to say that the very landscapes which create topophilia in some create topophobia in others, nor that landscape, affection and nostalgia are untutored by myth.

NOTES

1. I am extremely grateful to Tuija Lyytinen for drawing my attention to Seamon's (1993b) book of excellent essays.
2. If I were to include hunting as a sport I would have to concede that Appleton. (1974: 68) *does* devote a good deal of attention to this, viewing it an important linking theme between behaviour, landscape and aesthetics.
3. According to this view, the vaulter's pole, the skier's sticks, the cricketer's bat, the gymnast's rings and bars, or the tennis player's racket exemplify 'undoubted symbols of the erect, potent penis' (Balint, 1959: 29) and hence reinforce the athlete's confidence.Gender differences in sports participation, based on Freudian (Oedipal) concepts of *intrusion* (into space as in football which tends to be played by boys) and *inclusion* (as in receiving the ball in netball by girls) are given a spatial twist in the spurious suggestion that the boy's conflict with the father is 'decided on the football field in sublimated form' in the 'penetration' (i.e. intrusion) of the penalty area (Vinnai, 1973: 77).
4. I deal with this in the context of the British football stadium in Bale, 1992b: Chapter 3.
5. 'Fanzines' are 'fan magazines', often semi-published, fugitive and ephemeral. Their use in exploring the voice of the football fan is illustrated in Bale, 1992b.
6. This research showed that of top class Finnish athletes pleasant experiences in the natural environment (though not necessarily through sports participation) were obtained by 72 per cent of the women and 53 per cent of the men. Respective figures for unpleasant experiences were 44 per cent and 36 per cent. Of the total number of respondents 43 per cent perceived pleasant experiences in nature through sports competition or training (Lyytinen, 1993).

7

MYTH AND THE LANDSCAPES OF SPORT

If sports landscapes can be regarded as cultural images or ways of symbolising some of our surroundings, they can be studied across 'a variety of materials and on many surfaces – in paint on canvas, in writing on paper, [as well as] in earth, stone, water and vegetation on the ground' (Daniels and Cosgrove, 1988: 1, brackets added; Cosgrove, 1993: 7-9). By studying landscape representations in writings, paintings, films and other images, an insight is obtained into the culture that made them. Senses of place and identity are communicated, as is a sense of sport. The associations between sport, landscape and place are sometimes inferred by the most unlikely media. In a promotional display to lure tourists to the USA a baseball game is shown next to the Statue of Liberty. An advertisement for the Rover 800 coupé has a picture of the car in the foreground with a game of village cricket going on in the background, complete with country pub, thatched cottage, village church and surrounding woodland. The caption states that 'it's everything we know. It's everything we are'. On the back of an English £10 bank note is found an impression of a village cricket match at Dingley Dell and alongside a head and shoulders image of that place's creator, Charles Dickens. The analysis of such *iconography* 'concerns itself with the subject matter or meaning of works of art, as opposed to their form' (Panofsky, 1962: 3) and in such analyses symbolic values may be discovered which may have been unknown to the artist or author (Panofsky, 1962: 8).

In this chapter I want to focus on these kinds of sport landscape icons and interpret them as myths, after the manner of Roland Barthes (1973). In some cases, such an analysis deconstructs landscape images as if they were 'encoded texts'. According to James and Nancy Duncan (1992: 18), 'through Barthes's eyes one sees the world exposed and demystified; one's "natural attitude" towards the environment is shattered as the apparent innocence of landscapes is shown to have profound ideological implications', often justifying dominant values and severing the oft-assumed link between representation and reality. I will introduce these landscapes by looking, somewhat briefly, at English football (soccer) and American baseball. The images of the former conjure up landscapes of the inner city and the industrial north; those of the latter have an 'ability to archaicize America – famously exhibiting its *pastoral* spatiality' (Brown, 1991: 52, italics added). The bulk of the chapter, however, will concentrate on the mythical representation in print, on canvas and in other media, of the quintessentially English summer sport of cricket, a sport which arguably has spawned more books and paintings than any other.

BRITISH FOOTBALL AND THE INDUSTRIAL NORTH

Representations of the landscapes of British football in literary and artistic media are few and far between, especially in contrast to its summer companion, cricket. On the other hand, this assertion applies basically to high cultural forms such as stage plays, 'good' novels, poetry and paintings. When mass cultural forms such as boys' comics and television plays are included, football becomes more obvious as an element of the projected cultural landscape.

The most well known artistic representations of the British football landscape are probably those of the Salford artist, L.S. Lowry, whose paintings have represented both the external and internal views of the the stereotypical English football ground. In one of his most famous paintings, 'Going to the Match', the football ground is sited among nineteenth century terraced houses, factory chimneys forming a nearby horizon, with spectators striding to the ground in what can be nothing but an inner urban zone of a northern industrial city. Another northern artist, Harold Riley, presents a similar industrial image, terraced houses and factories forming the inevitable backdrop to the football ground.

Although professional football is played throughout Britain, writing which in part or in whole revolves around it tends to be set in the 'industrial north' of England. The climax of *The Card* by Arnold Bennett, in which a professional footballer plays a major part, is set in the north Staffordshire Potteries and would surely have been incongruous if set in Surrey. J. B. Priestley's writings were invariably set in the north of England, typified by Bruddesford United, the football club in *The Good Companions*. More recently, Hunter Davies's *Striker* does not have to start, like the life of his hero, in the traditional hotbed of English football, the north-east, but it does. Good journalism has also graphically described the stereotype. The following piece, by a *Guardian* writer, could only be applied to the north:

> ...there is a sparseness, a meanness about the ground. It is like a grey snapshot from the thirties ... the rawness of it proclaims a football town, subscribing to the male Saturday afternoon ritual which neither women's lib. nor television sport has gnawed its way into. (Cunningham, 1980: 15)

Boys' comics frequently have industry-football images projected in their cartoon strips. The legendary 'Roy of the Rovers' played for the geographically imprecise 'Melchester Rovers' but beyond the terraces the illustrations of his exploits depict factories and chimneys, not churches, village pubs, and trees. But in the adult comic, *Viz*, the surreal football cartoon, 'Billy the fish' is unambiguous in its north-eastern location. *The Manageress*, a television series about a woman football manager was set in Yorkshire; the BBCTV children's series about a boys' football team, *Jossey's Giants*, was set in the north-east; Michael Palin's comic portrayal of a football fanatic would not have worked, had it not been set in a stereotypical northern mill town. *Gregory's Girl*, a film about a girl footballer, is set in what many would agree to be the hotbed of British football culture, central Scotland. In one or two British films the football ground is presented almost incidentally as if to reinforce the northern image, especially in some of the 'new wave' films of the late 1950s and 1960s.

There are two points worth making about the dominance of 'industrial northernness' in these representations. First, it perpetuates the image of the inner city landscape of football. Although a detailed typology of the intra-urban location of British football grounds has yet to be formulated, it will be obvious to anyone who has visited more than a handful that the last thing that many of them could be called is inner-urban. Consider the grounds, for example, of Cardiff City, Leeds United, Bournemouth, Plymouth Argyle; they can hardly be called central in terms of intra-urban location.

Secondly, while *professional* football was established in the north and gradually diffused to embrace the rest of the country (Bale, 1978), the game was initially codified in the south of England, played in parks and commons around London in no way associated with regions of heavy manufacturing. Rather, it was Eton, Oxford and Cambridge which were its early homes (Marples, 1954). It was the Corinthians, the Royal Engineers and Oxford University who were the first FA Cup winners, not Blackburn Rovers, Aston Villa or Preston North End. However, the subsequent diffusion of the game was uneven and the professional league clubs do remain over-represented, in absolute and per capita terms, in the north of England. Overall, however, the playing of football *per se* does not have a particularly northern character. If amateur and recreational football are taken into account, it has been found that more people play football per head of the population in counties that are not particularly industrial or northern (Bale, 1982: 46-7). But the Lowryesque stereotype perpetuates the northern industrial image, something which must be regretted by those who favour and encourage the sport's *embourgeoisement*.

BASEBALL—PASTORAL GAME OF SUMMER ?

For many twentieth century American novelists, the crucible in which 'dissimilar characters are forced to shed their social antagonisms in pursuit of a common goal' is the baseball field (Goodman and Bauer, 1993: 233) but despite its urban origins in New York and Hoboken, New Jersey, baseball in the United States connotes, and is often connoted by, the pastoral and the rural (Guttmann, 1978: 100-8; Riess, 1989: 34). Indeed, Oriard (1991: 552) notes that for 'pastoral baseball fiction one can look at almost any baseball novel of the past four decades', citing Bernard Malamud's *The Natural* as the paradigm example. It is, according to the title of collected pieces of writing by columnist Roger Angell (1984), *The Summer Game*. Many writers have extolled the virtues of baseball as being reminiscent of the frontier, of the countryside in the city, of the rural idyll; it is sportified nostalgia. The movie, *Field of Dreams*, could have told essentially the same story in a suburban setting but the baseball park had to be in rural Iowa for the film to work on US audiences.

Many would support the view that 'at its heart, baseball is an agrarian game; it's the pastime that welds pasture to city' (Weil et al., 1992: 28). Even when the rural metaphors of 'park' and 'ground' began to be replaced by the more urban and technologically coded 'stadium' (with the erection of the Yankee Stadium in New York in 1923), the game continued to be 'perceived as the embodiment of traditional rural symbols, beliefs, and values relevant to the needs of urban America' (Riess, 1989: 221). Baseball creates the American ideal as well as the idyll. It has been said to simulate the American ideal of freedom (Giamatti, 1989: 83); it is also the family unit enjoying summer days on the bleachers; it is fathers playing ball with sons (Hall, 1985). It is the symbolic re-creation of the frontier spirit; after all, the baseball park has its infield – 'the urban core', and its outfield – the frontier; in both nineteenth century America and in the baseball park 'danger increases with distance' (Ross, 1973: 31). For the fan baseball has 'peace and contentment and the intimations of unity with his environment that may not be available to him outside the stadium' (Oriard, 1976: 33); it is a game played 'on a spacious green expanse in the bright light of day' (Rooney, 1974: 1); the scenic backdrop of the ball parks – their dirt and grassy fields – encouraged the feeling that the game was an idyllic pastoral refuge (Lipsky, 1981: 108). Indeed, the long-believed story of the rural origins of the game, in a cow-pasture in Cooperstown in up-state New York, itself turned out to be a myth. Today Cooperstown cashes in on the myth; indeed, the town is an urban simulacrum, the baseball myth being its *raison d'être* with no distinction being made between the real and the model. These rural images are argued to contribute in no small part to the attraction of baseball for fans and players though Novak (1988: 56) is one of the few American observers to actually use the word 'myth' when describing its rural image.

Baseball is double edged. The pastoral image may dominate but several observers have stressed that baseball's other landscape is both urban and quantified. As Lipsky (1981: 108) points out, the 'parks' cramped surroundings in narrow urban lots and their billboards emphasised that the escape (from urban life) occurred only within urban-capitalist borders'. And when you watch baseball in a high-tech, inner urban stadium with the players on a synthetic carpet, with electronic scoreboards, under floodlights on a cool April evening, where does the warm, rural evocation lie? Is it rural reverie that brings fans from southern Ontario to watch the Blue Jays play in the synthetic landscape of the Toronto Skydome? And surely the farmers who, as baseball fans, visit Kansas City have more than enough rurality every day of their lives to view the Royals Stadium as an agrarian myth; more likely it is an emblem of advancement and advanced technology (Mrozek, 1989: 204). In the city, therefore, the ballpark is 'an agrarian *illusion*, a splash of emerald in a chimney-stacked urbanscape' (Benson, 1989: xxv, italics added).

This alternative urban-advancement image is matched by the sport's mathematical image. There are few more quantified sports than baseball. Indeed, Bill Brown (1991: 55) has gone so far as to state that 'baseball's statisticity, rather than its pastorality, may make the game timeless, and timelessly American'; Novak (1988: 59) argues that what it satisfies in the psyche is an 'enormous love of order'. The game's scientific nature, its narrative as summarised in the box score, and the batting averages in the sports pages makes it 'seem central to, and no alternative to, the rise of a rationalised society'. Players, like workers in the factory, become 'objects of statistical knowledge' (Brown, 1991: 55). The image of quantification is also present in the physical landscape of base-ball. Although not as predictable and precise as many other sports, the geome-try of the baseball field is clear for all to see with the newer stadiums becoming more and more symmetrical (see Chapter 6). With its straight lines and dia-monds, right angles and radii, the arithmetic and statistics of the yearbooks and almanacs are matched by the field's geometry; it is 'a festival of angles and inches. A trigonometer's delight' (Novak, 1988: 61). Indeed, the growing spa-tial standardisation of stadiums violates one of the mythical attractions of the sport, 'that supreme frontier spirit – rugged individualism – which was found in unique individuals surviving in unique landscapes' (Oriard, 1976: 39).

A final interpretation is that the baseball field and its imagery does not sim-ply reflect the rationalism of modern north America but reflects the very work-places of those – the participants – who seek to escape them. Steven Gelber (1983) has pointed out that nineteenth century sources rarely communicated the rural aspects of the game (nor do twentieth century sources if my own casual observations of various baseball memorabilia shops and visual representations of the game found in the Baseball Hall of Fame in Cooperstown, are represen-tative) and if less concentration is placed on the role of nature and more on that of the players – and, I might add, the spectators – a somewhat different inter-pretation could be made, making its image something more than simply 'quan-tified pastoral' (Guttmann, 1978: 95):

> The game's attraction lay in its congruence with everyday life. It was popular because it was similar to, not because it was different from, day to day life. Baseball provided the male business worker with a leisure analog to his job. In the game he experienced social relationships and psychological demands similar to those he knew at work. Indeed, he was working at playing, and by doing so he was minimizing dissonance between those two aspects of his life. Baseball brought psychological harmony. *It appeared to be differ-ent from work because it was outdoor play, but underneath it was the same.* (Gelber, 1983: 7, emphasis added)

Gelber's allusion to the baseball game being basically 'the same' as the work place refers to the fundamental ordering of time and space both in the stadium and in the factory. In factory and park the worker, literally, knew his place. The trip to the ball park was, as interpeted here, nothing more than an extended tea break.

These brief overviews of football in England and baseball in north America set the scene for a more detailed examination of landscape imagery and sport. The image of English football quite explicitly links the sport to an urban-indus-trial base. The baseball landscape, on the other hand, has been summed up as being 'quantified pastoral' but the baseball park as a re(-)creation of rural America seems to me to be hardly proven. Both are essentially myths.

THE LIE OF THE LAND

I would guardedly argue that more has been communicated about the quintessentially English game of cricket, in various media, than any other sport –
including baseball. The remainder of this chapter looks in some detail at the
content of the landscape images of cricket which have been projected and suggests what they are, in fact, signifying.

Books, essays, plays, paintings, photographs, poetry, cartoons, postcards,
postage stamps, bank notes and advertisements communicate the English cricket landscape in a remarkably consistent way as being natural, rural and southern. The cricket landscape is invariably projected in writing, on canvas, on
stage and on celluloid as a nostalgic, rustic idyll. The doyen of English cricket
writers, John Arlott (1955: 7), said that cricket 'is as much a part of the pattern
of the English country as the green itself or the parish church. Two hundred
years ago landscape painters who often and clearly had no knowledge of the
game, would include a cricket match as inherent in the scene'. It has been
recognised that 'by the early part of this century cricket had come to play an
integral part in that strange, powerful formation of ideas about the English
countryside and its history which swims through the national imagination'
(Inglis, 1977a: 77). Today coffee table books containing glossy photographs
projecting the 'English countryside' often convey a similar image.

The nature of the landscape of cricket as projected by such media can be
aided by considering the variety of landscape elements which go to make up
the overall landscape ensemble of cricket. As noted in Chapter 6, in cricket the
landscape ensemble is afforded considerable significance by those seeking to
capture the essence and attraction of the game. What form does cricket's imaginative landscape ensemble take?

Consider the consistency of the following sample of descriptions. In the
poem 'The cricket pitch 1944', Brian Jones refers to the field 'ringed with
elms' (see Ross, 1981: 487); Neil Powell in 'The cricketers' watched the game
'from the woodland edge' (Ross, 1981: 489); Edmund Blunden's 'The season
opens' (Ross, 1981: 405) starts with the verse:

A tower we must have, and a clock in the tower,
Looking over the tombs, the tithe barn, the bower;
The inn and the mill, the forge and the hall,
And the loamy sweet level that loves bat and ball.

In 'Linden Lea' Edward Bucknell (Ross, 1981: 60) sites the cricket field within
'view of the Hall nestling among ancient trees, and an abundance of shade for
the spectators from other trees along one hedge. An open pavilion commanded
the ground from one corner, and another, sacred to the squire's wife and her
friends, was ensconced under a huge elm hard by'. One of England's premier
judges, Sir Norman Birkett (1957: 9), composed a cricket ensemble which
included a:

... small white painted pavilion of the village ground, the tins for the scoreboard, the horse with its big leather shoes pulling the roller, the wooden benches at intervals around the ground, the great spreading trees at the boundary's edge, the flowering hedgerows ...

Edmund Blunden (1985: 20) paints a peaceful picture when he urges the young cricketer, waiting for the next batsman to come to the crease, to 'glance from your post in the long field ... away to those farms and woods, spires and hills around you; rest your high spirits for a moment on the composure of that young mother with her sleeping baby, on the old white horse as still as if he were carved in chalk on the down'. The classic view is that 'of cricket set against a background of green trees, haystacks, barns, and a landscape of peace and plenty, remote from a world of busy getting and spending' (Arlott and Cardus, 1969: 24) while in *England their England* Macdonnell (1935) claimed the cricket ground as the essence of the *real* England, 'unspoilt by factories and financiers and tourists and hustle'. It is Macdonnell who, more emphatically than anyone else, captures the Kentish village cricket stereotype:

It was a hot summer's afternoon. There was no wind, and the smoke from the red-roofed cottages curled slowly up into the golden haze. The clock on the flint tower of the church struck the half-hour, and the vibration spread slowly across the shimmering hedge rows. ... Bees lazily drifted. White butterflies flapped their aimless way among the gardens. Delphiniums, larkspur, tiger-lillies, evening primrose, monk's hood, sweet peas, swaggered brilliantly above the box hedges, the wooden palings and the rickety gates. The cricket field itself was a mass of daisies and buttercups and dandelions, tall grasses and purple vetches and thistledown, and great clumps of dark red sorrel, except, of course, for the oblong patch in the centre – mown, rolled, watered–a smooth, shining emerald of grass, the pride of Fordenden, the Wicket. (Macdonnell, 1935: 107)

Indeed, to play in the shadows of an industrially-composed landscape ensemble would be considered by some observers of the cricketing scene to be nothing less than 'the fate' of the players so consigned (Frith, 1987: 43).

Representations of the English cricket landscape in painting and other forms of visual art also communicate the kind of rural idyll noted above. The majority of paintings of cricket are unambiguously rural in their settings (Bale, 1988). The idyll of pre-Victorian cricket with be-smocked and jovial rustics waiting to bat in the shade of the 'Red Lion' is typified by artists such as Ernest Prater (Frith, 1987: 64). Even during its so-called 'golden age', from the 1890s to 1914, cricket images harked back to a nostalgic idyll and an analysis of Gerry Wright's 'coffee table book' *Cricket's Golden Summer*, reveals how golden age players, though painted in authentic colours, are set 'in imaginary gardens done in the ruralist mode' (Simmons, 1990: 160). The result is typified by a representation of Wilfred Rhodes, a northerner who played in industrial Sheffield, Bradford and Huddersfield, but shown 'awkwardly in a garden of unusual floridity' (Simmons, 1990: 160). Today, in many representations which range from the modern greetings card (Figure 7.1) and the illustrated covers of virtually all cricket books (for example, Figure 7.2) to media which advertise the advantages of certain motor cars, bottles of English sherry (Figure 7.3), and real estate in the English village, the same cultural image of the landscape elements is constructed in convenient and accessible form.

Figure 7.1 *Watching Cricket* by Larry Smart, featured on a 1990s greeting card (Courtesy of Ling's Cards)

A model landscape

The landscape of cricket, elicited from writers, painters and others who have communicated remarkably consistent images of the game, permit the construction of a simple model of the English cricket landscape ensemble. Such an idealised representation (Figure 7.4) contains a number of distinct elements. Trees, shrubs, church, barn, marquee, woodland, chalk downland, spectators and players themselves far from exhaust the total. Added to these will be the field itself, the immaculately maintained 22 yard wicket contrasting with the greener outfield. Sight screens, scoreboards, parked cars, spectators' deck chairs and children playing beyond the boundary all add to the overall picture. To a degree, the image so projected is confirmed by a casual glance at many English village

Figure 7.2 Cover illustration of the *Penguin Cricketer's Companion* (Penguin edition, 1981)

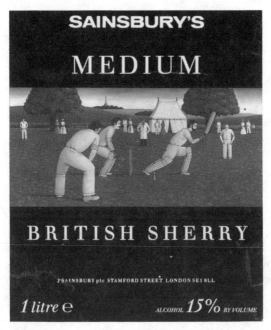

Figure 7.3 Merrie England, cricket and Medium British Sherry (Source: J. Sainsbury plc)

cricket grounds but this is not to deny the mythical nature of such landscapes, a subject I will return to later.

So far I have concentrated on village cricket; after all, this is part of the myth of Merrie England. Although the German observer of English sport, Rudolf Kircher (1928), believed that in top-class cricket 'the atmosphere of the village green is replaced by an audience of technical experts' and at that level the game was 'expert and artificial' (Kircher, 1928: 99), many of the major grounds (never called cricket 'stadiums' in England) at which county or professional cricket is played are projected as highly scenic locales. Worcester, arguably the most beautiful ground in the world, is also one of the most photographed, appearing in many books and calendars extolling the beauty of the 'eternal' English landscape. The backdrop is not the village church but the majestic gothic architecture of the cathedral but it is claimed that Worcester has developed facilities for top-level sport while continuing to give the impression of cricket as a meadow game (Kilburn, 1966). At a professional level, many English cricket grounds retain, in magnified form, the landscape elements of village grounds. Consider, for example, this cosy description of the Kent ground at Tunbridge Wells which has:

> ... a feeling of security and contentment. Much of this derives from the surroundings, for the ground is in a slight natural hollow and tightly enclosed all round by trees, through whose branches hardly a brick or chimney protrudes to spoil the view. And it is for one aspect of these surroundings that Tunbridge Wells is best known – the rhododendrums.

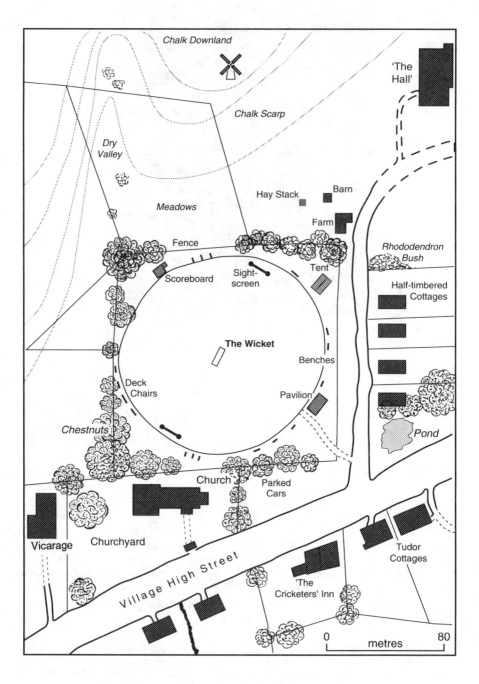

Figure 7.4 A model of the mythical English cricket landscape

Every year Kent play at Tunbridge Wells in early June, to coincide with the banks of mauve rhododendrums in flower. (Plumptre, 1988: 52)

In the case of many first class grounds the parish church is replaced by the cathedral, the village by the city, the farm by the factory. Each ground continues to be different, even if sometimes communicated in rather environmentally deterministic terms:

...does not the play of the side assume tone and colour from the scene? Yorkshire cricket has the aspect of Bramhall Lane and Leeds – dour, and telling of stern competitive life with smoke and real industry about ... Does not there come through the cricket at Sussex the brown and sunny flavour of Eastbourne and Hove when the time of day is noon and the earth seems humming with heat? The plain homeliness of the Midlands is expressed by Leicestershire cricket; it has no airs and graces, no excessive refinements. (Cardus, 1929: 55)

But even the many major grounds are projected as much-loved places, redolent of an unchanging England. They possess landscape elements which will 'not be easily destroyed. There will still be that sparkle of white wood, that sudden hush as the bowler delivers, the immemorial trees, the tents and flags, the smell of the grass, the measured pace of the match' (Sampson, 1981: 9-10).

Englishness and Southernness

The landscapes of cricket are projected as not only being bucolic and rural but as being overwhelmingly English and southern in location. The identification of cricket with the 'English way of life' was projected on film in Alfred Hitchcock's adventure, *The Lady Vanishes*, in which the archetypal Englishmen abroad, Caldicott and Charters, are much more concerned with the result of an England-Australia Test Match than with the intrigue and espionage surrounding them in late 'thirties Europe (Bergen, 1982: 126). More recently, in 1980s British cinema when national images have been for sale in the global movie market, cricket has been one such image used to bolster 'the iconography of heritage Englishness' (Higson, 1993: 116), so crucial in an 'image culture' (Elsaesser, 1993: 59). Among a list of 1980s British cinematic 'mythemes' are 'country house, ... white flannel, rules, and games' (Elsaesser, 1993: 65-6) while cricketing images aided the re-construction of 'Englishness' in the late 1980s films *Maurice* and *Another Country*, both typical reproductions of Englishness made during the Thatcher years. In the latter film, cricket practice at a 1930s private school is set among ivy-clad walls and mature yews (Higson, 1993: 111) and ends with the Moscow-domiciled English spy ('Guy Bennett'), surrounded in his drab flat with memories of England – including a cricket ball – being interviewed by a journalist who asks him what he misses of England. 'Bennett hesitates; choral music fades in, and he replies, "I miss cricket!" End of film' (Higson, 1993: 124).[1]

The cricket landscape could not be duplicated in countries to which the game was exported. Australia and other parts of the Empire could not adopt cricket precisely in the English form because 'their meadows are not precisely as English meadows, they have no long summer evenings, their society has never known the agricultural background based on a village community' (Milburn, 1966: 38). Instead of growing out of a landscape, facilities for cricket had to be created and the fact that cricket *had* been played at Moose Jaw, Saskatchewan, was seen by one observer as quite incongruous. At such a place:

> ...could there have been a pavilion and flags and a wrought iron weathervane incorporating stumps and a figure of Father Time ... umpires in long coats ... a pub ... a church with a tower and clock stuck not at ten to three but nearer four ... and not Rupert Brooke's epideictic honey but cucumber or sandwich spread for tea ... and a tree, spreading or weeping about the long-on boundary ... and the deck chairs ... and old vicars sleeping therein? Surely not in Moose Jaw. (Heald, 1986: 7)

In such writing we are urged to relate landscape to location and to believe that particular ensembles in particular locations could not conceivably be authentic but would, if so located, be simulacra – even kitsch or ersatz versions, like the English pub at Disneyworld. Taken further, cricket played in 'non-cricketing' countries or locations is frequently viewed in English cricket writing as a joke, reflecting a form of rabid Anglocentricism.

In England, cricket landscapes are projected as being dominantly southern in location. Cardus (1929: 27) 'heard folk from the south say of cricket at Sheffield that it is simply not cricket. Their preference has been for the game played with trees and country graciousness around'. This is a recurring theme in Cardus's writing and elsewhere he notes that 'a Lancashire and Yorkshire match is inconceivable at Tonbridge ... there is no nonsense about 'art for art's sake' in the Saturday afternoon matches in the hinterland of the northern counties' (Cardus, 1930: 173). Most cricket literature is set in the south-east. De Selincourt's *The Cricket Match* and R. C. Sherriff's *Badger's Green* both have downland locales. The former is set in Sussex and the latter in Hampshire. Much other cricket writing is set south of the Trent, most south of the Thames (Figure 7.5). Cricket (like 'Constable country'), projected as being located in and having the characteristics of 'the South Country', can be interpreted as a construction of the 'essential England, a metaphor which became compelling across the whole political spectrum from the later nineteenth century' (Daniels, 1993: 214).

The cultural image of English cricket, be it at the modest level of the village game or at the sophistication of élite sport, is one of quaintness, southernness, rusticity, heritage and nature. The cricket landscape as reflected in various media can be interpreted, like the English landscape itself, as an expression of English tastes and values (Lowenthal and Prince, 1965).

The making of the myth

From the kinds of representations of English cricket noted above, it is possible to interpret the cricket landscape, as projected by so many media, as a myth. I shall attempt to do this according to the ideas of the semiologist,[2] Roland

Figure 7.5 The distribution of places where cricket matches are mentioned in Alan Ross, *The Penguin Cricketers' Companion,* Penguin, London, 1981 (Source: Bale, 1986: 23)

Barthes (1973) and shall base my approach on that used in the analysis of another 'sporting' image, that of Landseer's nineteenth century painting, *Royal Sports on Hill and Loch* (Pringle, 1988; for another 'geographical' introduction, see Duncan and Duncan, 1992). Barthes argues for a relationship between two terms: a 'signifier' and a 'signified'. A third term, the 'sign' is the 'associative total of the first two terms' (Pringle, 1988: 143). The sequence of signifier, signified and sign appears again in myth (Figure 7.6). What is found here is a dialectic, or game of hide and seek, between meaning and form – which defines myth. The function of myth is therefore to make things look simple and uncomplicated or to mean something by themselves, hence establishing 'blissful clarity' (Barthes, 1973: 156).

Previous chapters showed cricket, like other sports, to be a cultural form, basically anti-nature and highly quantitative. The artificial character of the game is matched by the equally artificial and ordered nature of the 'typical' English landscape within which it is found – invariably the result of enclosure with land being 'transformed into a commercial space of regular, hedgerowed fields' (Short, 1991: 67). The cricket grounds and pitches, like the hedgerows, are carefully tended and, like the fields of pasture and arable, scientifically prepared; they are geometrically arranged with precisely measured wickets, creases and stumps. Data, statistics and records litter the pages of the annual copies of *Wisden.* What is more, and despite its southern origins, most cricket, per head of the population, is played in the industrial regions of northern

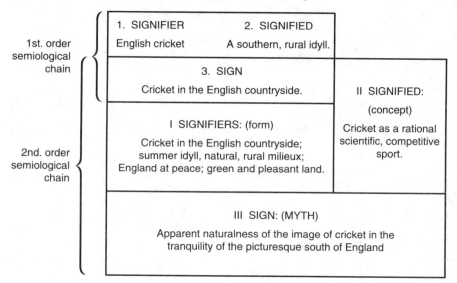

Figure 7.6 The cricket landscape myth

England, notably Yorkshire, where there are more than four times the national average per capita number of cricket clubs (Bale, 1982: 75). When projected in this way, these landscapes – manicured, synthetic and straight-lined – where considerable industry is expended and where considerable money is made, are very different from those which are principally communicated. Clearly, the second order sign (cricket's apparent naturalness) is a myth. But why should this 'mode of signification' have been communicated in view of the conflicting evidence?

It can be argued that the tastes which are reflected in the iconography of cricket landscapes are not necessarily those of the mass of the population but, as with many other landscape predilictions, 'of that minority who have been most active in creating English landscape taste and in moulding the landscape itself' (Lowenthal and Prince, 1965: 186). What is projected by the images of cricket is a landscape which is buccolic, picturesque, tidy and deciduous. Cricket is a northern as much as (arguably more than) a southern game but it is rare for industrial landscapes to form its backdrops. Soft, light, downland settings but no hard, dark mountainous or moorland backgrounds are projected. The southern bias in the coverage of cricket had not gone un-noticed by perhaps the greatest cricket writer of them all, the marxist historian C. L. R. James, who observed that the neglect of northern cricket in the sport's iconography 'passes comprehension. The only reason that makes sense to me is that it is wilful – the South does not want to know' (James, 1963: 130).

Many of the observations made about the image of baseball, noted earlier in this chapter, could be made about that of cricket. The propagation of a rural idyll surrounding a highly quantified and geometric game is arguably an example of 'the official imaginative life' (Inglis, 1977b: 503) offered to the British public by those forming 'the version of the English landscape which is so pow-

erful a component of ruling class culture' (Inglis, 1977b: 494-5). The iconography of cricket's landscape is a kind of post-nineteenth century dream – a
'dream of the post-industrial Garden of Eden' in which work is turned into cre-
ativity, regulation becomes sponteneity, resentment changes into delight. 'In
such unfettered providence, men and women dissolve the divisions of labour
and hateful class divisions which follow them, and live lives of joyful, cooperative praxis and poesis' (Inglis, 1992: 15). The English rural landscape
illustrates the English love of order and the orderliness of cricket therefore
harks back to times when physical and social boundaries were firmly marked
with everything in its place. The place of physical and moral order in cricket
provides something which is viewed as lacking in today's world (Lowenthal,
1991: 221; see also Daniels, 1993: 214-5).

If the milieux of the children's television puppet programmes such as
Camberwick Green and *Trumpton* were the official imaginative lives offered to
five-year olds (Inglis, 1977b: 503), then perhaps the cricket scene on the greetings card, or in the coffee table book of English country life, or on the bottle of
Sainsbury's sherry is that offered to 25 to 75 year olds. However, in order to
understand such a myth more fully it is necessary to relate it, not only to the
actual nature of cricket (the signified in the second order chain in Figure 7.6),
but also to the social, political, economic and cultural milieux within which it
flourishes (Pringle, 1988: 156). The imagery of cricket, I would argue, is in fact
part of what could be called the 'nostalgia industry' and contributes to a collage
of images contributing to 'national identity'. It was the cricket team which a
person supported that made up Norman Tebbit's notorious test of nationality,
and cricket is what Britain will always be, even if its future lies in Europe.
According to John Major a Britain dominated by Brussels in the mid-twenty-
first century would 'still be the country of long shadows on county (cricket)
grounds, warm beer, invincible green suburbs ... .'(*Independent on Sunday*, 25
April 1993: 24). Landscape, national identity and a particular kind of cricket
landscape are again intextricably mixed in the cartoonist's image of Major's
view of the eternal England (Figure 7.7).

Nostalgia is a potent force in popular culture, not only in recreating some
mythical 'golden age' but also in erasing history and stylising the present
(Cook et al., 1992: 71). It is not only for an age of subtopia, muggings, the
urban underclass, shopping malls and high rise blocks, that the English cricket
field (as projected) provides a reassuring image. The changing English 'countryside' itself, with its increasingly mechanised farming practices, prairie-style
fields and the associated removal of hedgerows, its encroaching golf courses,
and its lager louts, also requires a timeless 'antidote to the dreadful present'
(Lowenthal, 1985: 97). In the iconography of English cricket there is no sense
of class or racial tension, most obviously manifested in the English inner cities
in the long, hot summers in which the very cricketing scenes of a bygone
(mythical) ruralia are inevitably set. In the South Downs of de Selincourt's
Tillingfold the 'sweet air put gossip to shame and whose friendly peacefulness
made discontent remote'; in *England their England* Fordenden was 'unspoiled
by factories and financiers'; there 'the world stood still'; purged of the night-
mare of war, Badger's Green could return the public 'to normalcy and take
delight in the pleasure of simple things' (Howat, 1991: 9). These cricket

Figure 7.7 The rural cricket myth as a Major image of English eternalism (Source: *The Independent on Sunday*, 25 April 1993: 24)

images seek to reconstruct a land of the pastoral, 'freedom from necessity, the illusion that life can be a fairyland, but [appropriately in sports landscape images, in view of sport's temporal finitude] only for delimited periods' (Pugh, 1990b: 147, brackets added). As Roberts (1990: 239) notes, 'it is one of the basic ideological functions of all pastoral traditions to deflect or cover opposed class interests through the collective experience or memory of nature and the landscape'. Only on very rare occasions, as in Jerzy Skolimowski's film adaptation of the Robert Graves short story, *The Shout*, is the idyllic innocence of English cricket used as a source of deception for underlying menace (Bergen, 1982: 126). Generally, however, the view that most English landscape painting displays is 'unchanging rural bliss, an arcadia set in some past time when humans lived an easy and somehow "natural life" in a village community unscathed by technology' (Cosgrove, 1984: 264) neatly summarises the projected landscapes of cricket. This particular observation is all the more apt in view of the sport's quantitative, scientific and technologised character.

CONCLUSION

The sports landscape is represented in a wide variety of media. In many ways the landscape of cricket as communicated in print, poetry, novels, painting and film can be interpreted as both a mystification and a mythification of the 'reality' of modern British cricket. Cricket and baseball are attributed particular kinds of mythic landscapes in much the same way as the French *Guide Bleu* or the Hachette World Travel Guides 'hardly knows the existence of scenery except under the guise of the picturesque' (Barthes, 1973: 81; see also, Duncan and Duncan, 1992). In English cricket the industrial is made to look rural and the rational to look rustic, though I do not intend to suggest that such images have ever resulted from any conscious exercise to create such a myth. As has been noted in another context, 'there was no need for such measures given the apparent naturalness of the image' (Pringle, 1988: 157) – of cricket in Merrie England.

The sport-landscape representations which I have been discussing in this chapter are strong and pervasive and for many people these kinds of images are the only connection they ever have with sport. Today we can exist with minimal direct experience of our surroundings, relying on second-hand and packaged information, ideologically mediated, which create distorted cognitive maps and mental landscapes, hence opening the way for commercial (and political) manipulation of attitudes (Relph, 1989: 151). In their own small ways, the landscapes of sport illustrated in this chapter exemplify this point.

NOTES

1. Tennis on the lawn of the country house 'Windy Corner', is used in a similar way in that classic of British heritage cinema, *Room with a view*.
2. Barthes (1973: 120), describes semiology as 'a science of forms, since it   studies significations apart from their content'.

8

FUTURESCAPES OF SPORT: A WORLD OF SIMULATIONS?

Despite its myths, sportscape is a segmented, synthetic, specialised and spatialised landscape; it is also panopticised and mediatised. In its purest form it is a rational landscape writ large. Yet it has not reached an unambiguous state of modernity and people continue to resist some of the worst excesses of modernisation. The ambivalent character of the sports landscape can be summarised by returning to one of the subjects of Chapter 3, that is sport and nature, and to one of the themes of much of the rest of this book, sport and culture. Although sport is unquestionably a cultural phenomenon it remains a simulation of nature; it pushes nature as close as it can to culture and, in some sports, vice versa. This ambivalent character of sports landscapes is illustrated in Table 8.1. Like other ambivalent phenomena, being not quite what they seem, sports landscapes (and sport itself) are 'overflowing with meaning' (Fiske, 1989: 56). Some such 'meanings' have been explored in the previous pages of this book and will be explored further in this final chapter.

Towards post-modern sport?

Despite the many modernising tendencies in sports, people continue to obtain a positive sense of place from many sporting milieux. Space has not yet totally triumphed over place; nor are performers and audience totally exclusive of each other as the existence of numerous liminal zones in sports evidently testifies. It can even be argued that there are currents running through sports which oppose the tide of modernity and those who feel that the western world has entered a post-modern phase would argue that the tendency towards sameness and homotopia is being succeeded by heterotopia – where placelessness is being (re)placed. So what does the future hold for modern sports? What would the sports landscape be like in the Los Angeles of Ridley Scott's film *Blade Runner* or the London of Alan Ayckbourn's play *Henceforward*? What kind of sportscape is heralded by Disneyworld or EPCOT ('Experimental Prototype Community of Tomorrow')? And what sporting landscapes will be found in

Table 8.1 Examples of sports and sports landscapes as ambivalent categories (After Fiske, 1989: 57)

A	Ambivalent Category	Not A
NATURE	Cricket field	CULTURE
OUTDOOR	Stadium	INDOOR
ANIMALS	Horse racing	HUMANS
SWIMMING	Surfing	BOATING
NAKED	Athletic body	CLOTHED

cyberspace? In this final chapter I will hazard answers to these kinds of questions and seek to explore some possible alternative scenarios.

Such scenarios span a vast spectrum, from continued artifice and immurement to the sports landscape riding off on (another?) green wave and even embracing the *friluftsliv* philosophy of eco-activists. A worst case scenario might be that of 'nature's revenge' and the beginning of the end of certain sportscapes as a result of the very pollution of the human body and of the atmosphere (that is, inner nature [the body] and outer nature [the environment]) which the centimetre-gram-second-point philosophy of achievement sport has, in its own small way, helped to create and encourage (or, at least, not discourage). These are some broad possible futures. I will organise the rest of this chapter around a number of more detailed scenarios, illustrated by particular case studies. These are not meant to be mutually exclusive and are presented in the form which follows merely for convenience.

When talking about current and future trends I have found it difficult to avoid alluding to the 'post-modern', a term which is probably the most slippery of those used in this book and almost defies definition. In this chapter I am basically considering postmodernism as 'object' (that is, post-modern sports *landscapes*) rather than as 'attitude', though it is difficult to separate each of these 'manoeuvres' from each other (Cloke et al., 1991: 171). I can only really begin to talk about post-modern landscapes, however, when I have summarised the character of the modern sportscapes which post-modernity is reacting against. A well-cited schematic 'series of stylistic oppositions [may be used] in order to capture the ways in which postmodernism [in sports] might be portrayed in reaction to the modern' (Harvey, 1989: 42). Although applied initially to literature, Hassan's (1985: 123-4) scheme can be modified in order to commence a consideration of postmodernism and sports landscapes (Table 8.2). Many of the (simple) polarisations (which postmodernism actually seeks to break down) are caricatures to be sure, but some of them should by now be recognisable from allusions in previous chapters. For example, the purposefulness of modern sports and the functionalism of its landscapes contrast with the playfulness of the the postmodern and the multifunctional spaces which it occupies. In Chapter 4 I contrasted the 'distance' between the spaces in the modern sportscape with the participation and the breakdown of 'position' in the landscapes of postmodernism(s) while in Chapter 6 I contrasted Fordist track competitions with 'flexible' road racing.

Table 8.2 Some schematic differences between modernism and postmodernism in sports
(after Hassan, 1985: 123-4)

Modernism	Postmodernism
form	antiform
purpose	play
design	chance
hierarchy	anarchy
achievement	happening
distance	participation
totalisation	deconstruction
phallic	androgynous
Fordist	flexible
homotopia	heterotopia
race	run
nurture	nature

Several of the above oppositions have already been discussed. I touch on others in the remainder of this chapter. Sports landscapes of modernity are characterised by four basic characteristics; first, a tendency to colonise previous landscapes; secondly to become increasingly territorialised and segmented; thirdly to become more placeless, and fourthly to become increasingly technologised (Eichberg, 1988). The sports landscape has typically been a monocultural form of land use which I have called sportscape (Chapter 3). It is as specialised a use of land as motorways, retailing or factory farming. In its purest form, sportscape can be used for nothing but sport. Football stadiums, because of their sacred turf, can be used for little but football; rectangular swimming pools encourage serious swimming in straight lines, not frolicsome splashing and jumping, sliding and playing; it is difficult to use golf courses for running. These developments may be associated with what is broadly called modernisation – including the rationalisation of land use and its increasing specialisation. It is also associated with the spatial separation of players from spectators and the separation of one kind of spectator from another (see Chapter 4). Simple polarities are found in modern sports landscapes; these include indoor-outdoor; nature-artifice; work-leisure; public-private; monofuntional-multifunctional, old-new, and female-male. Many lack the ambivalence of the examples shown in Table 8.1. Post-modern landscapes of sports reject these polarities and place emphasis instead on ambiguity, ambivalence and contradiction, and a rejection of the neat and tidy world which modernist sport seeks to attain.

At the danger of oversimplifying, I will note that post-modern sports landscapes may elicit two possible reactions, namely (a) scepticism or (b) affirmation (Rosenau, 1992: 14-17). The former is essentially a pessimistic perspective, seeing the future in terms of meaninglessness and chaos, a post-modernism of reaction; the latter is more optimistic, seeing resistance and struggle as possibilities of a post-modern age. Another possible distinction is that between dystopian sports landscapes which would signal caution and those of a utopian character which would give cause for celebration (Wakefield, 1990: 98-

131). There are dangers here, however, of falling into the trap of dualistic thinking since such a wide ranging phenomenon as sport has the potential to generate both sceptical and affirmative reactions and is likely also to exhibit utopian and dystopian examples. And such a discussion assumes, of course, an absence of ambiguity about interpretations of dystopia/utopia.

I will start this final exploration by stressing the simularity of many land-scape tendencies in sports, and conclude with some counter-cultural and eco-logical perspectives.

A WORLD OF SIMULATIONS

In a sense all sportscapes are simulations of nature and the pre-modern land-scapes on which the antecedents of sports were played. We are reminded of the simularity of modern sports environments through the continued use of words like 'field', 'garden' and 'park' in the naming of sports places which may be made entirely of plastic, concrete, and steel. We are also reminded that the modern athlete is a simulation of the *amateur* by the continued use of the word 'player' in professional sports. But it can also be argued that the sportscapes of modernity promise to be replaced by sports landscapes of post-modernity, dis-solving many of the polarities noted earlier. Instead of being devoted *solely* to the achievement of better and better performances (though they will not neces-sarily retard them) these post-modern landscapes will accommodate sporting diversity; they will be various kinds of simulations of modern sports environ-ments but also ambiguous and contradictory in character. In some cases they will occupy the electronic world of hyper-space. At the same time it is possible that pre-modern forms, currently lying rather dormant or marginal to achieve-ment sport, may reassert themselves, producing a sporting world, not of post-modernity but of trans-modernity (Eichberg, 1991). There may also be various applications of technology which threaten/promise to bring about the end of sports landscapes as we know them.

North America has been called a land of artificial paradises (Baudrillard, 1988: 8) and what north America has today the rest of the western world fre-quently has (or craves for) tomorrow. North America is the engine which drives most parts of the machine of global popular culture and it is arguably in the US and Canada that the clearest hints and suggestions about some of the futurescapes of sport can be found. It should not be surprising, therefore, that several of the examples which follow come from north America.

'New old-fashioned'; a return to the vernacular

One group of landscapes seeks to retain their modern characteristic of mono-cultural land use but, at a superficial level, return to more traditional designs, attempting to draw on local custom, nostalgia and memories of yesteryear. In southern England in the county of Dorset (part of Thomas Hardy's Wessex) the delightful old town of Dorchester recently acquired a new football stadium for the town's non-league club. It is sited on the edge of the town, next to a supermarket and a large car park. In its suburban location and as part of a 'retail complex' (which encourages, in some cases, the use of the word 'tradium' rather than 'stadium') it reflects the modern tendency to segment urban space. In its design characteristics, however, it is more reminiscent of the pre/post-modern, with trees planted around it and a vaguely vernacular style characterising the buildings. Such buildings reject the functionalism of the 'concrete bowl' and return to ornament, colour and tradition – and in a not uninventive way. It is possible to 'reinterpret the syntax of the traditional temple form and use it on a boathouse in Henley. The festive polychrony of the Henley Regatta obviously forms the pretext for strong blues and reds which also relate to the colours of the site' (Jencks, 1987: 347). Quaintly reminiscent of a bygone age, such sports places are also examples of aesthetic populism – sports environments for Prince Charles.

Facilities which might be termed 'repositories of history' in the sense that they obviously mimic the past, are also exemplified by the 'new-old' development of Oriole Park baseball stadium at Camden Yards in Baltimore (Figure 8.1), opened in the Spring of 1992 to replace the city's old Memorial Stadium. Baseball writer George F. Will noted that 'every fan has a kind of memory of how a ballpark is supposed to look' (quoted in P. Brown, 1992: C6); and they know what a baseball place should be called – a 'field' or a 'park' – but not a 'stadium'. Oriole Park builds on these memories with history imploding back on itself. It is an attempt to return to a human scale of ballparks reminiscent of America's favourite baseball fields, Fenway Park and Wrigley Field (see page 80). It has an old fashioned bleacher section, brick arches and iron gates. Fans are close to the game, the grass field is not symmetrical and the resulting geometry makes it impossible to predict how the ball will play. The city is not shut out and 'from the ramps, there are vistas of Baltimore: the smokestacks, church domes and chimneys that give this gritty city its salt' (George F. Will quoted in P. Brown, 1992). The park is said to reflect traditional baseball values (see Chapter 7). It is located in the downtown, not in the suburbs. Fans were involved in the planning. It is built of steel rather than concrete and care has been taken over the detail of the building. Advertisements for Budweiser and Coca Cola are rendered in nostalgic style to fit the mood of the park. This is Disneyfied sportscape *par excellence* – a perfect model of simulation (Baudrillard, 1983: 23). In this new baseball park fans go back to the future. But although 'the contrast of this new ballpark with the Skydome in Toronto and other newly built antiseptic stadia could not be greater' (Lowry, 1992: 104), it does retain the characteristic of modernity by being used only for baseball.

These examples, Dorchester and Baltimore (another American example is Pilot Field, a baseball stadium in Buffalo, New York), involving as they do a return to vernacular styles of design, build on nostalgia as an antidote to modernity. They replace the anonymous concrete bowls or containerised stadium boxes, which may or may not be multifunctional, with 'modern-old fashioned' structures. They may also reflect the ways in which places seek to promote a distinctive image in order to create a sense of place in an increasingly placeless environment (Lash and Urry, 1994: 303). Although quaintly reminiscent of a bygone age and blurring the distinction between old and new,

Figure 8.1 Oriole Park, Baltimore, Maryland. Ornament is not a crime in such buildings (Photograph by Esto Photographs and Hellmuth, Obata and Kassabaum, Inc., Sports Facilities Group)

such developments are, nevertheless, a football ground and a baseball park respectively, not places for undefined, spontaneous play. They exemplify the ambiguity of the post-modern, typifying post-modernism as cosmetic and pastiche – simply a shift in surface appearance (Harvey, 1989). Paraphrasing Davis (1985:108-9), the concrete bowl romanticises the hegemony of corporate bureaucracy and mass production whereas Oriole Park is merely an almost standardised baseball stadium which has been gift-wrapped to the client's taste.

Golf and the great indoors

Reported as 'the ultimate golf course' (*The Guardian*, 7 November 1992: 19) and recently opened near Houston, Texas, 'Tour 18' consists of facsimile constructions of 18 of the best golf holes in the United States, sculptured as a 'real' cultural landscape. Such simulations include one hole at Pebble Beach, and others at Augusta and Oakmont. This is far from being the ultimate in golf landscape simulations, however. It may sound bizarre to suggest that golf (of all sports) totally overcomes nature when the natural environment in which it is played is neutralised and the sport – like so many others have done – moves indoors. In fact, it is now possible to play golf, using your own clubs, in a simulated indoor landscape, insulated from the natural elements in air conditioned 'comfort'. I am not talking here about a driving range which is essentially a facility for practicing golf but a form of golf where leagues and competitions of various kinds can take place.

If you drive along Highway 4 near London, Ontario, for example, you will discover, among factories and warehouses by the side the highway, an unimpressive containerised structure, typical of such facilities in north America and western Europe. It is called 'CaddyShacks' and, as the promotional leaflet states, once inside you can play 'real' golf (Figure 8.2). Golfers getting out of their parked cars are carrying their golf bags containing a wide variety of clubs. The outdoor temperature is about -7°C and a biting wind is sweeping across the Ontario lowlands. Entering the warmth of 'CaddyShacks' you encounter a cash desk and on one side of the building, a pool table and a row of seats and tables where people are enjoying a drink or snack under sunshades and umbrellas which keep off the simulated sunlight. Facing them are six booths about 10 metres long, each with an area for teeing off at one end and, at the other, a large, wall-sized television screen above a synthetic 'putting green' with one hole. It is within this area – about 10 metres by 5 metres – that an 18 hole game of competitive golf can be played. This is done by players selecting which of a number of famous golf courses they want to 'play on' and having paid the fee a picture appears on the screen showing the view from the first tee on the course of their choice. In turn they place their golf balls on a tee and drive them towards the view on the screen. On hitting the screen, built-in sensors calculate the velocity and trajectory of each ball and its flight continues, shown in simulated form as a white line on the screen. The distance covered and the deviation of the ball from the optimal direction is calculated and shown on a small screen. The second shot is then taken, with the appropriate club, from the point where the ball (would have) landed and the new scene on the screen shows the view from the second shot. The game proceeds in this way until the first hole is reached. When it is time to putt the ball into the hole a message on the screen informs the player where to place the ball near an actual hole in front of the screen. This is done by being told to select one of a series of numbers painted around the hole on the 'green'. The view from the second tee then appears and the game continues like this for eighteen holes, if required.

Outwardly, the place could be a tacky striptease joint; inside, the kitsch decor and individualised booths do nothing to reduce the impression that such a 'golf experience' is analogous in some ways to the world of pornography. Just as porn offers 'the simulacrum of a pan-erotic world where sex is always available' (Stam, 1988: 137), so CaddyShacks provides a simulacrum of the world of sport where you can always play golf. This example moves us closer still to a futurescape of simulation.

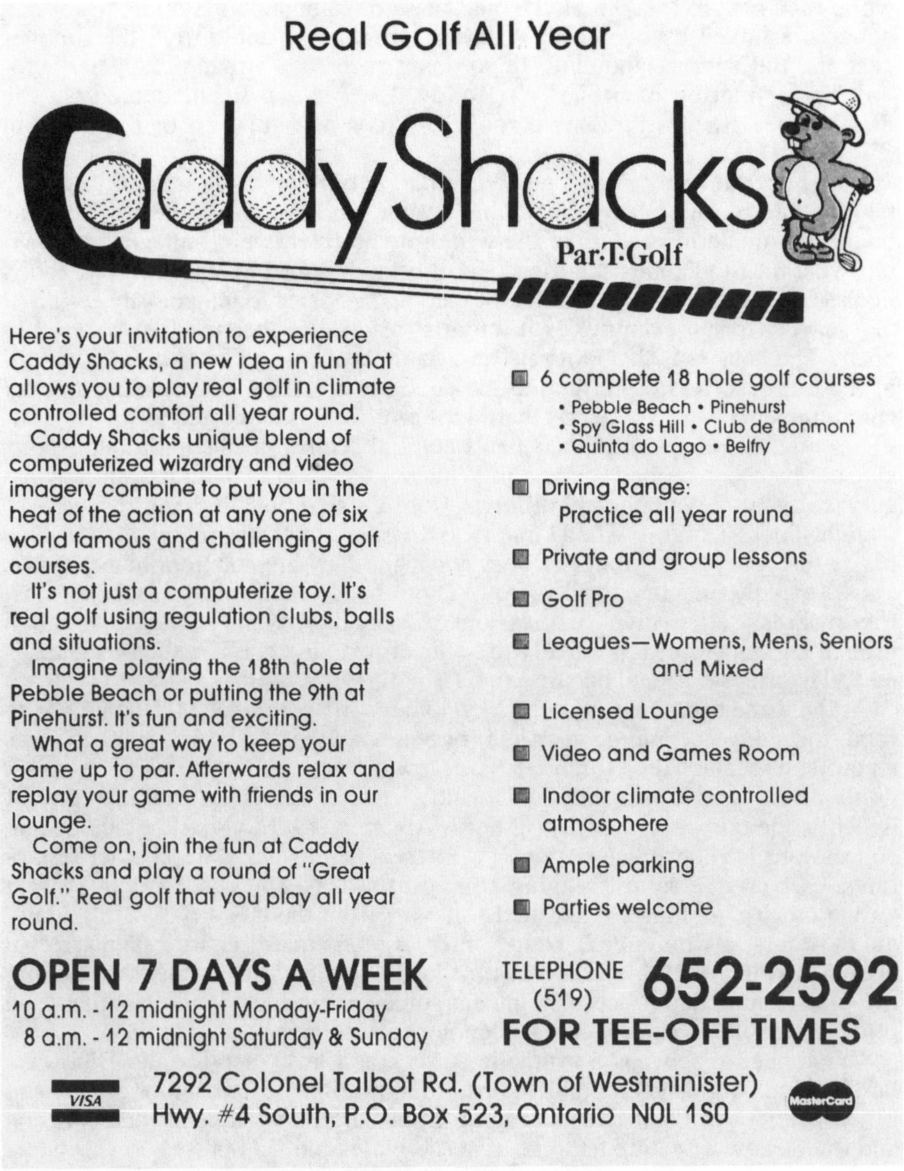

Figure 8.2 CaddyShacks, near London, Ontario

McDonald's World of Sports?

Near Union Station, just south of downtown Toronto, are two of the wonders of modern times. There is the CN Tower, the tallest free-standing structure in the world, and next to it is the SkyDome. These three buildings, station, tower and dome, are linked by overhead walkways, insulating people from the summer heat and the winter wind chill. In so doing such 'new urban prosthetics' provide 'a simulation of urbanity' (Boddy, 1992: 124). In the same way the SkyDome, with its retractable roof, provides a simulation of the stadium (Figure 8.3).

Built, on the one hand to replace urban dereliction with a sparkling new facility, and on the other to make money for the developers, the SkyDome is one of the modern wonders of the world of sports. It is not immediately obvious what the SkyDome actually is. Has it been designed for sport or for expositions? Is it an hotel or a collection of eateries? A place to temporarily reside or one to visit for an evening? Is it a tourist resort or a theatre? Is it covered or open? The answer is that, with its retractable roof (nature or artifice?), it is all of these things. It is, according to the publicity brochure, 'the world's greatest entertainment centre – like no other in the world'. It is dedicated to 'family fun' – different, therefore, from the 'men's cultural centres' as the traditional sports stadium has been termed (quoted in Whitsun: 1987, 243). With its gentle white curves it is also symbolically different from the traditionally hard, rectangular, straight-lined stadiums. The Dome is to a British football ground what a wine bar is to a pub. The former (Dome and wine bar) are 'metropolitan, middle class, sexually integrated and more likely to be tolerant of, or at least not hostile towards, "alternative" expressions of sexuality' while the latter (football ground and pub) are 'more likely to be local, working class, sexually segregated and overtly sexist and heterosexist' (Bondi, 1992: 164-5).

At the same time, however, the SkyDome is to sport what McDonald's is to food. Indeed, you could be mistaken for believing that the entire landscape was an outlet of McDonald's (Figure 8.3). A few extracts from the SkyDome media guide reveal that it has: four McDonald's counter service restaurants, one of which is the company's largest in north America; 19 'SkySnack' stadium-fare concessions; 48 'beverage stations'; a 350 seat Hard Rock Café; 3 other restaurants; 161 private suites, ranging from 10 to 40 person capacity; a 118 seat movie theatre; a climate controlled walkway from the city's rail station; daily guided tours; a fitness club with 5 international squash courts, sauna, recreational whirlpool, etc.; the 348 room SkyDome Hotel, 70 rooms overlooking the 'field'; and 1280 toilets. The media guide fails to include the fact that food prices inside the Dome are at least double those outside.

The stadium itself has a synthetic surface and hosts the Toronto Blue Jays baseball and Argonauts football teams. It has accommodated indoor cricket and a wide variety of other events ranging from fairgrounds, opera, rock concerts and trade shows. Seating and use of space is flexible, 53,000 seated spectators for football but between 10,000 and 70,000 for concerts and other events. The stadium has 43 pre-wired camera positions and the largest (33.6metres × 10.0 metres) video display board in the world (the 'Jumbotron') acting as a scoreboard and a video-replay screen, necessary in an age where television is the defining reality of sport (Goldlust, 1987). It is a classic example of an ambiguous landscape with the incongruous juxtapositionings of the modern and postmodern; but it is also an environment where sport is reduced to packaged consumption in an antiseptic, safe and totally controlled landscape. In other words,

Figure 8.3 The SkyDome, Toronto. The gentle curve of the 'entertainment complex' (above) or McDonald's world of sports (below)

the SkyDome is akin to a shopping mall, introducing as it does a variety of services, sources of fun, restaurants, hotels, fast-food and retail outlets. Like the mall it is safe and a place for the family, hence avoiding the need for heavy policing (it is self-policing). It is only superficially a sports stadium and like theme parks it operates as a disguised marketplace (Crawford, 1992: 16). The Dome, like many other elements of popular culture, blurs the distinction between leisure and commodification (Warren, 1993: 174). At one level it is a place to play and watch sport; but the fact that food and non-sport entertainment are at hand almost certainly contributes to its popularity. It could also be argued that the Dome is not really a landscape of sport at all but involves a return to a pre-modern tradition of mixed land uses, flexibility and multifunctionalism. It also blurs a number of polarities and exemplifies a privately owned 'public' cultural space created by modern technology (Crook et al., 1992: 66).

The SkyDome may be a paradigm of the post-modern sport place but the same blurring of land uses is found in many other, more ordinary stadiums. In London, for example, the new stadium for Millwall FC, completed in 1993, has been designed with flexibility of space use in mind (Darley, 1993: 43). The football stadium is no longer just a football ground. But the Dome, and other all-seat stadiums, changes the dialogical and tactile crowd into seated individuals. The scope for aimless strolling around the ground is virtually eliminated and in this respect the parallel with the shopping mall or the theme park (where *flânerie* is common) is not so applicable. This is not to say, however, that the 'individualised crowd' cannot display both euphoria and subtle forms of resistance through various carnivalistic antics.

The examples of CaddyShacks and the SkyDome illustrate aspects of the sports landscape which may be of considerable relevance in the future. Each typifies the continued immurement of sports – part of the interiorisation of much day to day life. It is argued by some that showsports such as track and field and even the various forms of élite level football will all be indoors in the next century. They will be additions to the rapidly growing number of dominantly indoor sports such as squash and badminton, ice hockey, the aerobics revolution and the body building phenomenon. Sports such as climbing, skiing, wind-surfing and moto-cross can today also take place indoors. In addition, these landscapes continue the well-developed trend towards the segmentation of sport space and the individualisation of people, treating them like things rather than human beings, placing them in small booths for squash or indoor golf, in 'fitness machines' (Borgers, 1988; Willis, 1990), or in numbered seats in stadiums rather than standing, socialising and inter-mingling on terraces. All this is invariably subject to subtle surveillance. At the same time CaddyShacks and the SkyDome are highly ambiguous structures, blurring the difference between sport, disport, desolation, stimulation, simulation, reality, indoors, outdoors, etc.

Water Worlds; surf in simulation

The desire to cater commercially for body cultural activities which deviate

from the achievement orientation of modern sport has been graphically illustrated by the changing nature of human 'water space'. Consider some changes
which have been happening to the swimming environment. The traditional rectangular pool alluded to in Chapters 2 and 3, the classic shape for sportised
swimming (but, because of the lack of suitable indoor alternatives, having to be
used by those who want to 'play-swim') has, in many cases, been either
changed or integrated into simulations of the pre-modern landscape of swimming – the multi-functional water worlds where sport or physical fitness is
replaced by bodily experiences. The new water worlds, whether those of a
municipal or commercial orientation, possess quite different shapes and functions from the rectangular swimming pool. They contain water slides and
chutes; simulated waterfalls and waves; they are of irregular and tortuous
shapes, unsuited for competitive racing but good for fun. In places like Florida
and Queensland such water worlds have returned to the outdoors. 'Wet 'n
Wild', for example, is set in, and visually dominates, the commercial strip of
International Drive in Orlando, Florida, and possesses huge chutes and slides
which are set among simulated 'beaches'. In Phoenix, Arizona, a simulated
world of future body culture includes an artificial surf beach where 'identical
waves roll in at identical intervals to wash upon imported sand' (Dovey,
1985: 39).

The changing worlds of water are matched by those of ice. The traditional
rectangular rink (see page 61) is being slowly replaced by 'leisure rinks' which
de-emphasise serious skating by incorporating artificial snow (sprayed by overhead nozzles), ice caverns and split levels (Bain and Pearson, 1991).

Virtual sport?

Television and/or computerisation is central to the running and organisation of
the modern sports milieux of not simply CaddyShacks, SkyDome and the programmed waves of the beach in the desert, but to most other modern sports
facilities. Gone are the days when television sport displayed indistinct, grainy
black and white images with clumsy camera control unable to capture crucial
goals in international soccer matches, and an absence of slow motion and
action replays. Indeed, some sports today exist as 'studio sports' with only
token live audiences. Whereas TV sport was traditionally considered second
best, the modern technology of high fidelity television, the split screen, fine
detail, the panoramic views of the field and the play back facilities, makes TV
sport better than the real thing. In fact, for some people 'mediated experiences
of sport on television' are the real thing (Goldlust, 1987: 173). Television has
become the defining reality of sport to the extent that a form of technology
intended originally for sports viewers in the comfort of their own homes is
today installed in the very stadiums where the games are held. Large TV
screens are now virtually obligatory elements of the big stadium landscape.
'The giant video screen is there to attract people to the stadium event and to
ensure that by attending they will not be deprived of the "television experience"' (Goldlust, 1987: 174). Visual access to the video screen becomes prime
seating; spectators used to seeing playbacks on TV find the sporting experience

reduced if such facilities are unavailable. Athletes in track races may also find the sport experience reduced without the large stadium TV screen on which they can observe their own progress *vis-à-vis* that of their opponents without turning round. Television has become the authoritative interpreter of the sporting experience (Goldlust, 1987: 174). So it is not necessarily the case that the more time people spend watching television, the less time they can spend in sports arenas (Adams, 1992: 118). In the fully bourgeoisified stadium, it would be possible for each spectator to possess a personal TV monitor to combine the 'real' stadium experience with the 'real' televison experience at the same time (Figure 8.4).

It has been stated that 'space is no longer in geography – it's in electronics' (Virilio, 1983: 115) and the polarity of the particular and the universal disappears as the particular becomes universal through communications and mass media (Rail, 1991: 747). People now ask 'did you see the game last night?' when they mean 'did you see the telecast of the game last night'. The improved quality of television receivers (the first live coverage in high definition TV was from the Albertville Winter Olympics in 1990) and the flexibility of global time-space relations which permit international sports events to be scheduled with the television viewer (rather than the athletes) in mind, encourage the use of unconventional landscapes for future-sport.

Consider, for example, the case of the final of the 1992 European football championship between Denmark and Germany, played in Gothenburg, Sweden. Although many Danish fans crossed the Sound to Gothenburg to watch the game in the Ullevi Stadium, many more watched the game in Denmark – most at home. But several thousands of Danes also watched the game in the open air, notably on huge TV screens erected in *Fælledparken*, a large area of grassed open space in the northern part of Copenhagen. Masses of people took to the

Figure 8.4 Sport as mediacracy or mediocrity? (Source: *The Guardian*, 15 August 1992: 12)

(Source: *The Guardian*, 15 August 1992: 12)

Fælled to watch the game, standing, shouting, mingling and falling over each other in the exhilaration of the Danish goals and victory. They were not confined in seats in a concrete stadium but were cavorting, carnival-like on the very ground where, ironically, folk football had flourished and early modern football in Denmark began – but they were watching the game on television. The reality in Gothenburg was impoverished by the simulation in Copenhagen. At the *Fælled* television really was a gathering place (Adams, 1992).[1]

The more likely (and certainly the more frequent) use of the home as the sole landscape of future-sport will, of course, be another stage in the progressive containment and segmentation of sport space as discussed in Chapter 4, furthering the trend towards domestication or privatisation of cultural consumption (Crook et al., 1992: 66). Landscapes of televisual sports possess a number of characteristics identified in a stimulating paper by Penz (1993). First, they are occupied by élite performers who provide the fastest, most spectacular and most demanding action. Hence, television sport is defined as élite sport. Slower, less spectacular sports are 'defined out' of the TV sportscape. Secondly, because television coverage concentrates on the sporting action, the peculiar characteristics of different sports places are sacrificed for intense coverage of action in sports spaces, one of which is much the same as any other. The placelessness of sport is therefore emphasised. Where details of place are included as a background to a mega-event, as in the case of the Wimbledon tennis tournament, they are all too often presented in sanitised, stereotypical and nostalgic terms (Blain, et al., 1993: 151). Thirdly, because television provides a global view instantaneously – the ultimate compression of time-space – its effects have been argued to create a shift in perspective. A temporal horizon replaces our spatial horizons; the depth of real time (of the sports telecast) triumphs over and replaces the depth of real space (as experienced in the stadium). Signs and images dominate an unmediated order of reality. The problem of sport broadcasting lies not in finding the best location but in finding the right time slot for an event (Penz, 1993). Hence, 'sport under postmodern conditions – sport's professional peak – appears to be geared to redouble the seductive and ephemeral play of signifiers which characterize the world of fashion and advertising' (Penz, 1993).

Let me now briefly link the televisualisation of sport with the subject of spectator involvement in the game (see Chapter 4). It is well known that fan support can become perverted into violence, as occurred most notably at the Heysel Stadium, Brussels in 1985. Here football was eclipsed by violence and in Baudrillard's (1993: 80) words, 'there is always the danger that this kind of transition may occur, that spectators may cease to be spectators and slip into the role of victims or murderers, that sport may cease to be sport and be transformed into terrorism: that is why the public must simply be eliminated, to ensure that the only event occuring is strictly televisual in nature'. In other words, in a Baudrillardian post-modern sport spectators are absent in case they are *more* than spectators – namely victims or killers – and where the authorities have 'suspended the public for an indeterminate period and expelled it from all stadiums to ensure the objective conduct of the match ... [in] ... a transparent form of public space from which all the actors have been withdrawn (Baudrillard, 1993: 80).

The banning of spectators from actual stadiums and arenas and furthering the domestic consumption of sports events might also solve one of sport's long-standing problems, that is the contravention of the idea of 'fair play' through the ability of spectators, through their aural and other forms of support and passion, to assist one team rather than another. In an empty stadium the world could watch on TV 'a pure form of the event from which all passion has been removed' (Baudrillard, 1993: 80). Alternatively, televisual techniques might create an audience digitally (Penz, 1993). Although sports bureaucrats rarely ban spectators from stadiums, some sports do attempt to stop them shouting during particular parts of a game, as in tennis (see page 89). And some sports laws do, of course, ban other 'unfair' forms of aural assistance from trainers or coaches. The present level of domestication of sport spectating might mark the beginning of the end of sports spectators as we traditionally know them and if this were to be the case another of the 'environmental' constraints on sport would have been removed. In such a dystopian scenario the machine would be a more appropriate metaphor than the theatre.

The shape of such a future is exemplified in the rare cases where spectators *are* already eliminated from sports events. The Real Madrid-Naples European Cup match in September 1987 was a game which took place in a empty stadium without spectators as a result of disciplinary action resulting from the excesses of Spanish supporters in a previous game. The match was, however, shown in full on television. Baudrillard (1993: 79-80) comments on this 'phantom football match' as:

> ...a world where a 'real' event occurs in a vacuum, stripped of its context and visible only from afar, televisually. Here we have a sort of surgically accurate prefigurement of the events of our future: events so minimal that they might well not need to take place at all – along with their maximal enlargement on screens. No one will have directly experienced the actual course of such happenings, but everyone will have received an image of them. A pure event, in other words, devoid of any reference in nature, and readily susceptible to replacement by synthetic images.[2]

Trash Sport

In the domestication of the sporting experience the distinction between sport and other forms of television entertainment becomes blurred. Already a number of television genres such as crime series and game shows display analogous excitement patterns to sports coverage, 'who is the murderer?' being replaced by 'who will win?'(Penz, 1993). Indeed, sports are not only being televisualised; televison entertainment is being sportised. Various 'shows' which may be described as (at least) sport-like, in that they involve the use of strength, physical fitness, competition, quantification and achievement, have been found to be highly attractive to TV audiences. In Britain these programmes have ranged across a wide spectrum – the fun-oriented and international *It's a Knockout* (*Jeux sans Frontieres* or *Spiel ohne Grenzen*) of the 1970s to *The Krypton Factor* and *The Strongest Man in the World*. More recently *Gladiators*, a toned-down version for UK viewers of *American Gladiators*, is virtually a cross between sports and game shows – perhaps sports-shows or kitsch sport. Such kitsch sports are often 'legitimate' sports which have been modified or carried to extremes with participants objectified through the use of show names (as in *American Gladiators*) or (as in the joviality of *It's a Knockout*) in the form of a nostalgic recreation of an imagined past (Clarke and Clarke, 1982: 79; Rinehert, 1992: 145). In *Gladiators*, the cultural referents of which are movies such as *Rollerball*, *Mad Max* and *Terminator 2* (Selway, 1992), competition takes place between the resident team and a team drawn from the public. Members of each team are undeniably fit and compete in what are obviously physical contests, staged in the national sports arena with a token audience. In Britain the total audience who watch the 'spectacle' from the comfort of their armchairs averages 10 million. Should this become the norm the traditional sport site will have been replaced by the sport sight [3.]

A final scenario for electro-sport is that heralded by the prospect of what has become known as 'virtual reality' (VR). The relationship between future-sport and the technology of VR has been explicitly explored by Rheingold (1992) who sees sports as one of several cultural fields which are ripe for incorporation into cyberspace. This is understood best by imagining:

> ...a wraparound television screen with three dimensional programs, including three dimensional sound, and solid objects that you can pick up and manipulate, even feel with your fingers and hands. Imagine immersing yourself in an artificial world and actively exploring it, rather than peering at it from a fixed perspective through a flat screen in a movie theater, or a television set, or on a computer display. Imagine that you are the creator as well as the consumer of your artificial experience, with the power to use a gesture or word to remold the world you see and hear and feel. (Rheingold, 1992: 16)

This is not a fictional description. The head-mounted displays and 3D computer graphics, input-output devices, and computer models that make up a virtual reality system make it possible for those who can afford it to become immersed in an artificial world 'and to reach in and shape it' (Rheingold, 1992: 16). This means that it would be possible to take part in a football game, a skiing event or a cricket match, experiencing the stadium or landscape ambience and that of the physical experience itself. The spectator becomes a player in the world that he or she has entered or even created as the boundaries between body and technology collapse.

ALTERNATIVE ALTERNATIVES?

The scenarios I have outlined so far have essentially been the outgrowth of technology, often applied in extravagant forms. They are characterised by the continued artificialisation and immurement of human movement culture, both of which I have shown to be typical of modern landscapes. However, other developments which may be termed post-modern also exist, in the sense that they seem to offer a form of resistance to the continued technologising of sports. Few examples, if any, of anarchist sports landscapes exist – simply because the basic tenets of anarchism and those of modern sports are mutually exclusive. In anarchism the notion of competition and profit is replaced by one of mutual aid in the meeting of 'needs' (Brietbart, 1975; Gallois, 1976) and the concept of anarchistic landscapes of sport is therefore something of a contradiction. Nevertheless, a number of body cultural activities which are vaguely anarchistic but also very close to sports, do appear to have emerged in recent years and represent utopian alternatives to the kinds of technological futures I described above. These are not folk-survivals such as knur and spell (page 98) but are alternative forms of sport-like activities, some, but not all, possessing an achievement orientation. Central to each, however, is the 'unconventional' and non-sportised landscapes on which they take place.

Clandestine sports; claiming back the streets?

'Confused drivers swerved off a road in County Durham [in north-east England] last week when they were greeted with the bizarre spectacle of horses and traps being raced at breakneck speed along a four mile stretch of the A693 [road]' (Merry, 1992: 5). This news item appeared as part of a report about the way in which Romany travellers raced horses along public roads and incurred the wrath of the police and automobile associations. Here was an example of a sporting activity taking over space for which it was not designed. It is not an isolated example of clandestine sports – those of disorder in contrast to the normal world of ordered and planned sportscapes. Such activities range from those which are dangerous to those which are safe; from those undertaken in relative isolation (e.g. climbing ruins) to those which are a form of display (street skateboarding).

In urban areas, the development of such sports is in part a response to the emergence of newer forms of urban space – the vast areas of open land such as hypermarket car parks, inner-urban derelict land and, as my earlier example showed, streets and pavements themselves, which, when not in use become available for sport-like activities. Such quasi-sports might be viewed as part of a boom in self-generated sports participation. Their landscapes are related to activities such as (a) *racing on wheels*, typified by supermarket trollys, old prams, small motor bikes or roller skates, on parking lots or in the streets and squares of the city; (b) *sliding* activities such as the use of plastic bags and cardboard boxes down grassy and earthy slopes respectively; (c) *throwing events* on wasteland, involving the use of stones and other objects, often with an unpredictable outcome (in Paris *mahgrebians* play what is obviously competitive *boules* on rough land near the Pompidou Centre while the most 'sportised' players have moved to specialised boulodromes [Camy et al., 1993: 176]); (d) *ball games* including the kicking of balls against walls and improvised forms of hockey; and (e) the *climbing* of trees or the scaling of buildings (Lefèvre, 1990).

Such activities in public spaces may be crudely sportised, tending towards the ethos of sport rather than recreation. Hence, informal races take place, skilled climbers of urban walls record in chalk their 'records', and ephemeral markings indicate the spatial limits of the 'sports' which colonise public spaces (Camy *et al.*, 1993: 180) as the urban environment is adapted to the wishes of the people. Urban time as well as urban space may be colonised; 'night jogging' in the streets of some cities is appearing as one of the latest innovations in the jogging genre (Camy, et al., 1993: 183).

Clandestine sports represent a counter-trend. Whereas the immurement of sport is well under way, the 'illegal' colonisation of space by subversive forms of movement culture remains rather limited. The so-called 'jogging revolution', regarded by some as 'post-modern' (Hansen, 1990), may initially have appeared somewhat subversive (in the style of the clandestine sports outlined above) but was quickly incorporated into the modern sport ethos of organised 'fun runs', road races or 'contained' on 'jogging trails' (see Chapter 5) and it remains to be seen whether such clandestine activities remain oppositional forms or become institutionalised and accommodated on landscapes specifically design(at)ed for them (Bach, 1993). At the same time it should be recognised that the numbers involved in using public spaces (apparently making a conscious choice of not using the huge number of specialised facilities which exist for sport-like activities) is not small. In the French city of Lyon, for example, it has been estimated that around 15,000 people use such spaces for body cultural activities; less than twice as many (25,000) use 'aerobics centres' (Camy et al., 1993: 177).

The quasi-accommodation of (what was) a clandestine sport is illustrated by an activity undertaken on the public space of the beach at Fiesta Island in San Diego, California. 'Over-the-line', as it is known, is a bat and ball game resembling softball which has been defined as 'an odd orgy of sports, spirits, sexism, sun and senselessness' (Curtis, 1989: 19). In many ways this 'sports symbol of San Diego' is like a folk-game. There are no admission charges for spectators who are not obviously segregated from the players, and the court is marked out on the beach – not by a tape measure but by the steps of a long time member of the local club. Neither is the tournament commercialised; it refuses sponsorship and it denies access to commercial food or drink vendors. Furthermore, over-the-line appears to sanction behaviour which is regarded as somewhat out of step with polite society. It seems to have elements of a sort of 'oppositional culture', not yet reduced to the ersatz carnival of 'The Cup Final' or the opening ceremony of the Olympics. It is certainly closer to Bakhtin's boisterous vulgarity than to polite sport with (the more polite) team names ranging from 'Runaway hormones' to 'Walking ads for birth control' (men) and from 'Three lying virgins' to 'Romancing the bone' (women).

Yet sportised elements clearly do exist in 'over-the-line'. An annual July 'Championship' event attracts 3,000 players and 80,000 spectators. And there is an 'over-the-line' players' association and so-called 'world championships', the 'sport' having spread to Mexico and Canada, as well as other US states. In these respects, together with the spatially-defined court marked out in the sand, the game resembles a modern sport. Yet it is not yet fully sportised; over-the-line is less anarchistic than the clandestine activities of the French hypermarket car parks, but less sportised than, say, trampolining. It is a new quasi-sport possessing the ambiguity of both the modern and the post-modern, similar characteristics being found in 'beach-volleyball' and 'street-basketball'. And in a sense some of the activities described above do possess elements of anarchist thinking, notably the absence of a governing body and the resulting absence of regulated and defined spatial parameters in which activities must take place.

At this stage I might note that Eichberg (1991: 122-3) argues that sportisation is only one form of the modernisation of movement culture. Another is physical education, or 'welfare sport' whose landscapes could be interpreted as a manifestation of placelessness because of their uniformity and standardisation, as with achievement sport. Another form of modernisation is that of the 'folklorisation' of sports, meaning the preservation of traditional sports, often for tourists (Eichberg, 1991). Such museumised games, because of their 'other-directedness' (tourist-oriented), could also be regarded as placeless or inauthentic (Relph, 1976: 118), though they may not require specialised landscapes on which to take place. A different development, however, is the emergence of totally new games, reminding us perhaps of pre-modern folk cultures, not in a nostalgic sense but rather as a vision for the future (Eichberg, 1991: 123). These would certainly shun the specialised and standardised landscapes of modern sports and include the alternative 'sports' movement associated principally with the 'hippy' years of the 1960s and early 1970s and such games are well documented through the advocacy of 'cooperative' sports by Orlick (1978). This movement is also exemplified by the 'zen' of running, touched on in Chapter 5 (page 114).

Ecological Architecture

By way of further contrast I will now look at Gerlev, a tiny village an hour away from Copenhagen in Denmark, where the local sports college (*idrætshøjskole*) has an unusual looking building sited on its campus. The building has been called a 'movement house' (Eichberg, 1993) and was completed in 1988; the terms sports hall or gymnasium have been deliberately avoided. The movement house at Gerlev was the result of a number of pressures and new movements – both physical and architectural – which were sweeping across Europe, and notably northern Europe, during the 1970s and 1980s. First, new kinds of movement culture in this period included such changes as the introduction of more expressive activities combining sport with body theatre, a shift in Danish gymnastic traditions from the rigid to the more experiential, and a growing emphasis on aesthetic activities including jazz and rock rhythms, juggling and acrobatics derived from the traditions of circus and the popular culture of laughter, and meditative experiences such as yoga. Many of the participants in these activities, according to Eichberg (1993), felt alienated in the square, rigid setting of the traditional gymnastic hall and while new, green-oriented activities such as running and skiing were able to move out into the open there was felt to be no appropriate space for the other new body cultures.

A second pressure came from movements among architects, notably those embracing the notion of 'ecological architecture'. New ideas, inspired by architects such as the Hungarian, Imre Makovecz, emphasised a move away from functionalism and towards new expressive forms of building, often incorporating local vernacular styles and using traditional, 'ecologically-correct', materials. Eichberg (1993) stresses the tendency in such movements to move away from the straight line of functionalism and adopt curved lines, an architecture full of surprises, often built on a self-help basis by local people. 'Soft' shapes and designs, using bricks and timber in contrast to the 'brutalism' of the concrete bowl stadium and the iron-clad sports-hall. In addition, a 'feminist architecture' has appeared with the rounded shapes, circles, ellipses, ovals, spirals and labyrinths, 'an alternative logic of female space' (Eichberg, 1993).

These movements, in body culture and in architecture, provide the context for the aforementioned Gerlev 'movement house'[4] which was built as a result of an architecture competition sponsored by the Danish Ministry of Culture in 1986. The competition attracted 26 entries and a rather unusual feature was that 5 of the 13 (38 per cent) published proposals (Riiskjær and Eichberg, 1989) were from women architects. This is proportionally much greater than the number of women (about 20 per cent) who are members of the Danish Architects' Association (Eichberg, 1993: 254). Many imaginative entries were received, often unconventional in style. The entries tended to avoid the functionalist 'modern rectangle' and several of the designs featured variations on traditional forms. The successful design resulted in a movement house which was a synthesis of a round movement space, a cubic house structure and a pyramid roof, constructed largely of timber. It is multifunctional, and its supporters claim that its usage and popularity have exceeded all expectations (Eichberg, 1993). While the movement house has apparently flourished, the 400 metre running track next door has become overgrown and has fallen into a state of disrepair; it is being claimed back by nature. The running track and movement house in the grounds of Gerlev college therefore symbolise the world of sport in microcosm with the alleged shift in emphasis from modern kinds of sporting landscapes to their post-modern alternatives.

At the same time, however, it should be noted that the 'movement house' is not an unambiguous structure and the popularity of the project may be the result of a 'honeymoon period' which the building may still be experiencing. Indeed, enthusiasm for it has been far from universal and it has not been without criticism. For example, it has been suggested that in a rectangular space the athlete in training has some angles to mentally cling to in order to obtain orientation (Eisen, 1992: 19).[5] The roundness of the building gives the impression of too much openness and an absence of any personal space with no corners or nooks and crannies to provide 'surprises' and symbolic (or actual) hiding places – or 'home'/'refuge' in the language of Balint or Appleton (Chapter 6). Contrary to the views of its advocates, this building may be more modern than post-modern (Kayser Nielsen, 1993b: 25).

Ecological alternatives to achievement sports are currently rather marginal phenomena which, in comparison with events such as the Olympics or World Cup, are of interest to a tiny proportion of the population. The implications for bringing about change in a landscape constructed on the mechanisation of the body, record seeking, competitiveness, and speed are profound. Yet around us in the everyday landscape we can see changes in values. The rejection of the cinder running tracks could not have been predicted 50 years ago; neither could the replacement of the rectangular swimming pools by water worlds. Shifts of emphasis within the 'trialectic' (page 6) have been taking place. What is more in question is the depth of such changes and their significance to both sport and society.

THE LAST SPORTS LANDSCAPE?

The final scenario for the future of the sports landscape rests on the assumption that nature could take its revenge on those who have exploited it. As several of the chapters in this book have shown, this includes a number of sports which have followed, in their own small way, the same direction as mainstream society in its exploitation of nature for its resources. What I am talking about here is the end of sports landscapes, not because they become multi-functional but because they become non-functional; in fact, they may no longer exist.

Various human actions create irreversible ecological impacts that simply eliminate existing sport landscapes from the earth's surface. I will call this 'nature's revenge'. In addition, sports landscapes could disappear as a result of 'planned withdrawal', the result of former participants undergoing a change of attitude towards participation in certain sporting activities and simply withdrawing their patronage from them. A variation on this scenario is that some sporting landscapes may no longer exist because the sports themselves have been subjected to legal prohibition.

Nature's Revenge

The Chernobyl disaster may, or may not, have been predictable. But there was always a risk and hence participating in sport close to such a facility becomes itself a risk. Following the disaster the sports landscapes in the environs of the nuclear reactor suffered immediate change. They were, literally, de-humanised. Tennis courts were closed, sporting activities in community facilities were discontinued and outdoor sports disallowed. Sport had become a high risk activity since 'according to health experts, everybody practicing sports in those days seriously endangered his or her health and well being' (Digel, 1992: 262). At Chernobyl running in nature had become un-natural.

On a less dramatic scale the human-induced changes in the physical environment have meant that in some sports the athletes have been at risk for some time. 'Sports, as a product of modern industrial society, is threatened by polluted nature', now out of control and threatening to create serious negative health effects (Digel, 1992: 262). Consider, for example, the case of training for running in city streets. Here we have the paradoxical situation of running through the exhaust fumes of industry and traffic, in which training for sport has backfired, resulting in possible long-term negative, rather than positive, effects on health.

At the same time, sport also contributes to pollution, damaging and destroying soil, air, plants, and animals. Skiing alone may cause the following ecological problems: destruction of natural vegetation, changes in the variety of plant species, shortening the growth period of vegetation, deterioration in root quantities, disintegration of protective forests, soil compression, chemical pollution of soil, desiccation of moors, increasing surface drainage and increasing the potential for landslides, soil erosion and avalanche hazards (Digel, 1992: 263). It has also been suggested that the continued growth of achievement sport is incompatible with the notion of sustainable development (Oittinen, 1993). Other sports contribute to litter and noise pollution, and are faced with increasing objections from residents' living next to nuisance-inducing sports facilities (Bale, 1992b: 126-32; Cachay, 1993). Sports are, therefore, increasingly coming into conflict with not only the natural but also the urban environment.

Of course, skiers themselves do not have a guilty conscience about skiing, even if they are enlightened and environmentally aware – as skiers tend to be in comparison with snowmobilers (Jackson, 1986), for example – because the factors contributing to the dying forests and eroded slopes include much more publicised factors such as toxic industrial fumes. So while there is doubt about their precise level of involvement, responsibility is passed around, distancing the skiers themselves for whom the dangers of mass skiing rarely become visible in the exercise of their sport (Digel, 1992: 260). Wildlife does not die as an immediate result of skiing, just as the lungs of athletes training in the inner city streets are not polluted to an extent that is immediately recognised. As a result, sports participants tend not to take responsibility for future generations. And disputes among experts justify our continued sporting activities.

In other cases, the predictions for the future are now being made. The classic example is that of global warming and in a number of papers coming out of the geography department at the University of Waterloo in Canada it has been argued that the effect of CO_2-induced warming may have the effect of raising winter temperatures, leading to a reduction in the snowfall and hence reducing the ski seasons, in turn leading to the virtual elimination of much of the ski industry. In the Lower Laurentian area of Québec, for example, it has been predicted that warming could lead to a reduction in the ski seasons by as much as 40 to 89 per cent (McBoyle and Wall, 1987). Predictions have shown that the state of Michigan will experience a 'minimum increase in winter temperatures of $6°F$ and a precipitation increase of 108 per cent of present day conditions as a result of trace gas warmings' (Lipski and McBoyle, 1991: 46). This would result in a reduction of the downhill ski season by about 60 per cent in the south and 30 per cent elsewhere in the state. These dramatic statistics would result in fundamental changes in the sporting and broader cultural landscapes of these regions.

These examples, of sport being affected by human-induced reversals of nature, may not immediately reveal that sport itself contributes to the pollution that could bring about its demise – or, at least, a reduction in the extent of sportscape – but nevertheless Digel (1992) has suggested that sport in its present form needs to be de-emphasised. Given the ecological threats facing sport, it may be in sport's own interests to start solving problems affecting it directly. The problem is that this might require the preliminary, but necessary conditions of 'a radical ecological transformation of the capitalist social and value system .... no less than a complete transformation of our lives, of our thinking, of our consciousness, steeped as it is in capitalist traditions would be required' (Rigauer, 1992: 68). A new, more ecologically-oriented sports landscape would reflect 'the rediscovery of slowness, and the art of taking one's time; ... the experience of non-measured space-time relations .. ., ways of individual and social sensitisation with respect for the environment' (Rigauer, 1992), a waning in the cult of the body, and much more, including the serious questioning of whether the construction of sports mega-projects can be justified in regions of over-abundance when elsewhere people are unable to satisfy their most basic needs. But the voluntary withdrawl from sportscapes looks unlikely, especially in the short term, despite the advocacy of some 'green' political parties. Young people are today mainly socialised in cities and are increasingly being attracted to recreational outlets in the urban environment – the very kinds of places which are already associated most with modern sport and its anti-ecological excesses (Telema, 1991).

The poor record of sport itself actively drawing back in order to reduce its negative impacts might be illustrated by the problems of banning the negative effects of 'pharmaceutical pollution' on the human body. The experience of the reaction to drug pollution of the human body is in many ways parallel to that of sport's pollution of the natural landscape. Quoting from a German newspaper, Hoberman (1992: 240) draws attention to the activities of the 'Green' Party in Germany which, in the 1980s, attacked 'medically hazardous training regimens, the biomechanical manupulation of athletes, the "Darwinistic" selection of national teams, the exploitation of children, and the "ruthless exploitation of the inherent limits of human nature" '. This quotation could easily be adapted to describe the manipulation of nature *per se*. The limited success in stifling steroid pollution is matched by the lack of success in curbing the pollution of the landscape of, and by, sport. According to some observers an international conspiracy, related not only to the globallly accepted model of achievement orientation but also to that of national sporting prestige, accounts for the continuation of entrenched pro-sport values. Such values could create the dystopian scenario of 'a dehumanized, robotlike athlete operating in a state of hypnosis, a creature either immune to pain or unable to stop it' (Hoberman, 1992: 283), performing, I might add, in a huge, windowless, concrete cell, accompanied only by other such athletes, a small number of officials and TV cameras – a synthetic landscape inhabited by synthetic 'beings'.

If sports are to be de-emphasised, with a resulting de-colonisation of sportscape it seems unlikely that sport will, itself, draw back. It cannot be argued that human beings are increasingly viewing themselves as part of nature. Legal regulations with effective and severe sanctions may be needed, therefore, especially in motor sports, a variety of water sports and most mountain sports (Digel, 1992: 265; Cachay, 1993: 320). The kind of statutory regulations might include imposing rules preventing dangerous sports, preventing the increase in the number of sports which conflict with the natural environment, prohibiting sports on nature reserves, stopping all advertising for skiing, and disassociating sports organisations from motor sports.

CONCLUSION

The often monofunctional landscapes of sports may be monuments to modernity. The ideology of achievement sport makes such landscapes necessary and with the increased 'economisation' of sport, the technical and functional character of such landscapes is likely to continue. Yet I believe, and I have tried to show, that these landscapes of achievement remain ambiguous and double-edged.

Far from specialisation and spatialisation being phenomena of the modern age, I demonstrated their presence in Greco-Roman, native American and medieval 'sports'. What is modern, of course, is the *standardisation* of the landscapes of national or global sports, derived from record-orientation, the myth of 'fair play', globalisation and rationalisation, and my basic thesis has been that modern sportscapes are archetypes of modernity, their rationalism born of the very (anti)nature of sport which encourages, more than most other forms of culture, the tendency towards placelessness. In their 'ideal' form, sportscapes would possess most of the criteria recognised by Relph (1976: 118) as being manifestations of placelessness. Indeed, many are already 'other-directed', uniform and internationally standardised, often lacking in human scale, and often undergoing continuous redevelopment ('improvement'). The erosion of nature and the replacement of geography by geometry have combined to create fields of achievement where sport has replaced disport and display has replaced play. At the same time, however, the modern landscape has witnessed continued resistance by fans and supporters to rationalisation, immurement and 'progress' and as a result place has not been totally replaced by space nor has the affection which people have for sports landscapes been eroded, though this affection is, of course, partial, gendered and mirrored by disaffection. Many sports landscapes possess a liminal character which has become central to participation. And the landscape of sport is not without its myths and the desire to romanticise and nostalgise what is often close to a geometric plane.

The future of the sports landscape is bound up in the future of sport and society. The modern sportscape with its rationality and its myths, its enclosed and segmented spaces, and its artifice and monoculture tell us a good deal about the character of sport itself; but, at the same time, it tells us that we live in an age of ambiguity. Perhaps it also reveals something about those who created it – and something about ourselves.

NOTES

1. In 'television as gathering place' (Adams, 1992), the receiver is regarded as   the television set and no reference is made to the huge TVscreens found in sports arenas and other public spaces. Yet when erected in parks and other places such screens surely place a new gloss on Adams's enticing paper.
2. A similar observation is made by Eco, 1987: 162.
3. The play on words is taken from Der Derian (1990: 307) who uses it to describe changes in war (from hand to hand conflict at the battle site to long range warfare by battle sight; for war read sport).

4. Eichberg (1993b) uses the term 'witches' house' *(hekse hus)* to describe this building. As the word 'witch' has negative connotations in English, I prefer the term 'movement house'. Not all Scandinavian feminists agree, however, that the word 'witch' is derogatory (Eichberg, 1993b: 253).
5. I am very grateful to Niels Kayser Nielsen for an English translation of part of this article.

BIBLIOGRAPHY

Adams, R., 1987, Same name, different game, *Sport Place*, 1 (2), 29-35.

Adams, P., 1992, Television as gathering place, *Annals of the Association of American Geographers*, 82 (1), 117-35.

Adams, R. and Rooney, J., 1984, Condo Canyon: an examination of emerging golf landscapes in America, *North American Culture*, 1, 65-76.

Adams, R. and Rooney, J., 1985, Evolution of American golf facilities, *The Geographical Review*, 75 (4), 419-38.

Allison, L., 1980, Batsman and bowler: the key relation of Victorian England, *Journal of Sport History*, 7 (2), 5-20.

Alt, J., 1983, Sport and cultural reification: from ritual to mass consumption, *Theory, Culture and Society*, 1, 93-107.

Angell, R., 1984, *The Summer Game*, Ballantine Books, New York.

Appadurai, A., 1990, Disjuncture and difference in the global cultural economy, *Theory, Culture and Society*, 2/3.

Appleton, J., 1975, *The Experience of Landscape*, Wiley, Chichester.

Appleton, J., 1984, Prospects and refuges re-visited, *Landscape Journal*, 3 (2), 91-103.

Appleton, J., 1990, *The Symbolism of Habitat*, University of Washington Press, Seattle.

Archetti, E., 1992, Argentinian football; a ritual in violence? *The International Journal of the History of Sport*, 9 (2), 209-35.

Arlott, J., 1955, *The Practice of Cricket*, Penguin, Harmondsworth.

Arlott, J., (ed.), 1977, *The Oxford Companion to Sport and Games,* Paladin, London.

Arlott, J., 1984, *Arlott on Cricket* (D. R. Allen, ed.), Collins, London.

Arlott, J. and Cardus, N., 1969, *The Noblest Game*, Harrap, London.

Arnaud, P., 1989, De l'eau vive a l'eau domestique: les usages sociaux de la natation et l'apparation de la natation sportive a Lyon au XIXe siècle, in *La Ville et le Fleuve,* Éditions de CTHS, Paris, 217-51.

Axthelm, P., 1970, *The City Game*, Harper and Row, New York.

Bach, L., 1993, Sports without facilities: the use of urban spaces by informal sports, *International Revue for the Sociology of Sport*, 28 (2/3), 281-97.

Bachelard, G., 1969, *The Poetics of Space*, Beacon Press, Boston.

Bain, A. and Pearson, A., 1991, Designed for leisure, in *Proceedings,* XVI Universiade FISU/CESU conference, Sheffield, 230-8.

Bale, J., 1978, Geographical diffusion and the adoption of professionalism in football in England and Wales, *Geography,* 63 (3), 188-97.

Bale, J., 1982, *Sport and Place,* Hurst, London.

Bale, J., 1985, Sportens rationelle landskaber, *Centring,* 6 (2), 100-9.

Bale, J., 1986, Sport and national identity: a geographical view, *British Journal of Sports History,* 3 (1), 18-41.

Bale, J ., 1988, Rustic and rational landscapes of cricket, *Sport Place,* 2 (2), 4-16.

Bale, J., 1989, *Sports Geography,* Spon, London.

Bale, J., 1990, In the shadow of the stadium: football grounds as urban nuisances, *Geography,* 75 (4), 325-34.

Bale, J., 1992a, Cartographic fetishism to geographical humanism: some central features of a geography of sport, *Innovation in Social Sciences Research,* 5 (4), 71-88.

Bale, J., 1992b, *Sport, Space and the City,* Routledge, London.

Bale, J., 1993, The spatial development of the modern stadium, *International Review for the Sociology of Sport,* 28 (2/3), 122-33.

Balint, M., 1959, *Thrills and Regressions,* The Hogarth Press, London.

Banes, S., 1987, *Terpsichore in Sneakers: Postmodern Dance,* Wesleyan University Press, Middleport, CT.

Bannister, R., 1957, *First Four Minutes,* Corgi Books, London.

Barish, J., 1966, The antitheatrical prejudice, *Critical Quarterly,* 8 (4), 329-48.

Barkley D. and Simmons, L., 1989, *Contribution of the Golf Industry to the Arizona Economy,* Technical bulletin 263, College of Agriculture, University of Arizona, Tuscon.

Barnes, T. and Duncan, J. (eds), 1992, *Writing Worlds,* Routledge, London.

Barthes, R., 1973, *Mythologies,* Paladin, London.

Bathrick, D., 1990, Max Schmeling on the canvas: boxing as an icon of Weimar culture, *New German Critique,* 51, 113-26.

Baudrillard, J., 1983, *Simulations,* Semiotext(e), New York.

Baudrillard, J., 1988, *America,* Verso, London.

Baudrillard, J., 1993, *The Transparency of Evil: Essays on Extreme Phenomena,* Verso, London.

Bennett, J., 1988, One man's Valley, *Voice of the Valley,* 1 (unpaginated).

Benson, M., 1989, *Ballparks of North America,* McFarland, Jefferson, NC.

Bergen, R, 1982, *Sport in the Movies,* Proteus Books, London.

Berking, H. and Neckel, S., 1993, Urban marathon: the staging of individuality as an urban event, *Theory, Culture and Society,* 10 (4), 63-78.

Berman, M., 1983, *All that is Solid Melts into Air,* Verso, London.

Billington, M., 1992, The lesson that art should learn from sport, *The Guardian,* 2 July, 24.

Birkett, N., 1957, Foreword, to A. Forest, *Village Cricket,* Hale, London.

Blain, N., Boyle, R. and O'Donnell, H., 1993, *Sport and National Identity in the European Media,* Leicester University Press, Leicester.

Blake, C., McDowell, S. and Devlen, J., 1979, *The 1979 Open Golf Championship at St. Andrews: an Economic Impact Study,* Scottish Academic Press, Edinburgh.

Blue, A., 1987, *Grace under Pressure: the Emergence of Women in Sport,* Sidgwick and Jackson, London.

Bly, R., 1993, *Iron John: a Book about Men,* Element Books, Shaftesbury.

Blunden, E., 1985, *Cricket Country,* Pavilion, London.

Boddy, T., 1992, Underground and overhead: building the analogous city, in M. Sorkin (ed.), *Variations on a Theme Park,* Noonday Press, New York, 123-53.

Bondi, L., 1992, Gender symbols and urban landscapes, *Progress in Human Geography,* 16 (2), 157-70.

Borgers, W., 1988, Von der motionsmaschine zum fitness-studio, *Breunpunkte der Sportwissenschaft,* 2 (2), 130-52.

Bourdieu, P., 1984, *Distinction: a Social Critique of the Judgement of Taste,* Routledge, London.

Bowden, M., 1994, Theaters of the world's soccer, in K. Raitz (ed.), *Theaters of Sport,* Johns Hopkins University Press, Baltimore (in press).

Bowen, M., 1974, Outdoor recreation around large cities, in J. Johnson (ed.), *Suburban Growth,* Wiley, Chichester, 130-52.

Bowen, R., 1970, *Cricket: a History of its Growth and Development Throughout the World,* Macmillan, London.

Bradby, D. and McCormack, J., 1978, *People's Theatre,* Croom Helm, London.

Brailsford, D., 1969, *Sport and Society: Elizabeth to Anne,* Routledge, London.

Brailsford, D., 1983, The locations of eighteenth century spectator sport, in J. Bale and C. Jenkins (eds), *Geographical Perspectives on Sport,* Department of PE, University of Birmingham, 27-60.

Brailsford, D., 1991, *Sport, Time and Society: the British at Play,* Routledge, London.

Brailsford, D., 1992, *British Sport: a Social History,* Lutterworth Press, Cambridge,

Braun, E., 1969, *Meyerhold on Theatre,* Eyre Macmillan, London.

Brecht, B., 1964, *Brecht on Theatre* (J. Willett, trans.), Methuen, London.

Breckle, S., 1992, review of Oekogeo, A. G. (1991), *Einfluss des orienteerunglaufes auf fauna und flora,* in *Scientific Journal of Orienteering,* 8 (6), 35-44.

Breitbart, M., 1975, Impressions of an anarchist landscape, *Antipode,* 7 (2), 44-49.

Brohm, J-M., 1978, *Sport: a Prison of Measured Time* (I. Fraser, trans.), Ink Links, London.

Brown, B., 1991, The meaning of baseball in 1992 (with notes on the post-American), *Public Culture,* 4 (1), 43-70.

Brown, P., 1992, Baltimore bows deeply to tradition, *The Globe and Mail* (Toronto), 19 March, C6.

Bulmer, L. and Merrills, R., 1992, *Dicks Out!,* Chatsby, Tunbridge Wells.

Burns, E., 1972, *Theatricality: a Study of Convention in the Theatre and in Social Life,* Longman, London.

Burns, R., 1989, Europe's artificial snow, *The Guardian,* 22 December, 34.

Cachay, K., 1993, Sport and environment, sport for everyone – room for everyone? *International Revue for the Sociology of Sport,* 28 (2/3), 311-23.

Callois, R., 1962, *Man, Play and Games,* Thames and Hudson, London.

Camy, J., Adamliewics, E. and Chantelet, P., 1993, Sporting uses of the city: urban anthropology applied to sports practices of the agglomeration of Lyon, *International Revue for the Sociology of Sport,* 28 (2/3), 175-85.

Cardus, N., 1929, *Days in the Sun,* Cape, London.

Cardus, N., 1930, *Cricket,* Longman, London.

Cardus, N., 1956, *Close of Play,* Collins, London.

Cardus, N., 1972, *Cardus on Cricket,* Souvenir Press, London.

Cashmore, E., 1990, *Making Sense of Sport,* Routledge, London.

Carter, J. and Krüger, A. (ed.), 1990, *Ritual and Record,* Greenwood Press, New York.

Catlin, G., 1973, *Manners, Customs and Condition of the North American Indians* (vol. 2), Henry G. Bohn, London.

Causey, A., 1989, On the morality of hunting, *Environmental Ethics,* 11 (4), 327-43.

Clarke, A. and Clarke, J., 1982, 'Highlights and action replays' – ideology, sport and the media, in J. Hargreaves (ed.), *Sport, Culture and Ideology,* Routledge, London, 62-87.

Clay, G., 1987, *Right Before your Eyes: Penetrating the Urban Environment,* Planners Press, Washington DC.

Cloke, P., Philo, C. and Sadler, D., 1991, *Approaching Human Geography,* Paul Chapman, London.

Cole, M. 1982, The beginnings of club cricket, *Wisden Cricket Monthly,* 6 (2), 2.

Collins, M., 1990, Review of J. Bale, 1989, *Sports Geography,* Spon, London in

Landscape Research, 15 (2), 32.

Cook, S., Pakulski, J. and Waters, M., 1992, *Postmodernization: Change in Advanced Society,* Sage, London.

Cooper, P., 1992, The 'visible hand' on the footrace: Fred Lebow and the marketing of the marathon, *Journal of Sport History,* 19 (3), 244-56.

Cosgrove, D., 1984, *Social Formation and Symbolic Landscape,* Croom Helm, London.

Cosgrove, D., 1985, Prospect, perspective and the evolution of the landscape idea, *Transactions of the Institute of British Geographers,* NS10, 45-65.

Cosgrove, D., 1989a, Geography is everywhere: culture and symbolism in human geography, in D. Gregory and R. Walford (eds), *Horizons in Human Geography,* Macmillan, London, 118-53.

Cosgrove, D., 1989b, Historical considerations on humanism, historical materialism and geography, in A. Kobayashi and S. Mackenzie (eds), *Remaking Human Geography,* Unwin Hyman, London, 190-205.

Cosgrove, D., 1990a, Environmental thought and action: pre-modern and post-modern, *Transactions of the Institute of British Geographers,* NS15 (3), 344-58.

Cosgrove, D., 1990b, Spectacle and society: landscape as theatre in pre-modern and post-modern cities, in P. Groth (ed.), *Vision, Culture and Landscape,* Berkeley Symposium in Cultural Landscape Interpretation, Berkeley, CA, 221-40.

Cosgrove, D., 1993, *The Palladian Landscape,* Leicester University Press, Leicester.

Cosgrove, D. and Daniels, S. (eds), 1989, *The Iconography of Landscape,* Cambridge University Press, Cambridge.

Cosgrove, D. and Domosh, M., 1993, Author and authority: writing the new cultural geography, in J. Duncan and D. Ley (eds), *Place/Culture/Representation,* Routledge, London, 25-38

Cosgrove, S., 1982, Football, theatre and social pleasure, in C. Jenkins and M. Green (eds), *Sporting Fictions,* Department of Physical Education, Birmingham University, Birmingham, 122-41.

Crawford, M., 1992, The world in a shopping mall, in M. Sorkin (ed.), *Variations on a Theme Park: the new American City and the end of Public Space,* Noonday Press, New York, 3-30.

Crook, S., Pakulski, J. and Waters, M., 1992, *Postmodernization,* Sage, London.

Csikszentmihalyi, M., 1988, Introduction, in M. Csikszentmihalyi and I. Csikszentmihalyi (eds), *Optimal Experience: Psychological Studies of Flow in Consciousness,* Cambridge University Press, Cambridge, 1-15.

Culin, S., 1907, *Games of the North American Indians,* US Government Printing Office, Washington DC.

Cullen, G., 1976, *The Concise Townscape,* Van Norstrand, New York.

Cuming, E., 1933, Sports and games, in A. Turberville (ed.), *Johnson's England,* (vol. 1), Clarendon Press, Oxford, 362-83.

Cunningham, J., 1980, The ups and downs of sporting life, *The Guardian,* 3 May, 15.

Curtis, J., 1989, The show and the sport, *Sport Place,* 3 (1/2), 1989, 18-23.

Daniels, S., 1988, The political iconography of woodland in later Georgian England, in D. Cosgrove and S. Daniels (eds), *The Iconography of Landscape,* Cambridge University Press, Cambridge, 43-82.

Daniels, S., 1989, Marxism, culture and the duplicity of landscape, in R. Peet and N. Thrift (eds), *New Models in Human Geography* (vol. 2), Unwin-Hyman, London, 196-220.

Daniels, S., 1992, Place and the geographical imagination, *Geography,* 77 (4), 310-22.

Daniels, S., 1993, *Fields of Vision,* Polity Press, Cambridge.

Daniels, S. and Cosgrove, D., 1988, Introduction: iconography and landscape, in D. Cosgrove and S. Daniels (eds), *The Iconography of Landscape,* Cambridge

University Press, Cambridge, 1-10.

Daniels, S. and Cosgrove, D., 1993, Spectacle and text: landscape metaphors in cultural geography, in J. Duncan and D. Ley (eds), *Place/Culture/Representation,* Routledge, London, 57-77.

Darley, C., 1993, Grounds for inspiration, *The Observer,* 15 August, 43.

Davis, M., 1985, Urban renaissance and the spirit of postmodernism, *New Left Review,* 151, 106-14.

Debord, G., 1987, *Society and the Spectacle,* Rebel Press (no place of publication indicated).

Delaney, T., 1991, *The Grounds of Rugby League,* Delaney, Keighley.

Delves, A., 1981, Popular recreation and social conflict in Derby, 1800-1850, in E. Yeo and S. Yeo (eds), *Popular Culture and Class Conflict, 1590-1914,* Harvester Press, Brighton, 89-122.

Der Derian, J., 1990, The (s)pace of international relations: simulation, surveillance and speed, *International Studies Quarterly,* 34 (3), 295-310.

Dickinson, D. and Dickinson, K., 1991, *Major League Stadiums: a Vacation Planning Reference,* McFarland and Co., Jefferson, NC.

Digel, H., 1991, Review of H. Eichberg, 1988, *Leistungsräume: Sport als Umwelt Problem,* in *International Review for the Sociology of Sport,* 26 (2), 69-81.

Digel, H., 1992, Sports in a risk society, *International Review for the Sociology of Sport,* 27 (3), 257-73.

Douglas, E., 1990, Impact on flora and fauna of the November classic 1988, held in the New Forest, Hampshire, England, *Scientific Journal of Orienteering,* 6 (2), 64-84.

Dovey, K., 1985, The quest for authenticity and the replication of environmental meaning, in D. Seamon and R. Mugerauer (eds), *Dwelling, Place and Environment,* Martinus Nijhoff, Dordrecht, 33-46.

Dovey, K., 1990, Old Scabs/new scars: the hallmark event and the everyday environment, in G. Syme, Shaw, B., Fenton, D and Mueller, W. (eds), *The Planning and Evaluation of Hallmark Events,* Avebury, Aldershot, 77-83.

Draper, P., 1976, Social and economic constraints on child-life among the !Kung, in R. Lees and I. DeVore (eds), *Kalahari Hunter Gatherers: Studies of the !Kung San and their Near Neighbours,* Harvard University Press, Cambridge, MA, 199-217.

Dryden, K. and MacGregor, R., 1989, *Home Game: Hockey and Life in Canada,* McClelland and Stewart, Toronto.

Duncan, J., and Duncan, N., 1992, Ideology and bliss, Roland Barthes and the secret histories of landscape, in T. Barnes and J. Duncan (eds), *Writing Worlds,* Routledge, London, 18-37.

Duncan, J. and Ley, D., 1993, Introduction: representing the place of culture, in J. Duncan and D. Ley (eds), *Place/Culture/Representation,* Routledge, London, 1- 21.

Dunleavey, J., 1981, Skiing: the worship of Ullr in America, *Journal of Popular Culture,* 4, 74-85.

Dunning, E. and Sheard, K., 1979, *Barbarians, Gentlemen and Players: a Sociological Study of the Development of Rugby Football,* Martin Robertson, Oxford.

Dwyer, T. and Dyer, K., 1984, *Running out of Time,* University of New South Wales Press, Kensington, NSW.

Eco, U., 1987, *Travels in Hyperreality,* Picador, London.

Edwards, J., 1979, The home advantage in sport, in J. Goldstein (ed.), *Sports, Games and Play: Social and Psychological Viewpoints,* Erlbaum, Hillside, NJ, 409-38.

Eichberg, H., 1977, The Nazi *Thingspiel*: theater for the masses in fascism and prolaterian culture, *New German Critique,* 11, 133-50.

Eichberg, H., 1982, Stopwatch, horizontal bar, gymnasium: the technologizing of sports in the 18th and 19th centuries, *Journal of the Philosophy of Sport,* 9, 43-59.

Eichberg, H., 1983, Kropskulturens trialektik, *Centring,* 4 (3), 129-39.

Eichberg, H., 1986, The enclosure of the body – on the historical relativity of 'health', 'nature' and the environment of sport, *Journal of Contemporary History,* 21, 99-121.

Eichberg, H., 1988, *Leistungsräume: Sport als Umwelt Problem,* Lit, Münster.

Eichberg, H., 1989a, Body culture as paradigm: the Danish sociology of sport, *International Review for the Sociology of Sport,* 24 (1), 43-60.

Eichberg, H., 1989b, The labyrinth – the earliest Nordic 'sportsground'? *Scandinavian Journal of Sports Sciences,* 11 (1), 43-63.

Eichberg, H., 1990a, Sport als umweltproblem? in J-M. Frei (ed.), *Sind Sport und Umwelt Vereinbar?* Schweizerischer Landesverband für Sport, Bern, 5-33.

Eichberg, H., 1990b, Stronger, funnier, deadlier: track and field on its way to the ritual of the record, in J. Carter and A. Krüger (eds), *Ritual and Record,* Greenwood Press, New York, 123-34.

Eichberg, H., 1990c, Race track and labyrinth: the space of physical culture in Berlin', *Journal of Sport History,* 17 (2), 245-60.

Eichberg, H., 1990d, Forward race and the laughter of pygmies: on Olympic sport', in M. Teich and R. Porter (eds), *Fin de Siècle and its Legacy,* Cambridge University Press, Cambridge, 115-31.

Eichberg, H., 1991, A revolution in body culture? Traditional games on the way from modernization to 'postmodernity', in J.-J. Barreau and G. Jaoun (eds), *Éclipse et Renaissance des Jeux Populaires,* Institute International Anthropologie Corporelle, Rennes, 101-29.

Eichberg, H., 1993a, 'Popular gymnastics' in Denmark: the trialectics of body culture and nationalism, *History of European Ideas,* 16 (4-6), 845-53.

Eichberg, H., 1993b, New spatial configurations of sport? Experiences from Danish alternative planning, *International Review for the Sociology of Sport,* 28 (2/3), 245-63.

Eichberg, H., 1993c, The social constitution of time and space as sociology's way home to philosophy. Sport as paradigm, Paper read at seminar of ICSS, Vienna, July.

Eisen, I., 1992, Rundt om vinklerne, *Gerlev Idrætshojskole Årsskrift,* 17-21.

Elias, N. and Dunning E., 1986, *The Quest for Excitement; Sport and Leisure in the Civilising Process,* Blackwell, Oxford.

Ellul, J., 1965, *The Technological Society,* Macmillan, London.

Elsaesser, T., 1993, Images for sale: the 'new' British cinema, in L. Friedman (ed.), *British Cinema and Thatcherism,* UCL Press, London, 52-69.

Elson, M., Buller, H. and Stanley, P., 1986, *Providing for Motorsports: from Image to Reality,* Sports Council, London.

Emslie, B., 1990, Bertold Brecht and football, or playwright versus playmaker, in G. Day (ed.), *Readings in Popular Culture,* Macmillan, London, 164-73.

Entriken, N., 1991, *The Betweenness of Place,* Macmillan, London.

Everitt, R., 1991, *Battle for the Valley,* Voice of the Valley, London.

Faarlund, N., 1973, Om verdigrunnlaget, friluftsliv og idrett, unpublished manuscript (quoted in Naess, 1989, p.178).

Fiske, J., 1989, *Reading the Popular,* Unwin Hyman, London.

Ford, S., 1991, Landscape revisited: a feminist reappraisal, in C. Philo (compiler), *New Words, New Worlds, Reconceptualising Social and Cultural Geography,* Department of Geography, St. David's University College, Lampeter, 151-5.

Foucault, M., 1979, *Discipline and Punish,* Penguin, Harmondsworth.

Foucault, M., 1980, *Power/Knowledge: Selected Interviews and Other Writings,* Harvester Press, Brighton.

Foucault, M., 1988, *Madness and Civilization,* Vintage Books, New York.

Frampton, K., 1985, Towards a critical regionalization; six points for an architecture of resistance, in H. Foster (ed.), *Postmodern Culture*, Verso, London, 16-30.

Frith, D., 1987, *Pageant of Cricket,* Macmillan, London.

Fuller, P., 1988, The iconography of mother nature, in D. Cosgrove and S. Daniels (eds), *The Iconography of Landscape,* Cambridge University Press, Cambridge, 11-31.

Furst, T., 1986, *The Image of Professional Baseball: the Sports Press and Ideas about Baseball in Nineteenth Century America* (PhD thesis, New School for Social Research), University Microfilms International, Ann Arbor.

Gallois, B., 1976, Ideology and the idea of nature: the case of Peter Kropotkin, *Antipode,* 8 (3), 1-16.

Galtung, J., 1984, *S*port and international understanding; sport as a carrier of deep culture and structure, in M. Ilmarinen (ed.), *Sport and International Understanding,* Springer-Verlag, Berlin.

Gardiner, E., 1930, *Athletics of the Ancient World,* Clarendon Press, Oxford.

Gelber, S., 1983, Working at playing: the culture of the workplace and the rise of baseball, *Journal of Social History,* 16 (4), 3-22.

Giamatti, A., 1989, *Take Time for Paradise: Americans and their Games,* Summit Books, New York.

Giulianotti, R., 1991, The Tartan Army in Italy: the case for the carnivalesque, *Sociological Review,* 39 (3), 503-27.

Goethals, G., 1978, Sacred-secular icons, in R. Browne and M. Fishwick (eds), *Icons of America,* Popular Press, Bowling Green, OH, 24-66.

Gold, M., 1984, A history of nature, in D. Massey and J. Allen (eds), *Geography Matters!,* Cambridge University Press, Cambridge, 12-33.

Goldlust, J., 1987, *Playing for Keeps: Sport, the Media and Society,* Longman Cheshire, Melbourne.

Golby, J. and Purdue, A., 1984, *The Civilisation of the Crowd: Popular Culture in England, 1750-1900,* Batsford, London.

Goodman, M. and Bauer, S., 1993, From Elysian fields: baseball as the literary genre, *The Sewanee Review,* 101 (2), 226-39.

Gregory, D., 1994, *Geographical Imaginations,* Blackwell, Cambridge, MA.

Grinnell, G., 1972, *The Cheyenne Indians* (vol. 2), Nebraska University Press, Lincoln (originally published in 1923 by Yale University Press).

Gruneau, R., 1993, The critique of sport in modernity: theorising power, culture and the politics of the body, in E. Dunning, J. Maguire and R. Pearton (eds), *The Sports Process*, Human Kinetics, Champaign, IL, 85-109.

Guttmann, A., 1978, *From Ritual to Record*, Columbia University Press, New York.

Guttmann, A., 1988, *A Whole New Ball Game*, University of North Carolina Press, Chapel Hill.

Guttmann, A., 1992, *The Olympics*, Columbia University Press, New York.

Haley, B., 1978, *The Healthy Body and Victorian Culture,* Harvard University Press, Cambridge, MA.

Hall, D., 1985, *Fathers Playing Ball with Sons,* Dell, New York.

Hamlyn, M., 1985, Instant cricket storms Lord's, *The Observer,* 4 November, 28.

Hansen, J., 1990, Kropsudfoldelser – fra sport til jogging; det moderne – det traditionsforandrede – det postmoderne, *Den Jyske Historiker,* 53, 81-96.

Hansen, J., 1991, Nordic sports under review, *The International Journal of the History of Sport,* 8 (2), 296-7.

Harris, H., 1964, *Greek Athletes and Athletics,* Hutchinson, London.

Harris, H., 1973, *Sport in Greece and Rome,* Thames and Hudson, London.

Harris, H., 1975, *Sport in Britain: its Origins and Development,* Stanley Paul, London.

Harvey, D., 1989, *The Condition of Postmodernity,* Blackwell, Oxford.

Hassan, I., 1985, The culture of postmodernism, *Theory, Culture and Society,* 2 (3), 119-32.

Hawtree, F., 1983, *The Golf Course: Planning, Design, Construction and Maintenance,* Spon, London.

Heald, T., 1986, *The Character of Cricket,* Faber, London.

Herva, H. and Lyytinen, T., 1993, Motivation for competitive sport of top level athletes in different sport events, paper presented at ICSS seminar, Vienna, July.

Hester, R., 1993, Sacred structures and everyday life, in D. Seamon (ed), *Dwelling, Seeing, and Designing: Toward a Phenomenological Ecology,* State University of New York Press, Albany, 271-97.

Hewison, W., (ed.), 1988, *Class war:* Punch *in the classroom,* Grafton Books, London.

Higson, A., 1993, Re-presenting the national past: nostalgia and pastiche in heritage film, in L. Friedman (ed.), *British Cinema and Thatcherism,* UCL Press, London, 109-29.

Hoberman, J., 1984, *Sport and Political Ideology,* Heinemann, London.

Hoberman, J., 1992, *Mortal Engines: the Science of Performance and the Dehumanization of Sport,* Free Press, New York.

Holt, R. 1989, *Sport and the British,* Oxford University Press, Oxford.

Hornby, N., 1992, *Fever Pitch,* Victor Gollancz, London.

Horne, D., 1986, *The Public Culture: the Triumph of Industrialism,* Pluto Press, London.

Howat, G., 1991, Sherriff of Badger's Green, *Journal of the Cricket Society,* 15 (2), 5-9.

Hudson, C., 1976, *The Southeastern Indians,* University of Tennessee Press, Knoxville.

Hyland, D., 1990, *Philosophy of Sport,* Paragon House, New York.

Inglis, F., 1977a, *The Name of the Game: Sport and Society,* Heinemann, London.

Inglis, F., 1977b, Nation and community: a landscape and its morality, *Sociological Review,* 25 (3), 489-514.

Inglis, F., 1992, Intellectual history and popular culture: the case of sport, *British Society of Sports History Bulletin,* 12, 1-22.

Inglis, S., 1983, *The Football Grounds of England and Wales,* Collins, London.

Inglis, S., 1990, *The Football Grounds of Europe,* Collins, London.

Jackson, E., 1986, Outdoor recreation participation and attitudes towards the environment, *Leisure Studies,* 5 (1), 1-23.

Jackson, P., 1988, Street life: the problems of carnival, *Society and Space,* 6, 213-27.

Jackson, J., 1957-8, The abstract world of the hot rodder, *Landscape,* 7, 22-7.

Jain, P., 1980, On a discrepancy in track races, *Research Quarterly for Exercise and Sport,* 51, 432-36.

Jakle, J., 1987, *The Visual Elements of Landscape,* University of Massachucetts Press, Amherst.

James, C., 1963, *Beyond a Boundary,* Hutchinson, London.

Jansma, K., 1991, Success and failure of institutionalisation: Frisian sports and games, in J.-J. Barreau and G. Jaouen (eds), *Éclipses et Renaissance de Jeux Populaires,* Institut Anthropologie Corporelle, Rennes, 77-88.

Jencks, C., 1987, *Postmodernism,* Academy Editions, London.

John, H., 1986-7, Das Schwimmfest in der Frühzeit des verbandssports (1878-1914/18), *Stadion,* 12/13, 171-6.

Johnston, R., 1991, *A Question of Place,* Blackwell, Oxford.

Katz, I., 1992, Nine killed at Le Mans, *The Guardian,* 27 April, 3.

Katz, C. and Kirby A., 1991, In the nature of things: the environment and everyday life, *Transactions of the Institute of British Geographers,* 16 (3), 259-71.

Kayser Nielsen, N., 1993a, Sports between rationalism and romanticism: patterns of movement in conflict, paper presented at the conference 'Body and nature – nature and body. Between construction and deconstruction', Odense University, December.

Kayser Nielsen, N., 1993b, Sport, landscape and horizon, paper presented at seminar on 'Sport, space, place and landscape', Keele University, July.

Kern, S., 1983, *The Culture of Time and Space, 1880-1918,* Weidenfeld and Nicholson, London.

Kilburn, J., 1980, County grounds of England, in E. Swanton and J. Woodcock (eds), *Barclays World of Cricket,* London.

King, H., 1986-7, Students of world records: pioneers of sports science, *Stadion,* 12/13, 305-7.

Kircher, R., 1928, *Fair Play: the Games of Merrie England,* Collins, London.

Kitto, H., 1951, *The Greeks,* Penguin, Harmondsworth.

Klein, M-L., 1993, Social-spatial conditions affecting women's sport: the case of the Ruhr area, *International Review for the Sociology of Sport,* 28 (2/3), 145-57.

Korsgaard, O., 1990, Sport as a practice of religion: the record as ritual, in J. Carter and A. Krüger (eds), *Ritual and Record,* 113-22.

Kuntz, P., 1973, The aesthetics of sport, in R. Osterhoudt (ed.), *The Philosophy of Sport,* Thomas, Springfield, IL, 305-9.

Lacey, M., 1992, The end of something small and the start of something big, in D. Bull (ed.), *We'll Support You Evermore,* Duckworth, London, 87-96.

Larsen, S. E., 1992, Is nature really natural? *Landscape Research,* 17 (3), 116-22.

Lash, S. and Urry, J., 1994, *Economics of Signs and Space,* Sage, London.

Lawrence, E. A., 1982, *Rodeo: an Anthropologist Looks at the Wild and the Tame,* University of Tennessee Press, Knoxville.

Lawrence, W., 1933, The drama and the theatre, in A. Turberville (ed.), *Johnson's England,* Clarendon Press, Oxford, 160-89.

Lean, G. and Keating, M., 1992, Alps scarred 'forever' by Olympics, *The Observer,* 9 February.

Lee, R., 1988, Modernization, in R. Johnston, D. Gregory and P. Haggett (eds), *The Dictionary of Human Geography,* Blackwell, Oxford, 302.

Lee, R. and DeVore, I, 1968, Problems in the study of hunters and gatherers, in R. Lee and I. DeVore (eds), *Man the Hunter,* Aldine Press, Chicago, 1-10.

Lefebvre, H., 1991, *The Production of Space,* Blackwell, Oxford.

Lefèvre, J-P., 1990, Ordre et désordre: analyse des espace sauvages de 'pratiques sportives clandestines' dans la région rouennaise comme témoignage di processus d'institutionalisation des pratiques et d'integration des jaunes, in B. Errais, D. Mathieu and J. Praicheux (eds), *Géopolitique du Sport,* Laboratoire de Géographie Humaine, Université Franche Comte, Besançon, 33-42.

Lester, T., 1980, Time to divide the field into zones, *Cricketer International,* 61 (3), 37.

Lewis, P., 1979, Axioms for reading the landscape, in D. Meinig (ed.), *The Interpretation of Ordinary Landscapes,* Oxford University Press, New York, 11-32.

Ley, D. and Olds, K., 1988, Landscape and spectacle: world's fairs and the culture of heroic consumption, *Society and Space,* 6 (6), 191-212.

Lipski, S. and McBoyle, G., 1991, The impact of global warming on downhill skiing in Michigan, *The East Lakes Geographer,* 26, 37-51.

Lipsky, R., 1981, *How we Play the Game,* Beacon Press, Boston.

Lobozeiwicz, T., 1981, *Meterologie im Sport,* Sportverlag, Berlin.

Louder, D., 1991, Etude géographique du sport en Amérique du nord: survol et critique, in B. Errais, D. Mathieu and J. Praicheux (eds), *Géopolitique du Sport,* Laboratoire de Géographie Humaine, Université Franche Comte, Besançon, 179-87.

Lovesey, P., 1979, *The Official Centenary History of the Amateur Athletic Association,* Guinness Superlatives, London, 1979.

Lowenthal, D., 1985, *The Past is a Foreign Country,* Cambridge University Press, Cambridge.

Lowenthal, D., 1991, British national identity and the English landscape, *Rural History,* 2 (2), 205-30.

Lowenthal, D. and Prince, H., 1965, English landscape tastes, *Geographical Review,* 55 (2), 186-222.

Lowerson, J., 1993, *Sport and the English Middle Class, 1870-1914,* Manchester University Press, Manchester.

Lowry, P., 1992, *Green Cathedrals,* Addison-Wesley, Reading, Mass.

Lutz, R., 1991, Careers in running: individual needs and social organization, *International Review for the Sociology of Sport,* 26 (3), 155-73.

Lynch, R., 1992, A symbolic piece of grass: crowd disorder and regulation on the Sydney Cricket Ground Hill, *ASSH Studies in Sports History,* 7, 10-48.

Lyngsgård, H., 1990, *Idrætens Rum,* Copenhagen, Borgen.

Lyytinen, T., 1993, personal communication.

MacAloon, J., 1981, *This Great Symbol; Pierre de Coubertin and the Origins of the Modern Olympic Games,* Chicago University Press, Chicago.

MacAloon, J., 1984, Olympic Games and the theory of spectacle in modern societies, in J. MacAloon (ed.), *Rite, Drama, Festival, Spectacle,* Institute for the Study of Human Issues, Pittsburgh, 241-80.

MacCannell, D., 1992, *Empty Meeting Grounds: the Tourist Papers,* Routledge, London.

Macdonnell, A., 1935, *England their England,* Macmillan, London.

McBoyle, G. and Wall, G., 1987, The impact of CO_2-induced warming on downhill skiing in the Laurentians, *Cahiers de Géographie de Québec,* 31 (82), 39-50.

McCormack, G., 1991, The price of affluence: the political economy of Japanese leisure, *New Left Review,* 188, 121-34.

McIntyre, D., 1985, Problems of the Melbourne test cricket pitch and their relevance to Australian turf pitches, *The Journal of the Sports Turf Research Institute,* 61, 80-134.

Magoun, F., 1938, *History of Football from the Beginnings to 1871,* Verlag Heinrich Pöppinghaus, Bochum-Langendreer.

Malcolmson, R., 1973, *Popular Recreations in English Society 1700-1850,* Cambridge University Press, Cambridge.

Malmberg, T., 1980, *Human Territoriality,* Mouton, The Hague.

Mangham, I. and Overington, M., 1987, *Organizations as Theatre: a Social Psychology of Dramatic Appearances,* Wiley, Chichester.

Marples, M., 1954, *A History of Football,* Secker and Warburg, London.

Marshall, L., 1976, *The !Kung of Nyae Nyae,* Harvard University Press, Cambridge, MA.

Martin, D., and Gynn, R., 1979, *The Marathon Footrace,* Charles C. Thomas, Springfield, MA.

Martin-Jenkins, C., 1984, *Cricket: a Way of Life,* Century, London.

Mason, T., 1980, *Association Football and English Society, 1863-1915,* Harvester, Brighton.

Mazrui, A., 1976, *A World Federation of Cultures: an African Perspective,* Free Press, New York.

McClelland, J., 1990, The numbers of reason: luck, logic and art in Renaissance conceptions of sport, in J. Carter and A. Krüger (eds), *Ritual and Record,* Greenwood Press, New York, 53-64.

Meinig, D., (ed.), 1979a, *The Interpretation of Ordinary Landscapes,* Oxford University Press, New York.

Meinig, D., 1979b, The beholding eye, in D. Meinig (ed.), *The Interpretation of*

Ordinary Landscapes, Oxford University Press, New York, 33-48.

Merry, J., 1992, Road racing gypsies give police a run for their money, *The Independent*, 24 May, 5.

Metcalfe, A., 1993, The development of sporting facilities: a case study of East Northumberland, England, 1850-1914, *International Review for the Sociology of Sport*, 28 (2/3), 107-19.

Milburn, J., 1966, Australia, in E. W. Swanton (ed.), *The World of Cricket*, Michael Joseph, London, 37-41.

Mitchell, R., 1988, Sociological implications of the flow experience, in M. Csikszentmihalyi and I. Csikszentmihalyi (eds), *Optimal Experience: Psychological Studies of Flow in Consciousness*, Cambridge University Press, Cambridge, 15-35.

Moen, O., 1990, *Idrottsanläggingar och Idrottens Rumsliga Utveckling i Svenskt Stadsbyggande under 1900-talet*, Handelhögskolan, Gothenburg.

Moen, O., 1992, *Från Bollplan till Sportcentrum*, Byggforskningsrådet, Stockholm.

Moen, O., 1993, Facilities for sports and physical training, in H. Aldskogius (ed.), *Cultural Life, Recreation and Tourism*, National Atlas of Sweden, Stockholm, 48-53.

Moon, Y. and Shin, D., 1990, Health risks to golfers from pesticide use on golf courses in Korea, in A. Cochran (ed.), *Science and Golf*, Spon, London, 358-63.

Moorhouse, H., 1989, Models of work, models of leisure, in C. Rojek (ed.), *Leisure for Leisure*, Macmillan, London, 15-35.

Morgan, R., 1985, The Tuscan game of Palla. A descendent of the medieval game of tennis, *Stadion*, 11 (2), 176-92.

Morgan, W., 1980, *Prehistoric Architecture in the Eastern United States*, MIT Press, Boston.

Mosher, S., 1991, Fielding our dreams: rounding third in Dyersville, *Sociology of Sport Journal*, 8 (3), 272-80.

Mossiman, T., 1985, Geo-ecological impacts of ski-piste construction in the Swiss Alps, *Applied Geography*, 5, 29-38.

Mrozek, D., 1989, review of J. Chandler, 1988, *Television and National Sport*, in *Journal of Sports History*, 11 (2), 202-5.

Murphy, M. and White, R., 1978, *The Psychic Side of Sports*, Addison-Wesley, Reading, MA.

Murray, C., 1992, *The Soccer Crowd: Match Day at Manchester City*, MUS Publishers, Stockport.

Murrie, D., 1986, Determination of wind assistance in athletics: are the measurements at Meadowbank Stadium valid? in J. Watkins, T. Reilly and L. Burwitz (eds), *Sports Science* (Proceedings, VIII Commonwealth and International Conference on Sport, PE, Dance, Recreation and Health), Spon, London, 387-92.

Mützelberg, D. and Eichberg, H. (eds), 1984, *Sport, Bewegung und Ökologie*, Studienganges Sportwissenschaft der Universität Bremen, Bremen.

Nabakov, P., 1981, *Indian Running: Native American History and Tradition*, Ancient City Press, Santa Fe, NM.

Naess, A., 1989, *Ecology, Community and Lifestyle*, Cambridge University Press, Cambridge.

Nagbøl, S., 1990, At bade er regionalt, nationalt of overnationalt – Helgoland på Amager, in J. Hansen, N. Kayser Neilsen and L. Ottesen (eds), *Kropskultur og Idræt*, Idrætshistorisk Årbog, 6, Odense Universitetsforlag, Odense, 24-32.

Nagbøl, S., 1993, Enlivening and deadening shadows, *International Review for the Sociology of Sport*, 28 (2/3), 265-80.

Needle, J. and Thomson, P., 1991, *Brecht*, Blackwell, Oxford.

Nesmith, C. and Radcliffe, S., 1993, (Re)mapping Mother Earth: a geographical perspective on environmental feminisms, *Society and Space*, 11, 379-94.

Nielson, B., 1986, Dialogue with the city; the evolution of baseball parks, *Landscape,* 29 (1), 39-47.

Norberg-Schultz, C., 1979. *Genius Loci: the Phenomenology of Architecture,* Rizzoli, New York.

Novak, M., 1988, *The Joy of Sports,* Hamilton Press, Lanham, MD.

O'Riordan, T., 1981, *Environmentalism,* Pion, London.

Oates, J., 1987, *On Boxing,* Garden City, New York.

Oittinen, A., 1993, The right of common access to nature, paper presented at ICSS seminar, Vienna, July.

Olwig, K., 1992, Sexual cosmology; nation and landscape at the conceptual interstices of nature and culture or: what does landscape really mean? *Man and Nature Working Papers,* 5, Humanities Research Centre, Odense University, Odense.

Oriard, M., 1976, Sport and space, *Landscape,* 21 (1), 32-40.

Oriard, M., 1981, Professional football as cultural myth, *Journal of American Culture,* 4 (3), 27-41.

Oriard, M., 1991, *Sporting with the Gods; the Rhetoric of Play and Game in American Culture,* Cambridge University Press, Cambridge.

Orlick, T., 1978, *Winning through Cooperation,* Hawkins and Associates, Washington DC.

Osterhoudt, R. (ed.), 1973, *The Philosophy of Sport,* Thomas, Springfield, IL.

Ottesen, L., 1990, På hjemmebane, in J. Hansen, N. Kayser Nielsen and L. Ottesen (eds), *Kropskultur og Idræt,* Idrætshistorisk Årbog, 6, Odense Universitetsforlag, Odense, 33-48.

Ottesen, L., 1992, Home field as home, unpublished paper, Centre for Sports Research, Copenhagen University.

Oxendine, J., 1988, *American Indian Sports Heritage,* Human Kinetics, Champaign, IL.

Panofsky, E., 1962, *Studies in Iconology: Humanistic Themes in the Art of the Renaissance,* Harper and Row, New York.

Pardon, S., 1896, *Wisden Cricketers' Almanac,* Wisden and Co., London.

Penz, O., 1990, Sport and speed, *International Review for the Sociology of Sport,* 25 (2), 157-67.

Penz, O., 1991, Ballgames of the north American indians and in late medieval Europe, *Journal of Sport and Social Issues,* 15 (1), 43-58.

Penz, O., 1992, Mediasport, in R. Horak and O. Penz (eds), *Sport: Kult und Kommerz,* Verlag für Gesellschaftskritik, Vienna.

Penz, O., 1993, Ephemeral sport, paper presented at ICSS seminar, Vienna, July.

Peyker, I., 1993, Sport and ecology, in S. Riiskjær (ed), *Sport and Space: New Challenges to Planning and Architecture,* Council of Europe, Copenhagen, 71-7.

Philo, C., 1986, 'The same and the other'; on geographies, madness and outsiders, *Occasional Paper,* 11, Department of Geography, Loughborough University, Loughborough.

Philo, C., 1992a, Foucault's geography, *Society and Space,* 10, 137-61.

Philo, C., 1992b, personal communication.

Pietarinen, J., 1991, Principal attitudes towards nature, in P. Oja and R. Telema (eds), *Sport for All,* Elsevier, Amsterdam, 581-7.

Plumptre, G., 1988, *Homes of Cricket,* Macdonald, London.

Pocock, D., 1981, Sight and knowledge, *Transactions of the Institute of British Geographers,* NS6 (4), 385-93.

Pocock, D., 1988, The music of geography, in D. Pocock (ed.), *Humanistic Approaches in Geography,* Occasional Paper, 22, Department of Geography, Durham University, Durham, 62-71.

Porteous, D., 1985, Smellscape, *Progress in Human Geography,* 9 (3), 356-78.

Porteous, D., 1990, *Landscapes of the Mind: Worlds of Sense and Metaphor,* University of Toronto Press, Toronto.

Price, R., 1989, *Scotland's Golf Courses,* Aberdeen University Press, Aberdeen.

Pringle, T, 1988, The privation of history: Landseer, Victoria and the highland myth, in D. Cosgrove and S. Daniels (eds), *The Iconography of Landscape,* Cambridge University Press, Cambridge, 146-61.

Pugh, S., 1990a, Introduction: stepping into the open, in S. Pugh (ed.), *Reading Landscape: Country–City–Capital,* Manchester University Press, Manchester, 1-6.

Pugh, S., 1990b, Loitering with intent: from Arcadia to the arcades, in S. Pugh (ed.), *Reading Landscape: Country–City–Capital,* Manchester University Press, Manchester, 145-60.

Punter, J., 1982, Landscape aesthetics: a synthesis and critique, in J. Gold and J. Burgess (eds), *Valued Environments,* Allen and Unwin, London, 100-23.

Quanz, D., 1992, Stadionlabatorium – messstation einer aufkommenden wissenschaft vom sport im kaiserreich, *Brennpunkte der Sportwissenschaft,* 6 (1), 5-21.

Quercetani, R., 1964, *A World History of Track and Field Athletics, 1864-1964,* Oxford University Press, London.

Quercetani, R., 1991, *Athletics: a History of Modern Track and Field Athletics (1860-1990),* Vallardi, Milan.

Quilis, A., 1991, Le terrain de rugby; jeux et enjeux de l'espace, in B. Errais, D. Mathieu and J. Praicheux (eds), *Géopolitique du Sport,* Laboratoire de Géographie Humaine, Université Franche Comte, Besançon, 33-42.

Rail, G., 1991, The dissolution of polarities as a megatrend in postmodern sport, in F. Landry, M. Landry and M. Yerlés (eds), *Sport – the Third Millenium,* Les Presses de L'Université Laval, Sainte-Foy, 747-51.

Raitz, K., 1987a, Perception of sport landscapes and gratification in the sport experience, *Sport Place,* 1 (1), 49-62.

Raitz, K., 1987b, Place, space and environment in America's leisure landscapes, *Journal of Cultural Geography,* 8 (1), 49-62.

Redmond, G., 1973, A plethora of shrines: sport in the museum and hall of fame, *Quest,* 19, 41-8.

Rees, R., 1993, *Interior Landscapes,* Johns Hopkins University Press, Baltimore.

Relph, E., 1976, *Place and Placelessness,* Pion, London.

Relph, E., 1981, *Rational Landscapes and Humanistic Geography,* Croom Helm, London.

Relph, E., 1985, Geographical experiences and being-in-the-world: the phenomenological origins of geography, in D. Seamon and R. Mugerauer (eds), *Dwelling, Place and Environment,* Nijhoff, Dordrecht, 15-38,

Relph, E., 1987, *The Modern Urban Landscape,* Croom Helm, London.

Relph, E., 1989, A curiously unbalanced condition of the powers of the mind: realism and the ecology of the environmental experience, in F. Boal and D. Livingstone (eds), *The Behavioural Environment,* Routledge, London, 277-88.

Rheingold, H., 1992, *Virtual Reality,* Mandarin, London.

Riesman, D. and Denny, R., 1971, Football in America: a study in culture diffusion, in E. Dunning (ed.), *The Sociology of Sport,* Cass, London, 152-87.

Riess, S., 1989, *City Games: the evolution of American Urban Society and the Rise of Sports,* University of Illinois Press, Urbana.

Rigauer, B., 1981, *Sport and Work* (A. Guttmann, trans.), Columbia University Press, New York.

Rigauer, B., 1992, The 'true value' of sport is its commodity value: a critical discourse of ideology, *Innovation in Social Sciences Research,* 5 (4), 63-69.

Rigauer, B., 1993, Sport and the economy, in E. Dunning, J. Maguire and R. Pearson (eds), *The Sport Process: a Comparative and Developmental Approach,* Human Kinetics, Champaign, IL, 281-305.

Riiskjær, S., (ed.), 1993, *Sport and Space,* Council of Europe, Copenhagen.

Riiskjær, S. and Eichberg, H. (eds), 1989, *Bevægelse i Arkitekturen,* Forlaget Bavnebanke, Slagelse.

Rimmer, P., 1992, Japan's 'resort archipelago' : creating regions of fun, pleasure, relaxation and recreation, *Environment and Planning A,* 24 (11), 1599-625.

Rinehert, R., 1992, Sport as kitsch: a case study of the American Gladiators (abstract), *Proceedings* of the North American Society for Sport History, 144-5.

Risse, H., 1921, *Sociologie des Sports,* August Reher, Berlin.

Roberts, J., 1990, The greening of capitalism: the political economy of the Tory garden festivals, in S. Pugh (ed.), *Reading Landscape: Country City Capital,* Manchester University Press, Manchester, 231-45.

Rohé, F., 1974, *The Zen of Running,* Random House, New York.

Rooney, J., 1974, *A Geography of American Sport; from Cabin Creek to Anaheim,* Addison-Wesley, Reading, MA.

Rooney, J., 1975, Sports from a geographic perspective, in D. Ball and J. Loy (eds), *Sport and Social Order,* Addison-Wesley, Reading, MA, 51-115.

Rösch, H. E., 1986, *Sport und Geographie,* Düsseldorfer Sportwissenschaftliche Studien, 1, Instituts für Sportwissenschaft, University of Dusseldorf.

Rose, G., 1993, *Feminism and Geography: the Limits of Geographical Knowledge,* Verso, London.

Ross, A., (ed.), 1981, *The Penguin Cricketer's Companion,* Penguin, Harmondsworth.

Ross, G., 1898, Tennis, in Suffolk, Earl of, Peek, H. and Aflalo, F. (eds), *The Encyclopaedia of Sport* (vol. 1), Lawrence and Bullen, London, 457-62.

Ross, M., 1973, Football and baseball in America, in J. Talimini and C. Page (eds), *Sport and Society,* Little, Brown and Co., Boston, 102-12.

Ruddell, E. and Hammit, W., 1987, Prospect-refuge theory: a psychological orientation for edge effects in recreation environment, *Journal of Leisure Research,* 19 (4), 249-60.

Sack, R., 1983, Human territoriality: a theory, *Annals of the Association of American Geographers,* 73 (1), 55-74.

Sack, R., 1986, *Human Territoriality,* Cambridge University Press, Cambridge.

Sampson, A., 1981, *Grounds of Appeal,* Hale, London.

Samuels, M., 1979, The biography of landscape, in D. Meinig (ed.), *The Interpretation of Ordinary Landscapes,* Oxford UP, New York, 51-88.

Sandell, K., 1991, Ecostrategies and environmentalism – the case of outdoor life and *friluftsliv, Geografiska Annaler,* 7B (2), 133-41.

Sandiford, K., 1984, Victorian cricket technique and industrial technology, *The British Journal of Sports History,* 1, (3), 272-85.

Sang, J., 1993, Sport and the Global System: the case of Athletics in Kenya, unpublished paper, Keele University.

Sansome, D., 1989, *Greek Athletics and the Genesis of Sport,* University of California Press, Berkeley.

Sayer, M., 1989, Dualistic thinking and rhetoric in geography, *Area,* 21 (3), 301-5.

Schechner, R., 1973, *Environmental Theater,* Hawthorn Books, New York.

Schechner, R., 1985, *Between Theater and Anthropology,* University of Pennsylvania Press, Philadelphia.

Schechner, R., 1988, *Performance Theory,* Routledge, New York.

Seamon, D., 1993a, Different worlds coming together, in D. Seamon (ed.) *Dwelling, Seeing and Designing: Toward a Phenomenological Ecology,* State University of New York Press, Albany, 219-46.

Seamon, D., (ed.) 1993b, *Dwelling, Seeing and Designing: Toward a Phenomenological Ecology,* State University of New York Press, Albany.

Selway, J., 1992, Never mind the quality, how about those pecs?, *The Observer,* 29 November, 65.

Shannon, D. and Kalinsky, G., 1975, *The Ballparks,* Hawthorn Books, New York.

Shaw, G. B., 1915, Preface, in H. Salt (ed.), *Killing for Sport,* Bell, London, xi-xxxiv.

Shearman, M., 1897, Athletics, in Suffolk, Earl of, Peek, H. and Aflalo, F. (eds), *The Encyclopaedia of Sport* (vol. 1), Lawrence and Bullen, London, 47-68.

Shields, R, 1991, *Places on the Margin: Alternative Geographies of Modernity,* Routledge, London.

Shilling, C., 1993, *The Body and Social Theory,* Sage, London.

Shore, B., 1993, Marginal play: sport at the borderlands of time and space, paper read at ICSS seminar, Vienna, July.

Short, J., 1991, *Imagined Country: Society, Culture and Environment,* Routledge, London.

Simmons, J., 1990, The golden age of cricket, in G. Day (ed.), *Readings in Popular Culture,* Macmillan, London, 151-63.

Simpson-Housley, P. and Scott, J., 1993, Poles apart? The Terra Nova and Fram Antarctic expeditions and Judeo-Christian attitudes towards nature, *Transactions of the Institute of British Geographers,* NS18 (3), 395-400.

Sinclair, A. and Henry, W., 1893, *Swimming,* Longmans, Green, London.

Skolimowski, H., 1987, Forest as sanctuaries, in E. Paakola et al. (eds), *Metsäluonnon Kautta Henliseen Kasvuun,* Kriittinen Korkeakoulu, Helsinki, 105-12 (quoted in Telema, 1991: 615).

Slowikowski, S., 1991, Burning desire: nostalgia, ritual and the sport-festival flame controversy, *Sociology of Sport Journal,* 8 (3), 239-57.

Smith, D., 1981, People's theatre – a century of Welsh rugby, *History Today,* 31 (3), 31-6.

Smith, P., 1979, *Architecture and the Human Dimension,* Eastview Editions, Westfield, NJ.

Snyder, E., 1991, Sociology of nostalgia: sport halls of fame and museums in America, *Sociology of Sport Journal,* 8 (3), 228-38.

Snyder, E., 1993, Responses to musical selections and sport: an auditory elicitation approach, *Sociology of Sport Journal,* 10 (2), 168-82.

Sorkin, M., 1992, See you in Disneyland, in M. Sorkin (ed.), *Variations on a Theme Park,* Noonday Press, New York, 205-32.

Sprawson, C., 1993, *Haunts of the Black Masseur: the Swimmer as Hero,* Vintage, London.

Springwood, C., 1992, Space, time and hardware individualization in Japanese baseball: non-western dimensions of personhood, *Play and Culture,* 5 (3), 280-94.

Stam, R., 1988, Mikhail Bakhtin and left cultural critique, in E. Kaplan (ed.), *Postmodernism and its Discontents,* Verso, London, 116-45.

Stone, G., 1970, American sports: play and display, in E. Dunning (ed.), *The Sociology of Sport,* Cass, London, 47-65.

Stone, G., 1972, Introduction, in G. Stone (ed.), *Games, Sport and Power,* Transaction Books, New Brunswick, NJ, 1-17.

Tarasti, L., 1988, The significance of the environment for sport, *Sport Science Review,* (no volume number), 40-3.

Taylor, Lord Justice, 1990, *Hillsborough Stadium Disaster: Final Report,* HMSO, London.

Telema, R., 1991, Nature as motivation for physical activity, in P. Oja and R. Telema (eds), *Sport For All,* Elsevier, Amsterdam, 607-15.

Terauds, J., 1985, *Biomechanics of the Javelin,* Academic Publishers, Del Mar, CA.
Tester, K., 1991, *Animals and Society: the Humanity of Animal Rights,* Routledge, London.
Thomas, K., 1983, *Man and the Natural World; Changing Attitudes in England 1500-1800,* Allen Lane, London.
Thornes, J., 1977, The effect of weather on sport, *Weather,* 32, 258-67.
Thrift, N, 1981, Owners' time and own time: the making of a capitalist time consciousness, 1300-1800, in A. Pred (ed.), *Space, Time and Geography,* Gleerup, Lund, 56-84.
Tomlinson, A., 1992, Shifting patterns of working class leisure; the case of knur-and-spell, *Sociology of Sport Journal,* 9 (2), 192-206.
Tuan, Y-F., 1961, Topophilia: personal encounters and the landscape, *Landscape,* 1 (1).
Tuan, Y-F., 1968, Discrepancies between environmental attitude and behavior: examples from Europe and China, *Canadian Geographer,* 12 (2), 176-91.
Tuan, Y-F., 1971, Geography, phenomenology and the study of human nature, *Canadian Geographer,* 15 (2), 181-92.
Tuan, Y-F., 1974, *Topophilia,* Prentice-Hall, Englewood Cliffs, NJ.
Tuan, Y-F., 1975, Geopiety: a theme in man's attachment to place, in D. Lowenthal and M. Bowden (eds), *Geographies of the Mind,* Oxford University Press, New York, 11-39.
Tuan, Y-F., 1979, *Landscapes of Fear,* Basil Blackwell, Oxford.
Tuan, Y-F., 1982, *Segmented Worlds and Self,* University of Minnesota Press, Minneapolis.
Tuan, Y-F., 1984, *Dominance and Affection: the Making of Pets,* Yale University Press, New Haven.
Tuan, Y-F., 1986, *The Good Life,* University of Wisconsin Press, Madison.
Tuan, Y-F., 1989, *Modernity and Imagination: Paradoxes of Progress,* University of Wisconsin Press, Madison.
Turner, B., 1984, *The Body and Society: Explorations in Social Theory,* Blackwell, Oxford.
Ullman, E., 1974, Space and/or time: oportunity for substitution and prediction, *Transactions of the Institute of British Geographers,* 63, 125-39.
Unwin, T., 1992, *The Place of Geography,* Longman, London.
Vanderzwaag, H., 1972, *Toward a Philosophy of Sport,* Addison-Wesley, Reading, MA.
Veijola, S., 1993, Bodyguards and bodybenders of sexual difference: female protagonists constituting space and knowledge, paper read at ICSS seminar, Vienna, July.
Vinnai, G., 1973, *Football Mania,* Ocean Books, London.
Virilio, P., 1983, *Pure War,* Semiotext(e), New York.
Von Korsfleisch, S., 1970, Religious Olympism, *Social Research,* 37 (1), 231-6.
Vuolle, P., 1991, Nature and environments for physical activity, in P. Oja and R. Telema (eds), *Sport For All,* Elsevier, Amsterdam, 597-606.
Wagner, P., 1981, Sport: culture and geography, in A. Pred (ed.), *Space, Time and Geography,* Gleerup, Lund, 85-108.
Wakefield, R., 1990, *Postmodernism; the Twilight of the Real,* Pluto Press, London.
Warren, S., 1993, 'This heaven gives me migraines'; the problems and promise of landscapes of leisure', in J. Duncan and D. Ley (eds), *Place/Culture/Representation,* Routledge, London, 173-86.
Webster, F., 1940, *Sports Grounds and Buildings,* Pitman, London.
Webster, P., 1993, Vélodrome survivors look back on French treachery, *The Guardian,* 17 July, 15.
Weil, D., Halberstam, D. and Richmond, P., 1992, *Baseball: the Perfect Game,* Rizzoli, New York.

Weiss, P., 1968, *Sport: a Philosophic Inquiry,* Southern Illinois University Press, Carbondale, IL.

Whiting, J., 1968, Are hunter-gatherers a cultural type?, in R. Lee and I. DeVore (eds), *Man the hunter,* Aldine, Chicago.

Whitsun, D., 1987, Leisure, the state and collective consumption, in J. Horne, D. Jary and A. Tomlinson (eds), *Sport, Leisure and Social Relations,* Routledge, London, 229-53.

Wickham, G., 1992, Sport, manners, persons, government: sport, Elias, Mauss, Foucault, *Cultural Studies,* 6 (2), 219-31.

Willett, J., 1977, *The Theatre of Bertold Brecht,* Methuen, London.

Willis, P., 1982, Women in sport in ideology, in J. Hargreaves (ed.), *Sport, Culture and Ideology,* Routledge, London, 117-35.

Willis, S., 1990, Work(ing) out, *Cultural Studies,* 4 (1), 1-18.

Wilson, A., 1992, *The Culture of Nature,* Blackwell, Cambridge, Mass.

Wilt, F., 1959, *How they Train,* Track and Field News, Los Altos, CA.

Wimmer, M., 1976, *Olympic Buildings,* Edition Leipzig, Leipzig.

Winningham, G. and Rienert, A., 1979, *Rites of Fall: High School Football in Texas,* University of Texas Press, Austin.

Winters, C., 1980, Running, *Landscape,* 24 (1), 19-22.

Wright, J., 1966, *Human Nature in Geography,* Harvard University Press, Cambridge, MA.

Young, P., 1968, *A History of British Football,* Stanley Paul, London.

Zelinsky, W., 1988, Where every town is above average: welcoming signs along America's highways, *Landscape,* 30 (1) 1-10.

Ziemilski, A., 1965, Scepticism au siècle du sport, *Recherches Internationales à la Lumiére du Marxisme,* 48, 9 (quoted in Brohm, 1978).

Zurcher, L. and Meadow, A., 1970, On bullfights and baseball: an example of interaction of social institutions, in E. Dunning (ed.), *The Sociology of Sport,* Frank Cass, London, 175-97.

INDEX